HAITI
(1995–2000)

THE BLACK BOOK
ON
INSECURITY

PROSPER AVRIL

Haiti (1995 - 2000): The Black Book on Insecurity

Universal Publishers/uPUBLISH.com
USA • 2004

ISBN: 1-58112-533-X

"As a gift of God, human life is sacred. It deserves respect. Nobody has the right to destroy it or to use it as he pleases".

(*Conférence Episcopale d'Haïti – Présence de l'Eglise en Haïti*, p. 321.)

Books by Prosper Avril

1. Le Tir Au Fusil
   Rifle Marksmanship
   Presses Nationales d'Haïti, 1979
   Port-au-Prince, Haïti (160 pages)

2. Vérités et Révélations - Tome I
   Le Silence Rompu (Breaking the Silence)
   Imprimeur II, 1993
   Port-au-Prince, Haïti (264 pages)

3. Vérités et Révélations - Tome II
   Plaidoyer pour l'Histoire (A Plea for History)
   Imprimeur II, 1994
   Port-au-Prince, Haïti (264 pages)

4. Vérités et Révélations - Tome III
   L'Armée d'Haïti, Bourreau ou Victime? (The Haitian Army, Guilty or Not?)
   Imprimerie Le Natal, 1997
   Port-au-Prince, Haïti (484 pages)

5. From Glory to Disgrace
   The Haitian Army 1804 - 1994
   Universal Publisher/UPublish.com, 1999
   U.S.A. (414 pages)
   ISBN 1-58112-836-3

6. An Appeal to History
   The Truth about a Singular Lawsuit
   Universal Publisher/UPublish.com, 2000
   U.S.A. (304 pages)
   ISBN 1-58112-784-7

7. Haïti (1995 - 2000)
   Le Livre Noir de l'Insécurité (The Black Book on Insecurity)
   Imprimerie Le Natal, 2001
   Port-au-Prince, Haïti (383 pages)
   ISBN 99935-621-0-6

TABLE OF CONTENTS

PORTRAITS OF VICTIMS

After page 146

1. Mrs. Mireille Durocher Bertin, lawyer, founder of a political party, journalist, professor at the State University, assassinated by gunfire in broad daylight on March 28, 1995.

2. M. Michel Gonzalès, businessman, Manager of Haiti Air Cargo, assassinated by gunfire in broad daylight on May 22, 1995.

3. General Max Mayard, Officer of the Haitian Army (FAD'H), former Assistant-Commandant of the Army, assassinated by gunfire in broad daylight on October 3, 1995.

4. M. Hubert Feuillé, deputy of the legislative body, assassinated by gunfire in broad daylight on November 7, 1995.

5. Reverend. Antoine Leroy, Pastor and staff member of a political party, assassinated by gunfire in broad daylight on August 20, 1996.

6. Mrs. Micheline Lemaire Coulanges, Business woman, Entrepreneur, assassinated by gunfire in broad daylight on

December 22, 1997.

7. M. Jean Pierre-Louis, Catholic Priest, parish priest of Mont-Carmel Church at Bizoton, Port-au-Prince, assassinated by gunfire in broad daylight on August 3, 1998.

8. M. Jimmy Lalanne, Physician, assassinated by gunfire in his office, in broad daylight, on February 27, 1999.

9. M. Yvon Toussaint, Physician and Senator at the Haitian Parliament, staff member of a political party, assassinated by gunfire in broad daylight on March 1ˢᵗ, 1999.

10. M. Roland Décatrel, businessman and entrepreneur, assassinated by gunfire in broad daylight on August 31, 1999.

11. M. Jean L. Dominique, agronomist, journalist, owner and manager of Radio Haiti Inter, assassinated by gunfire in broad   daylight on April 3, 2000.

12. M. Ary Bordes, Physician, former Minister for Public Health,   assassinated by gunfire in broad daylight on May 6, 2000.

After page 234

1. Journalist Jean L. Dominique with the author (July 1989).

2. Miss Christine Jeune, Police Officer at the Haitian National Police (PNH), assassinated by gunfire in obscure conditions on March 19, 1995.

3. Boris Pautensky, a 6 year-old child kidnapped at his school on May 28, 1996.

4. Mrs. Erla Jean-François, Mayor of the City of Chansolme (North-West), assassinated by gunfire in broad daylight on May 30, 1996.

5. M. Joseph Rony C. Charles, director at PROMOBANK in Cap-Haitian, assassinated by gunfire in broad daylight on August 5, 1996.

6. M. Louis Emilio Passe, former deputy of the Haitian Legislative body, assassinated by gunfire on October 16, 1997.

7. M. Roger Cazeau, retired colonel of the Haitian Army (FAD'H), former Commandant of the Haitian Air Force, assassinated by gunfire on June 14, 1999.

8. Sister Marie Géralde Robert, nun, Manager of a Health Center at Côtes-de-Fer (Southwest), assassinated by gunfire on November 17, 1999.

9. Colonel Jean Lamy, Councelor to the Haitian National Police (PNH), assassinated by gunfire on October 8, 1999.

10. Brother Hurbon Bernardin, of the Christian Institution's Brothers, assassinated at Vallée de Jacmel on November 30, 1999.

11. Mrs. Carmen Boisvert Alexandre, 74 years old, a scholar, tortured and assassinated at her home on July 25, 2000.

12. M. Patrice Gousse, young Manager and Entrepreneur,

assassinated by gunfire in broad daylight on September 17, 2000.

13.M. Jean-Rood Guerrier, Engineer, former deputy at the Haitian Legislative body, assassinated by gunfire on December 20, 2000.

14.Colonel Jean Lamy, Counselor at the Haitian National Police, assassinated y gunfire on October 8, 1999.

FOREWORD

In civilized societies, the phenomenon of insecurity can appear in several forms. Various forms in which it can occur come readily to mind: social insecurity, unpredictable road conditions, unreliable food supplies, etc. The insecurity that concerns us in this book is that which arises from the violent behavior of people towards other people, violence that attacks a person's life, property, physical integrity and inheritance.

The members of any human society will certainly often suffer from the misdeeds and deviant behavior of some within their community. In such cases, the penal systems that operate within the society will intervene to correct the misdeeds and to maintain the confidence of the public in the reliability of their system of protection against the actions of criminals and gangsters.

However, when there is an excessive escalation of violence—homicide, voluntary aggravated assault, invasion, burglary and other violent acts—then insecurity becomes entrenched and life is characterized by a permanent feeling of fear, anguish and concern that invades the human soul and disturbs the daily routine. This situation becomes alarming in more ways than one, for when the sensitivity of the population to violence grows, and when the brakes that are intended to restrain the violent behavior are not firmly applied or are slow to operate, then insecurity is transformed into a social and political phenomenon.

This, unfortunately, is the situation in which the Haitian people have been struggling for too long already: living in a latent state of insecurity—that is, with a permanent lack of security.

What is security?

Security is the "trustful and quiet state of mind of someone who believes that he is protected from danger" (*Larousse*), or "the situation of someone who feels himself protected from danger, who is reassured" (*Petit Robert*).

Reading these simple definitions, it is easy to understand the great importance that is attached to the notion of safety in the life of a person or a nation. It is impossible for a person to develop, socialize freely, travel, work, sleep, or relax without this legitimate feeling of being protected from danger. Moreover, since any nation is made up of free men and women, the very existence of the State is threatened when a climate of insecurity persists at its core, destroying the trustful and peaceful spirit of the citizens who comprise its population.

This opinion is well expressed by the French political theorist Sébastian Roché, who writes:

Security is a collective good by excellence. The State has constituted its power on its capacity to guarantee it. Therein lies the foundation of its legitimacy. (*Sociologie*

Politique de l'Insécurité [*Political Sociology of Insecurity*], p. 228).

Over the last six years, Haiti has lost a considerable number of its sons and daughters, who were pointlessly mown down by blind violence. Intellectuals, teachers, engineers, doctors, priests, pastors, members of religious orders, business people, police officers, soldiers, ordinary citizens, politicians, artisans, workers, peasants, school children, infants, young and old men and women, journalists, bankers, and others whom we still do not know—all have fallen, killed by the specter of violent death that now haunts all the corners and recesses of Haiti, a country where it was formerly so good to live.

In addressing this problem, what is so exasperating is the veil of the anonymity that often covers this delinquency, this criminal activity in Haiti. Most of the time, no personal or social relation appears to bind or oppose the aggressor and the victim; these crimes thus seem to be blind and pointless.

Considering the paramount importance of the notion of safety for any human being, and in view of the increasing seriousness and extent of criminal activity throughout the country and the consequent threat to its institutions and its integrity, we thought that it was imperative for every Haitian to understand the many aspects of the plague constituted by insecurity, in order to be able to fight it effectively and preserve the country from catastrophe. We believe that it is essential to place before the national conscience a collection of documents and facts concerning the phenomenon—a "white paper", although in the circumstances we should rather call it a "black paper"—so that at a glance every Haitian can evaluate the situation, determine the problem and help to solve it.

To achieve this task, we have made extensive use of opinions expressed by Haitian intellectuals and thinkers on the subject, and information provided by the Haitian press—data that is freely accessible to everyone—in order to reflect as closely as possible the true everyday life of the nation.

By providing the reader with a compilation of facts and data on events that occurred during the period referred to, and by proposing solutions to the thorny problem of insecurity in Haiti, the author of *Haiti (1995–2000) – The Black Book on Insecurity* has a noble goal in mind. His intention is to make a contribution to the reconstruction of the Haitian nation by attempting to inspire influential leaders and responsible governments with a resolve capable of motivating them to work together to find, as quickly as possible, effective ways of working towards the eradication of this "evil that spreads terror" among Haitian families.

We trust that this work of research, analysis, compilation and proposal of solutions will not be a "shot into the air". May it succeed in stirring all the daughters and sons of Haiti, whether eminent intellectuals or humble citizens, to stop, once and for all, this train of death that mindlessly destroys everything in its way: lives, promises, hopes and dreams. May Haiti, the Pearl of the Antilles, be released from the specter of insecurity and regain its former good reputation, and may the Haitian people soon find again the once-famous smile that they lost a long time ago.

Prosper Avril

INTRODUCTION

February 7, 1986! A date that heralded great changes for Haiti! Efforts towards correcting the drifting of the past! On this day—February 7, 1986—the Haitian people celebrated the advent of a new era characterized by freedom of expression, freedom of political choice and respect for individual freedom, within a secure State guaranteeing peaceful streets and homes. This public peace was essential to the great and much desired economic revival, which would eventually receive the support of the international community. Thus, after the collapse of the Duvalier regime, the Haitian people expected an improvement in the conditions and quality of their life.

What is the result now at the end of the year 2000, fourteen years after the emergence of this hope?

After 1986, Haiti experienced a series of frustrating twists and turns in the achievement of a transition to a stable and democratic government. Several transitory governments followed one after another at the helm of the State without being able to end the transition period and establish a legitimate government. Drowned in the tumult of popular claims exacerbated by the action of political leaders acting in the shade; overcome by a misinformation campaign that succeeded in discrediting all the heads of State after Duvalier; destroyed or weakened by destabilizing actions, *coups d'état* and attempts at *coup d'état*: the various governments prior to 1990 failed in their efforts to establish in Haiti the tranquil climate necessary to launch the country on a path to genuine democracy.

Hope reappeared after the elections of December 1990, when candidate Jean-Bertrand Aristide, profiting from popular favor, became the legitimate president of Haiti. Relieved, everyone thought that the country was finally going to enjoy a respite. This was far from the case as genocide was committed before the inauguration of the elected president, in reaction to the insane venture of Dr. Roger Lafontant who tried vainly to seize the presidential Palace on the night of January 6–7, 1991.

The euphoria of the December 16, 1990 victory then melted to mass hysteria on the morning of January 7, 1991, when the army quashed the Lafontant *coup d'état*. Partisans of the president-elect, benefiting greatly from the action of the Haitian Army (FAD'H), occupied the streets. That day, they lynched or "necklaced" a large number of compatriots under the approving or tolerating eyes of the military, who feared appearing favorable towards the condemnable initiative of the usurper Lafontant. This carnage was thus perpetrated with total impunity. Haitians could even watch fanatics publicly exhibiting incinerated limbs of their victims on state television.

From that day on, the division of the country into two distinct camps was reinforced. The slogan *"Makout pa ladan"* ("Macoutes, stay outside"), current since the fall of M. Jean-

Claude Duvalier, was reinstituted with greater force, the term "Macoute" signifying all those who had had relations with the Duvalier governments, whether from near or afar.

Thereafter, a Manichæan cleavage of Haitian society into "good" and "bad" poisoned the political atmosphere of the country at the national level. Directed by the Constitution itself, which for ten years refused them access to elected office, the former partisans of the Duvalier regime were publicly vindicated on the least pretext. Once installed, the new and legitimate government was not going to embarrass itself by unscrupulously and wrongfully accusing them of crimes or plots at random.

In fact, after 1986, it was impossible to establish a stable and secure environment in Haiti. Although it occurred in unfavorable circumstances, a unique opportunity to create a tranquil political and social climate in the country arose in 1994, on the occasion of the second landing of US troops in Haiti, which was solicited—with contempt for any nationalist feeling—by President Jean-Bertrand Aristide in order to regain power.

A success without a fight, this military operation—undertaken in Haiti on September 19, 1994 and dubbed *Uphold Democracy*—was to carry out a precise mission comprising three quite distinct parts: (1) to force the departure of the regime founded by the military after the overthrow of President Aristide in 1991, (2) to restore Jean-Bertrand Aristide to his position and (3) to create a secure and stable environment in Haiti.

While the Haitians had the shame of this occupation to

expunge, they expected at least to profit from the welcome aftermath of having a safe country, ready to be launched on the path of modernization and of accelerated and durable development, thanks to the restoration of peace, to the investments of foreign entrepreneurs and the Haitian private sector, and also to the massive assistance promised by the international community.

Unfortunately, in the year 2000—six years after the execution of the *Uphold Democracy* operation—political stability and the promised social peace have not materialized. Nowadays, the country is still deprived of the vital institutions essential to the correct functioning of a democracy—a legitimate parliament, undisputed city halls, a constitutional electoral council, an independent legal system, and so on—and in this environment, the Haitian people live in a latent state of insecurity.

Safety, this "trustful and quiet state of mind of someone who believes he is or feels himself protected from danger", is no longer within the reach of the Haitians. Read a description of the situation, composed as an inventory at the beginning of the new millennium, by Jean L. Prophète:

> Be alert! Be very prudent! Do not go out in the evening. Do not ride in a taxi. Do not trust immigration officers. If they ask you for your address, give them a false one. Especially do not display your money. Go out with only the minimum necessary. Leave at your home your passport, your credit cards, all your important papers as well as your precious jewels. Distrust all human contact of which you are not absolutely sure. Fear all tinted-glass vehicles, devious pedestrians and especially suspicious motorcyclists. Be always on

your guard, continually vigilant, continually attentive. Avoid as much as possible the downtown area. Avoid the road of Carrefour, overcrowded, cluttered, and stressful, like a pagan Calvary. To go into the countryside, travel during the day. It is highly recommended to travel in convoy. It is severely forbidden to go alone at night. (*Inventaire de Fin de Siècle* [*Inventory of the End of the Century*], p.19).

This opinion reflects the current perception of life in Haiti. To go to work, to manage a business, to use the national highways, to visit the markets or supermarkets, to go to the bank, to the movies, to surprise parties or to walk at moonlight in the capital or in the province constitutes a risk in Haiti today! Moreover, this report is not the fruit of an overly fertile imagination. In the first month of the period covered by this study—January 1995, four months after the execution of *Uphold Democracy*—the daily newspaper *Le Nouvelliste* also drew attention to the malady:

A very poorly restrained wind of violence is blowing over the capital and some cities of the province. As proof, there has not been a day without someone, somewhere, being a victim of the prevailing climate of insecurity. And so, acts are committed day and night by gangsters, by assassins, by robbers armed with firearms or knives; fear and worry perspire on the face of every individual among the population. (*Le Nouvelliste*, January 30, 1995, p. 1.)

Today, it is distressing to note that in spite of all the efforts and sacrifices that have been endorsed by the Haitian people, and notwithstanding the billion dollars invested in Haiti by the United States under the heading of assistance to this country, all the surveys, investigations and research projects indicate that the quality of the life in Haiti was better before 1986.

What happened? Why could Haiti not regain domestic peace after its return to constitutional order as restored by the *Uphold Democracy* operation in 1994? Why has the insecurity, especially political, that has prevailed during the three years of the *coup d'état*, far from disappearing, rather invaded every sector of national life and spread throughout the entire country? What is the extent of the damage? Can the Haitians, by themselves, hope to reverse the situation?

To answer these questions, we shall attempt to examine in depth the phenomenon of insecurity in Haiti between 1995 and 2000. We shall provide an overview of the quality of the country's leadership, beginning from the rupture of the democratic process by the 1991 *coup d'état*. We shall analyze the political choices made by government authorities after the return to constitutional order in 1994. Then we shall clarify the factors that favored the development of insecurity in Haiti. Finally, following the publication of a non-exhaustive list of those who suffered violent deaths during each year of the period 1995–2000, we shall share with the reader some ideas that we propose as our modest contribution to the eradication of this evil.

We sincerely hope that after the publication of this book, a step will have been made towards pricking the conscience of all Haitians and their partners in the international community regarding the phenomenon of insecurity in Haiti, so that finally, in safety, peace and order, the country can look forward to harmonious and enduring development, bearing in mind the compelling image of the dreams of the martyred people of Haiti.

CHAPTER I

THE YEARS OF AMBIGUOUS LEADERSHIP

On February 7, 1991, amidst the euphoria and joy of a people in search of a better life, the whole world greeted the advent of the priest Jean-Bertrand Aristide to power in Haiti. This event was hailed by the international press as unique in the annals of Haitian history. The press enthused that for the first time (as they thought), a Haitian president had been chosen by means of free and democratic elections. The atmosphere of joy was tangible.

However, on the very day of the inauguration of the newly elected president, the atmosphere of celebration was sullied by a disconcerting incident: Father Jean-Bertrand Aristide had not finished being girded with the presidential sash and pronouncing the solemn oath "to respect the constitution and the laws of Haiti" before the government prosecutor of the time, M. Bayard Vincent, dared to hand an arrest warrant to the immediate past president, Mme Ertha Pascale Trouillot, in the very environs of the Legislative Palace.

This bizarre incident alone put in jeopardy the future of the new government, because it clearly indicated an attitude of vengefulness; it was an initiative that would affect the sound leadership of the State, which was so necessary for the economic revival of the country. Seven months later, a bloody *coup d'état* took place, initiating a period of political repression that could only be ended by a second military occupation of Haiti.

A. The *Coup d'État*

Thus, on the very day of the inauguration of President Aristide, the political climate of the country became cloudy, and then during the following days was quickly and completely darkened by a series of governmental actions that could only be described as anti-democratic: the illegal, arbitrary and humiliating imprisonment of the former head of state, Justice Ertha Pascale Trouillot, in the National Penitentiary; daily occupation of the streets by violent crowds, verbal and physical aggression against members of Parliament, arson of buildings owned by political and trade-union organizations, the hardening of political speech, etc.—many acts that could only culminate, on September 30, 1991, in a brutal rupture of the democratic process, which would again call everything into question by instigating a state of anarchy, exacerbated intolerance and latent repression in the land.

The arrest of Mme Trouillot undoubtedly constitutes a prelude to the failure of the first eight months of the Aristide government. This act, representing a deliberate decision, indicated the strategy that this new regime intended to adopt in the management of its internal policy, which was, in fact, one of revenge. When one realizes that the government prosecutor still depended on a minister of Mme Ertha Trouillot at the time of drafting the warrant for her arrest, one understands that this initiative had been planned before the ceremony of inauguration of the new head of state, and so involved disloyalty by a public servant.

The FAD'H also, which had worked in a perfectly orderly manner towards the success of the recent elections, was harshly hit on the same day, during the same ceremony. On February 7, 1991, while the new president was delivering his inaugural message, he coldly announced the dismissal of the officers of the military staff, who had been invited by the protocol office to attend the inauguration ceremony. This was done in the presence of government officials, the general public, foreign ambassadors and guests.

Following the installation of the government, a wind of revenge blew over the nation. In addition to the former president, Ertha Trouillot, former ministers—including Anthony Saint-Pierre—and civil servants of former regimes—including Fritz Joseph, René Maximilien and others—were arrested and jailed. The legal pretext of "plotting against the interior safety of the State" was resuscitated and become a fashionable slogan.

The political climate in Port-au-Prince was thus overheated. An inexpressible fear came over all the voters who had not appeared to be in favor of the new regime. Intolerance was even exercised against members of the political opposition—former partisans or allies of the Lavalas movement, who had contributed to the new leaders' accession to power.

In August 1991, with this frame of mind prevailing, the headquarters of the United Democratic Confederation (KID), was ransacked and destroyed under the auspices of the rigid fanatics of the ruling party. The KID party was a branch of the National Front for Change and Democracy (FNCD), the coalition that had been used as a promotional banner for the candidacy of M. Jean-Bertrand Aristide. At the same time, and under the same conditions, the building of the Autonomous Center for Haitian Workers (CATH), a trade-union organization also involving people who were close to those in power, was burned down. This tense atmosphere was used as a backdrop for the execution of the *coup d'état* on the night of September 29, 1991, which overthrew the legitimate government and had the most dramatic consequences for Haiti.

With the democratic process thus broken down, the military, acting with constraint, decided to hand the reins of power to the Supreme Court Justice, having obtained from Parliament a resolution confirming the presidential vacancy, in an effort to give a constitutional varnish to the anti-democratic action undertaken.

But the international community did not approve the *fait accompli*. It had invested too much in the 1990 elections in Haiti to endorse such a catastrophe, which it treated as a slap in the face of the New World Order. From the start, it proclaimed the return of the deposed president to power.

The partisans of President Aristide wanted to react to the *coup d'état*; their reactions were repressed violently, with a pitiless severity.

B. Oppression After the *Coup d'État*

On the night of the *coup d'état*, hundreds of citizens lost their lives. A report of the US State Department estimates the number of victims at between 300 and 500. (*Notes on Haiti*, US State Department Office of Inter-American Affairs, April 3, 1997). Then commenced a regime of repression against the enemies or adversaries of the putschists and against the Lavalas activists. The latter had organized some pockets of resistance inside the country, to oppose the military rule.

Encouraged by the firm position of the international community with respect to the *coup d'état*, the partisans of the exiled president intensified their mobilization inside Haiti, thus preventing the newly installed government from consolidating its position. Military outposts (Chantal, Camp-Perrin, Morency, and Fort Platon in the South) were attacked by Lavalas militants using small arms.

To limit the destabilizing effect of these militants, slum areas were leveled by the military, resulting in many deaths, degrading the image of the military and provoking an exodus of the inhabitants into the countryside and to the coast. Consequently, in December 1991, the international community began to impose economic sanctions on Haiti in an effort to bring down the military regime.

Regarding the management of public affairs during these three years, the situation was even more ambiguous. In the United States, a Haitian government in exile headed by M. Jean-Bertrand Aristide was functioning with Haitian funds in US banks, without regular control of the legislative branch of power that was situated in Port-au-Prince, and without the procedures established by the laws concerning finance and public accountability. In Haiti, another government that appeared to be official was ensuring the effective functioning of the State.

However, the military staff officers did not allow the bureaucrats, summoned by them to help in the management of the country, to have real autonomy. Customs, the Internal Revenue Office and public administration in general were barely functioning. Meanwhile, the embargo was devastating. Electricity, public transport and other activities were literally paralyzed by the lack of fuel following the imposition of international sanctions. External assistance was frozen, normal provisioning of the country suspended, the export of commodities reduced to nothing.

Inside the country, the populous districts were constantly in turmoil. Raboteau in Gonaïves, La Fossette in Cap-Haitian and Ste Hélène in Jérémie had become centers of revolt. The Lavalas militants possessed firearms, including homemade ones. Faced with such a situation and considering the possibility of a resistance characterized by armed struggle, the military government resorted to an even more severe repression that did not achieve their desired result. On the contrary, following a persistent rumor announcing the launching, by the partisans of the president-in-exile, of an operation called *fè koupe fè*, ("only steel can cut steel"), the repression escalated to alarming proportions. Military operations were launched in slum areas to attack these centers of Lavalas resistance.

The *Report of the National Commission of Truth and Justice*, covering two years (1995–1997) of investigation into violations of the right to life committed during the three years of the putschist regime's management (1991–1994), is damning. It says:

> According to collected testimonies, violations of the right to life, including summary or extra-judiciary executions and massacres (defined by the Commission as the summary execution of at least three persons in the same event satisfying the criterion of unity of time and place), are listed statistically under the heading of executions, together with forced disappearances, which can be assumed to be summary executions. Like death threats, they are considered as attempted violations of the right to life. The consequences of the execution attempts constitute also an infringement of the right to physical integrity in most of the cases. A victim who survives the attempt is often injured, sometimes mutilated.

> The Commission analyzed 1348 cases of violations of the right to life, among them 333 forced disappearances, 576 summary executions, and 439 attempts at summary execution. In every administrative region of the country, cases of extra-judicial execution, of death by torture, or of disappearance were discovered.

This sustained aspect of the oppression illustrates the context of all the other cases of violation and indicates the absence of a brake to stop the violations of human rights. The administrative regions of the West (principally Port-au-Prince), of the North and of the Artibonite (especially Raboteau) were the most harshly hit.

It is in the region of Port-au-Prince that the right to life has been the most seriously affected: one rediscovers that three quarters of the cases of disappearance and close to half of the reported summary executions were carried out there. A statistical study was made of the records of the *Hospital of the State University of Haiti* (HUEH) over a ten-year period (1985–1995). This hospital is the only one in the region of Port-au-Prince that has a public morgue. Its records were a useful source of information.

The statistical analysis of these files indicates how, during the reference period, the number of political assassinations increased sharply in comparison with the preceding years. From the statistical point of view, the difference is highly significant and shows that the average number of victims has more than doubled—increasing from an average of ten deaths a month during the preceding years to about 24 deaths a month.

Furthermore, this period shows the highest number of assassinations of the last ten years, during which there were a number of non-democratic regimes in Haiti. (www.haiti.org: *Rapport de la Commission Nationale de Vérité et de Justice* [*Report of the National Commission of Truth and Justice*], Chapter V, B.1.)

Thus, the National Commission of Truth and Justice counted 909 cases of Haitians who were victims of violent death ("summary executions and forced disappearances") during the three years of the putschist regime. In addition, 439 attempts at summary execution were counted. The Commission highlighted certain cases of spectacular assassinations of very important personalities, such as that of businessman Antoine Izméry, minister Guy Malary and Father Jean-Marie Vincent.

However, it should be carefully noted that this insecurity was of a specifically political nature. Despite the general increase in misery caused by the drastic and unjust imposition of an economic embargo on the country, and despite the nightly complete darkness caused by the almost total absence of electric power in the principal cities, citizens who were not involved in politics did not feel threatened by a general insecurity. People were able to go about their business without feeling that they were living in a state of permanent danger.

Admittedly, the *Report of the National Commission of Truth and Justice* does record — under the label of "political repression" — the sporadic occurrence of arbitrary provocations and retaliations, mainly in the populous districts where resistance was very active, and also in the communal sections (that is, rural administrative divisions) placed under the authority of the section chiefs (senior rural police officers).

The situation of nascent political violence under the military regime did not improve at all during these three years. On the contrary, it continued to worsen, leading to the assassination of Father Jean-Marie Vincent in broad daylight on August 28, 1994, three weeks before the landing of the US troops in Haiti.

Finally, having considered the serious violations of human rights in Haiti, having especially taken into account the high number of "boat people" sailing regularly for the US coast, and in view of the total chaos with which the country was threatened, the United Nations approved, at the request of President Aristide, the landing on Haiti of 23,000 troops, mainly from the famous 82nd US Airborne Division, for the purpose of restoring constitutional normality to Haiti.

The foreign troops—dubbed "the Multinational Force"—landed on September 19, 1994 and were charged with the mission of neutralizing the small but unruly Haitian Army of 7,000 soldiers, of restoring the legitimate president to office and of establishing a "secure and stable environment" in the country. This was the *Uphold Democracy* operation.

C. The *Uphold Democracy* Operation

On July 3, 1993, to resolve the Haitian crisis, a significant document notable for its new and unique character was signed under the auspices of the United Nations by the exiled president of Haiti, M. Jean-Bertrand Aristide, and the commander-in-chief of the Haitian Army, General Raoul Cédras. This initiative aimed at the peaceful restoration of constitutional order in Haiti — a solution that could, however, never be applied because of the reticence of the two main protagonists.

One year after the signing of this document, in a letter dated July 29, 1994, President-in-Exile Jean-Bertrand Aristide informed the general secretary of this eminent international body that "the moment has come for the international community, a principal witness of the Governors Island's Agreement, to take prompt and decisive action, under the authority of the United Nations, in order to allow its complete application." (Prosper Avril, *From Glory to Disgrace*, p. 300.) It was the green light awaited by the United Nations to justify the use of force in the settlement of the crisis, born in the *coup d'état* of September 30, 1991, for the benefit of President Aristide.

On September 19, 1994, the landing of the occupation forces, in a deafening din of helicopters, tanks and fighters, was successfully effected in the cities of Port-au-Prince and Cap-Haitian.

The Haitian Army did not offer any resistance to the deployment of the foreign forces. On September 18, 1994, the day before the landing, a delegation consisting of former US president Jimmy Carter, US senator Sam Nunn and former head of the US armed forces, General Colin Powell, had obtained from the Haitian *de facto* president, Emile Jonassaint, a guarantee that the operations would proceed without a fight, that there would be no response from the Haitian soldiers. He kept his word.

Further to this, former US president Jimmy Carter (representing current president Bill Clinton) and *de facto* Haitian president Emile Jonassaint signed a document titled "Agreement of Port-au-Prince". This agreement offered capitulation of the Haitian Army in return for the promise of a general amnesty for those responsible for the *coup d'état*. However, the Haitian government did not live up to this promise, in spite of the vote in Parliament, on October 6, 1994, approving a law of amnesty for the authors of the *coup d'état* and their accomplices.

In the days following the landing, the GIs proceeded to disarm the Haitian troops. After the first moments of frustration and worry had passed, the Haitian soldiers calmly awaited a decision regarding their future. They fully obeyed the orders of the Haitian military staff officers, and confidently awaited the outcome of corresponding negotiations concerning them, which was to be "no reprisals". An incident that occurred at Cap-Haitian, in which ten Haitian soldiers were killed by US troops—by mistake, according to the US leadership—did not affect their behavior. The defeated Haitian commander-in-chief, General Raoul Cédras, personally accompanied the chief of the expedition, US general Hugh Shelton, on a tour of all Haitian military garrisons to ensure that the operation would proceed without further incident.

At this significant stage, General Cédras passed the command to General Jean-Claude Duperval and on October 12, 1994 left the country, bound for Panama, in the company of the army chief-of-staff, General Philippe Biamby, in accordance with the guarantees offered to them before their departure. According to *Haïti Progrès*, "General Cédras had the benefit of several special recommendations for admission to Panama, beginning with that of President Aristide himself who made a direct request to his Panamanian counterpart, Ernesto Balladares." (*Haïti Progrès*, October 19–25, 1995, p. 3).

Colonel Michel François, the chief of the Port-au-Prince

police force, not having benefitted from the same favors, had left the country the day before, by his own means, bound for the Dominican Republic.

The first goal of the program had been accomplished. The military chiefs, having been defeated without a fight, had left the country. The US Army, in the person of General Hugh Shelton, temporarily assumed political power in Haiti. General security was assured by the US troops, vested with the authority of the State. The return of President Jean-Bertrand Aristide in Haiti was imminent.

D. The Promises of a Return

On October 15, 1994, Operation *Uphold Democracy* moved into its second phase. President Jean-Bertrand Aristide returned triumphantly aboard a US Air Force plane to Haiti, a country weakened morally, structurally and economically. The temporary commander of the Haitian Army, General Jean-Claude Duperval, was at the airport to greet President Aristide, who, very willingly and without turning a hair, accepted military honors from a battalion of the army. Everything went smoothly and in perfect order.

At the time of the landing of the US troops in Haiti, while a feeling of shame oppressed the national elites, the country in general was facing a distressing situation, characterized primarily by the many catastrophic effects of the embargo: scarcity of fresh consumer goods, degradation of the environment, systematic reduction of forest reserves, acceleration of mountain erosion and the process of desertification. At the socioeconomic level, the country was seriously afflicted by the impossibility of meeting the demands of public health and especially by the increase in unemployment, a consequence of the closing of industries that involved subcontractors and employed more than 30,000 paid workers, thus affecting the livelihoods of almost 300,000 people when collateral effects are considered.

Moreover, electricity and drinking water were scarce, and the road network and the communication system—non-existent in several parts of the country—functioned unpredictably at the national level. Agricultural production regressed rapidly. The per-capita income reached a very low level. Basic commodities did not arrive from overseas.

Added to this situation of shortage at the national level were a heightening of the division among Haitians and a concern close to panic on the part of citizens who had expressed opposition to the return of President Aristide.

This was the general political, economical and social scene on the day before President Jean-Bertrand Aristide's return to Haiti. With the re-establishment of constitutional order, everyone hoped for an end to this situation of uncertainty and stagnation, for the revival of the economy, for the resumption of external assistance and for a more positive attitude from the international community.

Thus, if the arrival of the foreign troops in Haiti disturbed the patriotism of more than one Haitian, many secretly comforted themselves with expectations of the end of the embargo nightmare and the beginning of a period of political and social peace in Haiti.

On October 15, 1994, Port-au-Prince awoke decorated with a thousand colors. An aircraft of the presidency of the United States was bringing President Aristide back to the country, in preparation for the second, most significant, phase of *Uphold Democracy*. The crowd rejoiced jubilantly, even deliriously. M. Aristide had just contradicted the Haitian proverb: "One cannot return an egg to the belly of a hen after she has laid it". Indeed, the egg had been returned to the belly of the hen.

The plane landed at the International Airport in Port-au-Prince. After honors had been presented by a military battalion, a convoy of helicopters with President Aristide on board headed towards the National Palace, occupied since September 19, 1994 by US troops. On arriving there, the repatriated Haitian president, under the powerful protection of the claws of the Eagle, elatedly climbed the steps of the platform set up on the porch of the Palace. There, foreign delegations, members of the diplomatic corps, representatives of the countries known as friends of Haiti (USA, France, Canada, Argentina, Venezuela), officials of the Malval government, special guests and the staff of the army were already waiting, all in their allotted seats. Outside the Palace, hanging on to the iron fences, the people waited joyfully to hear the speech of their leader.

However, these enthusiastic supporters were disappointed at not being able to see M. Aristide directly during his speech, because he was standing behind a bulletproof glass screen for the sake of his safety, regardless of how this was assured, in theory, by the GIs and US Intelligence Service agents.

On this day, October 15, 1994, there was a renaissance of hope for the Haitian people. With the firmly pledged support of the international community, there was no doubt that the country would enjoy a new beginning. The entire nation hung on the restored president's every word, savoring this message of hope, on which depended the future of the Haitian people.

This speech, distributed in several languages, was indeed a message of hope. Here are the most relevant fragments:

Today is October 15. Today is the day on which the sun of democracy has awoken never to sleep again. Today is the day in which the light of reconciliation shines in the morning, at noon and in the evening. In the morning, I promise abundant security; at noon, yet more security; and in the evening, security that requires no payment.

Security generates peace; peace is the atmosphere that allows political parties to develop, to multiply themselves, to flourish in complete liberty. This is the atmosphere that allows senators, representatives, mayors and members of Communal Sections Administrative Councils (CASECs) to fulfill their missions according to the prescriptions of the Constitution.

...

The individual efforts of all world citizens committed to democracy share responsibility for the great hope for the future that today symbolizes. You who traveled with us home to Haiti demonstrate that our journey with the people of Haiti continues. Your words, your energy, your enthusiasm, your spirit are rewarded at this momentous first step towards lasting peace. With you, again and again, we shall continue to say "No!" to violence! "No!" to vengeance! "Yes!" to reconciliation!

Today we embark on a new beginning, ready to share peace, reconciliation and respect among all our citizens. The success of this mission in this small corner of the universe will reflect the kind of new world order that we can create.

…

Today, with the day and the night reconciled, a new future is opened to us. We have found together—women and men, poor and rich, military and civilian, minors and adults—an era of tolerance and justice, and we weave interlaced bonds of love and solidarity. (*Haïti en Marche*, October 19, 1994, p. 16.)

The heated, exclusive language of 1991 had disappeared and given way to moderate, inclusive speech from the restored president. The slogans: "'Yes!' to reconciliation, 'No!' to revenge" were hammered out in several languages, so that the change of course should be perfectly clear to all Haitians and also to foreigners who were concerned about the struggle of the Haitian people for a better life. Moreover, President Aristide judged it necessary and useful to strike some poses while asking the multitude to repeat in Creole these magic words, which they did willingly.

M. Aristide preached "safety for all, safety in the morning, at noon and in the evening, abundant safety". "Not a single drop more of blood should fall on the land of Haiti", he exclaimed.

Everyone was fascinated. The man seemed truly to have changed, to the satisfaction of everyone. The *Haïti Observateur*, a weekly magazine hitherto very critical of President Aristide, expressed this frame of mind unequivocally in its leading article. Under the title "Finally, Reconciliation!" this journal made the following relevant remarks at the time:

> We are relieved when we note that at his arrival in Port-au-Prince last Saturday (15 October), President Aristide, restored to office, repeated more than once the magic word—"reconciliation"—and said he is opposed to "vengeance".
>
> We applaud the priest-president as well as the Haitian bishops, who, from now on, find themselves on the same wavelength—that of reconciliation. We hope that President Aristide will be able to convince his supporters about the advantages of a rule of law, a society which functions under the rule of law, instead of a country submitted to the law of the jungle.
>
> We dare to believe that President Aristide will succeed this time. Nevertheless, the peasant in us makes us recall the wisdom of our humble brothers and sisters, who use their beautiful Creole proverbs to express profound truths: "It is easy to take a snake to school, but to make it sit is another story". May President Aristide, who understands well the psychology of snakes, display his ability to discipline them! (*Haïti Observateur*, October 19–26, 1994, p. 14.)

However, in this environment of excessive confidence, an event that deserved attention occurred on the very next day. On the evening of October 16, the rumor circulated that the new commander of the army, General Jean-Claude Duperval, was planning a *coup d'état* against M. Aristide. Mobilized by unknownmasterminds, groups of partisans, already over-excited by the return of their leader, occupied the streets in a threatening manner. It was like Attila at the gates of the city. Anything could happen.

Fortunately, an official statement from the army headquarters, and the intervention of the US occupation forces quickly restored calm. However, during the night, making someone's catchphrase a reality, the crowd destroyed, set fire to, or ransacked the military stations and outposts throughout the country. At Gonaïves, several houses of former partisans of the putschist regime were looted, among them the home of General Duperval's mother. Analyzing this outrageous event, a perceptive person could discern the outlines of a message that portended a dark future for the country, because, as the *Haïti Observateur* had observed, the actions of the zealous supporters of the president contradicted the speech of reconciliation that he had made the day before.

However, the presence of the foreign soldiers in Haiti was intended to prevent the repetition of such misdeeds. Indeed, the troops of the Multinational Force were to remain in Haiti for a certain period to establish "a secure and stable environment" in the country. After that, they would be replaced by another detachment from the United Nations, which would then have the mission of maintaining the established climate of security.

The presence of the US soldiers in the land, guaranteeing peace in the streets and among families, brought relief to everyone, the role of these troops, known to all, being to allow all Haitian citizens, winners and losers, to be able to go about their business freely and in complete safety.

On this last point, the political community felt so secure that new political parties arose to life. The Unified Front for the National Liberation of Haiti (FULNH) of Raphaël Bazin, the Movement for National Integration (MIN) of Mireille Durocher Bertin, and the Institutional and Reformist Convergence (CRI) of Paul Arcelin announced their entry in the political arena to take part in the democratic struggle. It was in this environment, in November 1994, that a group of citizens founded the Reformist Coalition for the Development of Haiti in Democracy and Order (CREDDO) Party of which we are the leader. Had not President Aristide himself wished, in his message of return, to see "political parties ... develop, multiply and function in complete freedom"? Every Haitian citizen was thus well prepared to accept the rules of the democratic game and to comply with them.

Unfortunately, the atmosphere of festivity and reconciliation evaporated very quickly. In January 1995, President Aristide executed his first act of revenge by announcing, during a press conference, the dismantling of the Armed Forces of Haiti. This deliberate political decision was the first in a series of initiatives that would soon be seen as detrimental to the future of the young Haitian democracy and that would have an unquestionably negative effect on the problem that concerns us in this book: the phenomenon of insecurity in Haiti.

CHAPTER II

UNFORTUNATE POLITICAL CHOICES

In an article published at the beginning of 1995, journalist Pierre-Raymond Dumas was wondering what the future would be like if the people and politicians of Haiti did not take certain steps to prevent and fight the phenomenon of insecurity that threatened to spread throughout the whole country. He wrote:

> Faced with a community that is on the verge of a police vacuum, faced with this army broken into small pieces, a word comes obsessively to mind and is on everyone's lips—a word that must be used with caution: insecurity. This word has become, little by little, like the phrase "the high cost of living", the obligatory theme of all political speech whether in the Lavalas camp or the opposition....
>
> The return of President Aristide to power seems to have put an end to—or perhaps muted—the permanent agitation, the *dechoukaj* ["uprooting", referring to the kind of widespread violence that attended the ending of the Duvalier regime]. For the moment, the random *dechoukaj* is over; it is making room for consensus, national reconciliation, pluralism and tolerance, for respect for the right to vote. All the speeches testify to this big change in society. What will the future be like under such conditions? Its

characteristics can already be perceived. Appeasement should be the axis, the major theme. Family, urban life, decentralization and management of leisure, political relations and employment, the State: It is a question of whether to build what everyone now wants or to rebuild what is in ruins....

It is not fears and silences that are required, but intentions. It will be a question of creating professional policemen.... A police force worthy of the name is necessary to control the ravaging effects of drug trafficking, gangster activity, to guarantee the maintenance of public peace ... ("Insécurité et Demain?" ["Insecurity and Tomorrow?], *Le Nouvelliste, December 30, 1994–January 2, 1995,* p. 22.)

Haitian intellectuals thus seemed to have perceived clearly the path that needed to be taken by the authorities and society in order to halt the progress of the growing insecurity that gained more ground in Haiti each day: consensus, reconciliation, pluralism, tolerance, respect for the right to vote. The political choices facing those in power remained a determining factor for the success or failure of any program of economic and social recovery of the country.

Any democratic regime must be based on honest electoral competition, an independent judiciary, political pluralism, a parliamentary opposition (whether a majority or a minority), a free, unfettered press, a non-partisan police force, respect for personal freedom, tolerance, and the free functioning of national institutions.

However, in January 1995, those in power clearly

demonstrated their adoption of a political policy that did not tally with these premises. The implementation of this policy, beginning with the unilateral, unconstitutional and arbitrary decision of the executive branch of government to abolish the army as a national institution, was also characterized by intolerance towards their political partners, the politicization of the existing judicial and police services, the indecent manipulation of the electoral system to the exclusive profit of the ruling clique, and many other changes that could only have a negative impact on the security of the Haitian population.

A. The Dismantling of the Army

Well before 1994, President Jean-Bertrand Aristide had announced the policy that he intended to apply concerning the Haitian armed forces on being restored to power. This is what he wrote in 1993:

> It is also necessary that we rebuild the army and the police: a task as overwhelming as it will be to overcome the divorce between them and the people. The leading groups, who are guilty of crimes against humanity, must be brought to justice. A great many soldiers who have been abused and brainwashed were panicked by a fear of unemployment or of the disintegration of their institution. Others were afraid or found no other solution but to obey. Some deserted, and some officers were demoted or dismissed by the general staff.

> The people have always been victimized by the army. In the name of love, because I have been faithful to the cause of non-violence for twenty years, I have opposed the law of retaliation. I have acted and I will act to create a commission of inquiry to restore and purify the army; the commission will determine responsibility without judging

the army collectively. The victims know me. We will have to create the means for this change: those who drive the tanks and those with empty stomachs who cry out their need for dignity should know they are part of the same family.... (*Aristide, An Autobiography*, p. 163).

Moreover, on his return to the country on October 15, 1994, President Aristide did not hesitate to express confidence in the Haitian military once more. In the speech that he delivered on this historical occasion, he addressed them in these terms:

Officers, non-commissioned officers, soldiers, I come to bring you the spirit of peace. Together, hand in hand, we shall rebuild our country, through reconciliation. The whole world watches Haiti very closely. We are an example to all who champion the realization of good causes. Violence, no! Revenge, no! Reconciliation, yes! (*Haïti en Marche*, October 19, 1994, p. 20.)

President Aristide finally confirmed this frame of mind after his return to Haiti, during a press conference held at the National Palace on October 19, 1994. *Le Nouvelliste* reported the president's words as follows:

"I am the president of those who fought for my return and of those who did not want the return," said the Head of State, who took advantage of this meeting with the press "to plead many times for reconciliation between all Haitians and the creation of a legitimate opposition, while asserting in 11 points that the professionalization of the Armed Forces and the separation of the police and the army remain the priorities of his program". (*Le Nouvelliste*, October 20 1994, p. 1.)

However, contrary to these numerous assertions, in January

1995, President Aristide announced his decision to dismantle the Armed Forces of Haiti (FAD'H), confusing the military institution with the men who serve in it. This decision, a serious challenge to the Constitution and the laws then in force, was relayed by the defense minister, General Wilthan Lhérisson, in a manner suggesting that it concerned something trivial: "The army does not exist any more", he said casually, echoing President Aristide. In fact, this government decision, significant though it may seem, was authenticated by no official document.

The dismantling of the FAD'H necessarily harmed the plan for the security of the whole country. Why?

The army has had to deal with a broad variety of tasks in Haitian society. Indeed, it is the overly general character of its mission that has endangered its existence at this turning point in the nation's history and that has also been used as a pretext to charge the Haitian military institution with responsibility for every evil in the country. What was the role of the FAD'H in the Haitian community prior to 1995?

The constitutional and lawful mission of the FAD'H includes land, sea and air defense; protecting families, stores and industrial facilities; defending strategic facilities (the dams at Péligre, the telecommunications stations, the airports); policing the cities and the rural areas; guarding the borders; and more. At the same time, the army of 7,000 soldiers was charged with the task of fighting narco-traffickers and smugglers, ensuring the reliable operation of the navigational aids in the Haitian ports and the telecommunication stations throughout the country, and many other services whose continuity had to be assured.

However, no consideration was made of the danger to general safety that this brutal rupture in the culture of the country represented, nor of the patent vacuum that the absence of an army was creating in Haiti, a country brought to the baptismal font by the military. The vacuum persisted for a long time and so had a negative impact on the safety of the whole population.

Not only was the decision to dismantle the army abrupt, but also the files of the army disappeared after the 1994 invasion and are still beyond the reach of those in charge of national security. This incomparable loss means that from the very beginning, the new security forces have been deprived of a valuable instrument that would help their investigators enormously in their job of tracking down the perpetrators of crimes and offenses.

Not only was this considerable portion of the nation's memory displaced, but also all of the files concerning the nation's security from a strategic perspective, as well as from a political or criminal perspective, were reported as missing. The plans for the defense or protection of the country, the inventory of important sites that must be protected, the files of dangerous criminals, the cryptographic files representing several years of patient compilation, all had vanished or were no longer available. The new security forces were obliged to start again from scratch.

Concerning the security of the cities and of the countryside, the prolonged indecision was fatal. The delinquents had time to proliferate. Vulnerable commercial and industrial enterprises were for a time obliged to provide themselves with their own surveillance systems or to hire a private company for this purpose. Many private homes and schools had to encumber their budget with a provision for their protection, one of many factors that substantially raised the cost of living.

Thus, a new phenomenon was born in Haiti, and a new class of businessmen has made its appearance: the security merchants. The companies or agencies of safety have proliferated. No commercial enterprise risks operating without security agents posted at its door. Government officials everywhere, at every level of public administration, are flanked by bodyguards, a state of affairs that formerly was seldom seen. Today, everyone feels it necessary to fill as much as possible the great vacuum created by the absence of the military.

As for the countryside, it has been left to its own devices. The absence of the structures that formerly ensured the surveillance of crops and of rural life leaves the peasants without assistance. Harvests, cattle, chicken coops and irrigation rights are no longer protected from the actions of gangsters, delinquents or profiteers. The law of the jungle applies, with everyone having to manage for themselves. Consequently, peasants are often compelled to dispense justice for themselves.

Admittedly, there was much abuse in the countryside that needed to be corrected. The section chief, who headed the rural police, was a true autocrat. With the communal section deprived of a court, the task of judging litigation between peasants (concerning the destruction of harvests by cattle, conflicts in the distribution of irrigation times, etc.) fell to the section chief, and there was no possibility of appealing against his decisions. Needless to say, such a system led to corruption and abuse and had to be corrected. However, surely a responsible political power could have made the necessary corrections without creating this dangerous vacuum that affects the safety of the peasants? Moreover, now with the communal section deprived of police protection, those who fill the vacuum, being members of political groups but lacking any legal mandate, often exhibit the same reprehensible behavior towards the peasants as the former section chiefs did.

In general, the dominant position of the Haitian Army in society constituted the fundamental cause of the perpetration of a number of abuses that were blamed on members of the military institution. This fact was well known, and, from both a national and an international perspective, everyone desired the formation of an army separate from the police force in Haiti. Thus, considering the problems existing at the time, ordering the dismantling of the institution guarding the national flag is simply an aberrant idea which could not help but lead to a general insecurity.

Furthermore, it is not possible to conceive the establishment of a rule of law in Haiti without respect for the Constitution, a constitution put into force after a popular referendum in March 1987 in which the participation exceeded 80%, and in which more than 90% of the votes cast during a poll approved it—a constitution that prescribes the existence of a military force.

Incidentally, here is an opinion published in 1994 in a pro-Aristide newspaper:

> The law concerning the separation of the police force from the army, a constitutional requirement, was foreshadowed last July in the Governors' Island Agreement and in the Pact of New York, in accordance with the 1987 Constitution. Everything was signed and approved by the protagonists of the Haitian crisis. All Haitian institutions must work diligently towards the implementation of this constitutional principle. For this purpose, a bill was submitted to the examination and vote of the Haitian Parliament. No one, regardless of his or her authority, can be exempted from extending due respect to the directions of the Constitution or can disparage it. The new law is a constitutional requirement. Authority must remain with the Constitution. (*16 décembre Magazine*, February 1994, p. 3.)

We are of the same opinion. As the geographer George Anglade said: "Unquestionably, our executive functions urgently need to be redistributed between the presidency controlling the army, and the government controlling the police". (*Cartes sur Table,* Volume I, p. 18.) This is the voice of reason, because if—as some would have us believe—the abuses committed by members of the army were a consequence of the harmful character of the institution itself, then these abuses would have ceased following the dismissal of the army. Given the persistence of such a situation after the replacement of the FAD'H by the National Police Force of Haiti (PNH), one must concede that the source of the evil is somewhere other than in the nature of the military institution.

B. The Policy of Intolerance

At the announcement of the dismantling of the FAD'H, observers understood *ipso facto* that the appeasing speech delivered on October 15, 1994 was only a decoy. Two months after this decision, intolerance revealed its harmful presence during the brutal assassination, in broad daylight, of lawyer Mireille Durocher Bertin, a prominent figure among those opposed to the Aristide government.

However, two days after the perpetration of this odious crime, which national and international opinion classified as a political crime, the same speech of reconciliation, decorated with a promise to hold free and honest elections, was repeated by President Aristide at the time of the historical visit to Haiti by the president of the United States, Bill Clinton. Taking into account the political crime just committed in Port-au-Prince, this speech was perceived as a renewed personal commitment by President Aristide, in the presence of the leader of the most powerful nation on the planet, to promote tolerance and to return to the path of reconciliation. Here is a fragment of the speech:

> All men are born equal; their creator has provided them with certain inalienable rights, such as the right to life, to liberty and to the pursuit of happiness. To share this happiness around the democratic table, the sun of reconciliation has shone from October 15 until today and will continue to shine. Reconciliation is, and remains, the pivot around which orbit justice, peace, respect, human dignity and economic progress. Accordingly, we walk resolutely towards the organization of free, honest and democratic elections. If democracy were a river, the principle "one man, one vote" would be the bridge.

(*Le Nouvelliste*, April 3, 1995, p. 14.)

Thus, President Aristide made a threefold commitment, to tolerance, national reconciliation, and credible elections open to all without distinction.

However, at the time of the elections scheduled for that year, the spirit of intolerance was even more evident. It made a brazen appearance during the formation of the Provisional Electoral Council (CEP) charged with the mission of organizing this poll. The CEP, which fell short of conformity with the Constitution, could have been the product of a consensus, which would give it a democratic appearance. But the government did not consider any of the suggestions formulated by the political parties, all of which were excluded from participation in the formation of this new council.

In addition to this patent intention of excluding others from the electoral process, actions were initiated against some political leaders under cover of false and fanciful accusations. The phrase "plot against the interior safety of the State" was again haphazardly applied to impose silence on political adversaries of the Lavalas regime, forcing many into exile.

After the transfer of power on February 7, 1996, the same policy of intolerance was adopted by M. René Préval, who was elected, with a low percentage of popular participation, to the presidency of the Republic. The slogan *"Makout pa ladan"* ("Macoutes, stay outside") reappeared. Any person expressing a political opinion different from that preached by the ruling party was ostracized. Even stubborn opponents of the Duvalier regime, such as Pastor Antoine Leroy, were labeled "Macoutes". This atmosphere of intolerance was clearly evident in the US State Department's report on human rights for 1996. Here is a fragment:

> In August [1996] police arrested 15 former soldiers, 2 party activists, and 2 other persons meeting at the Port-au-Prince headquarters of an opposition political party, the Mobilization for National Development (MDN); in February, police had harassed MDN party members outside the capital. The authorities later charged those arrested in August with threatening state security. Over the next 2 months, police arrested several other MDN members and former soldiers on similar charges and issued a warrant for the arrest of the party's secretary general, Hubert de Ronceray. In September police also arrested a less well-known opposition political figure, Carmen Christophe, a former mayor of Port-au-Prince. The leader of the opposition political party CREDDO, former military ruler Prosper Avril, likewise faced a warrant for his arrest on similar charges. The authorities also conducted illegal searches with the apparent intent of harassing opposition political figure Duly Brutus and members of his family. (U.S. Department of State, *Haiti Country Report on Human Rights Practices for 1996*, released by the Bureau of Democracy, Human Rights, and Labor, January 30, 1997.)

Partisans or former allies of the current regime who dissociated themselves from the Lavalas movement were not spared. The plainest example is the case of M. Léon Jeune, former minister and the person prematurely selected, in 1995, as the *dauphin*, or successor, to M. Aristide as president of the Republic. An armed commando raided his home at night and arrested him.

The protests raised at the time of the elections of April 6, 1997 again confirmed the fact that the government had not deviated one iota from its policy of intolerance. This policy, accompanied by intransigence on the part of the authorities, was the cause of the rejection of the results of this poll by the Haitian political parties and the civil society, which accused the regime of wanting to monopolize the whole political arena, ignoring even former Lavalas allies. This situation created a deadlock that would last until the end of the mandate of the deputies and two thirds of the senators, in January 1999, culminating in a serious political crisis.

In February 1997, at the expiry of the ten-year period stipulated in the Constitution for the exclusion from public affairs of former partisans of the Duvalier regime, President René Préval made no democratic speech inviting those against whom this constitutional provision was directed to come forward and participate fully, now as rehabilitated citizens, in the construction of the State. On the contrary, the political parties having been solicited to take part in workshops sponsored by the International Republican Institute (IRI) in 1998, President Préval publicly criticized this initiative, in his official speech on the occasion of the Day of the Flag in Arcahaie on May 18, 1998, denouncing the presence of certain Duvalierist political groups at these democratic meetings. President Préval described the initiative of the political leaders in meeting at such a conference as an ideological *coup d'état* against his authority.

Thus, no ideology that differed from that of the ruling party was allowed to emerge. The highest political authority of the country officially condemned the very principle of ideological pluralism. Faced with this public demonstration of intolerance, the Haitian Conference of Political Parties (CHPP), which developed from these workshops and to which 26 leaders of various political persuasion were signatories, was effectively dissolved. A few months later, the IRI would also be forced to terminate its program and leave Haiti.

According to the views of the Lavalas party, there can be no question either of sharing power or of democratic succession. Consequently, there can be no question of honest and credible popular consultation. Their acknowledged principle is that of only one catechism: the Lavalas creed. All opponents or adversaries who dissent from this creed are threatened or have to live in a considerable state of danger.

By this time, the attitude of intolerance—the source of insecurity and instability—far from improving, was conversely radicalized. Now it has been accentuated even further by combining with a new approach: a demonstration of politically motivated violence towards the political parties by the popular organizations (OP), forcing everyone to endorse the views of the government.

Into this situation has been born an unfamiliar and macabre new phenomenon, popularly dubbed *"chimère"* ["chimera"], referring to the "fabulous fire-breathing monster of mythology with the head and torso of a lion, the abdomen of a goat and the tail of a dragon" (*Petit Robert*). The *"chimères"*, a new breed of anarchists, troublemakers in the pay of the legitimate authorities, are used like shields or infantry to intimidate citizens and to sow terror among the population whenever the government wants to impose on the nation an idea or insane political project. Nowadays, it is common for them to be involved in verbal threats or aggression against political leaders, arson of private property, destruction of private motor vehicles, disruption of the business of street traders, assaults and crimes against citizens, disruptive incursions into public offices and even courts, etc.—and all with impunity!

Sometimes, even state properties are not spared—for example, in cases of fire or the ransacking of electoral materials or offices, vehicles, or police stations. In 1999, a senior police officer from the town of Mirebalais was killed after being submitted to the torment of *"pèlebren"* ("necklacing"). In 2000, another officer was almost assassinated the same way in the center of the capital, Port-au-Prince. The main problem is that whereas in the past the "Macoutes" had some chiefs to whom one could sometimes complain to obtain redress, no one knows where to go or whom to address after having suffered harm caused by these "chimères".

In an article published on September 26, 2000, M. Jean-Claude Bajeux, a former minister for culture in the Aristide government, exposed the gravity of the situation:

> The speech of violence is always present on the waves of our radio stations. It contaminates all kinds of claims. We have heard people saying, "If the street is not white tomorrow morning, it will become very red". Even declarations concerning "peace" are formulated in

a context that makes them threatening and fear-provoking. A leader of one popular organization threatened to eliminate all opposition during the following five years. He even enumerated the leaders who would be the target of this "elimination". What exactly is the content of these euphemisms: "to neutralize", "to eliminate", "to remove", "to draw aside", "to put aside", and in Creole, "to dismantle"?

This type of speech is all the more worrying in that it is followed by no effort from the political godfathers of these militants to correct these deviations, and to take advantage of the opportunity to "teach a lesson". ("Pour Qui sont ces Serpents ...?" ["Who are the Serpents For?"], *Le Nouvelliste*, October 3, 2000, p. 15.)

This text illustrates well (as if it were still necessary) the role and importance of these "chimères" in this regime of intolerance, and the laxity of the legal authorities in addressing the problem. It clearly indicates the pure and simple repudiation, by the Lavalas regime, of ideological pluralism, multi-partisanship and the principle of democratic succession.

On top of everything else, this policy of intolerance is supported, naturally, by the law-enforcement agencies—police, courts and prisons—which are used as a Damoclean sword suspended over the heads of citizens who promote doctrines contrary to the ones that are espoused by the Lavalas party.

C. Control over Law Enforcement

Another factor supporting criminal activity in Haiti is the control that the executive branch of power has exerted over the police force and the courts. After the re-establishment of the legitimate government in October 1994, a reform of the national law-enforcement agencies was initiated in Haiti with the assistance of the international community. The task to be performed was immense, arduous and exciting; but far from accomplishing this reorganization with objectivity and impartiality, the restored executive chose rather to put the law-enforcement agencies at the service of its own interests.

1. Control over Justice

Since 1994, the desire of the executive to control the law-enforcement agencies to achieve its own political ends has been obvious. Until 2000, citizens who obtained release orders from the examining magistrate, and people released after jury trial, were kept in prison on the orders of the executive, which did not approve of the courts' decisions. As an illustration of the scandalous character of such behavior by the executive, we mention the case of M. Bob Lecorps. This Haitian citizen, after being declared "not guilty" by a jury and released by the court in June 1996, was kept in prison on the personal order of President René Préval. On being informed that the jury had issued a "not-guilty" verdict, the President declared to the media that he did not approve the jury's decision. M. Lecorps did not regain his freedom until four years later, in January 2000, again on the personal order of the president.

Often judicial enquiries are blocked, protracted or simply never commenced. It frequently happens that arrested delinquents are released without explanation. Sometimes suspects are identified within governmental institutions but the law-enforcement agencies take no action. The executive is able to exert control over the justice system at several levels:

Initially, at the level of the government prosecutor or the Attorney's office. Through this authority, the executive exerts an absolute grip on the freedom of the citizen who may be arrested at any time on a legal pretext and held in custody. By this institutional means also, the executive often manages to keep citizens who have obtained release orders from the examining magistrate, or even those whom the courts have declared to be innocent, in prison for political reasons.

Subsequently, at the level of the examining magistrate. Through this authority, the executive can prolong preliminary investigations. While this judicial enquiry proceeds, the citizen will be deprived of his freedom, sometimes for two, three or even four years, without his case ever being brought before the court.

Then, at the level of the judges. More than 13 years after the promulgation of the Constitution, the procedures for legally appointing judges still have not been implemented. Making full use of its *de facto* power to appoint and remove judges at will, the executive takes advantage of this situation, treating them like vassals.

Finally, at the level of the prisons. Many citizens who have never been brought before a judge or condemned by a court have been detained in prison, under the authority of the ministry of justice, for political reasons.

This situation, at the very least alarming, is well highlighted in a report of the US State Department on the state of human rights in Haiti, dated February 1999:

> The authorities have been known to use the criminal justice system to retaliate against politically undesirable persons and have detained such persons in open defiance of court orders for their release. Persons detained in this manner also may be involved in private disputes with influential political figures. As of year's end, the ICM [Civil Mission International] was tracking 67 cases in which due process was not followed or persons apparently were detained for political reasons. During the year, the authorities failed to execute release orders issued by judges in at least seven high-profile and politically sensitive cases. (U.S. Department of State, *Haiti Country Report on Human Rights Practices for 1998*, released by the Bureau of Democracy, Human Rights, and Labor, February 26, 1999).

2. Control over the Police Force

With regard to the police force, the question of its independence and of its non-political nature has posed a problem since its formation. It should be remembered that in 1994, when the new Haitian police force was being organized, the organizers had the bad idea of recruiting the personnel for the new institution from among the Haitian boat-people who were being detained behind the barbed wire fences of the refugee camp in Guantanamo, Cuba. Everyone knows that these refugees were mostly savage partisans of President Aristide, then in exile, who had taken to the sea as "boat people" during the putschist regime. Thus, the new Haitian police force—supposedly a non-political institution—included, from its inception, political activists and supporters of a political leader who fostered the project to return to effective power.

Consequently, the new police force got off to a very bad start with regard to the non-political nature of the institution and its neutrality in the execution of its duties. It was destined to become an armed force at the service of one man or political party. Subsequently, although no political affiliation was officially required of the applicants as a selection criterion when joining the police force, attentive observers will recall that the first graduates of the Academy of Police in 1995 publicly promised allegiance to the Lavalas movement. They were asked to conclude their oath with the Lavalas' slogan: *"Yon sèl nou fèb, ansanm nou fò, ansanm ansanm nou se Lavalas"*. ("Alone, we are weak, together we are strong, all of us together, we are the floods"). Thus, the new institution had plainly and publicly affirmed its allegiance to a political movement.

By observing the evolution of the police force, one can see that the effects of this bad beginning persisted in the years following its inception. The police force was too often implicated in illegal although official acts, which displayed the devotion of many of its members to political masters. At worst, some of them were often shown to be involved in reprehensible activities, ranging from drug trafficking to massacring citizens.

The politicization of the police force is well highlighted by

Mr. Adama Dieng, an independent expert from the United Nations. After a mission carried out in Haiti from July 27 to August 8, 2000, he wrote this in the report that he addressed to the Secretariat-General:

> Another example that reinforces the tendency towards politicization of the police is the case of the incidents which occurred at Maïssade on 11 and 12 July 2000, and which allegedly included illegal arrest and detention, maltreatment and destruction of property. These events were the subject of an investigation conducted by advisers to MICAH (Human Rights section). Their investigation showed that the Maïssade incidents were the work of members of the Espace de concertation and members of Fanmi Lavalas. They also injured persons and damaged houses. The investigators noted that searches and arrests made on the basis of information provided by members of Fanmi Lavalas were directed only at members of the *Espace de concertation*. No homes of members of Fanmi Lavalas were searched. The police did not even question, much less arrest, the individuals implicated in the attacks carried out on the afternoon of 12 July. (United Nations, *Report on the situation of human rights in Haiti*, Document A/55/335 (28 August 2000), Section III, par. 23.)

This is as if to say that the police force was at the service of *Fanmi Lavalas* ["Lavalas Family"].

At the time of the elections of May 21, 2000, the active participation of the PNH in electoral fraud for the benefit of the same party, *Fanmi Lavalas*, was also denounced, a fact reported by other political parties, by the president of the CEP, and recently by police officers as recorded in the Dominican press (*El Siglo*). This public implication of police interference in the electoral process leads us to consider another question in our study: the political control exerted over the national electoral institution by the current government.

D. Control over the Electoral System

The *coup d'état* of September 1991 having constituted a barrier to the democratic process, it was necessary to await a return to constitutional order, which occurred in 1994, before hoping that fair elections might finally be held in Haiti. More than ever, this was the moment to make the right choice: the creation of a new and independent electoral system capable of ensuring neutrality between the candidates at the elective functions of the Haitian administration.

But what did we observe?

Far from following the path indicated by the Constitution for the formation of the provisional electoral council, or otherwise consulting with all the political parties to find a compromise acceptable to the majority, an arbitrary approach was adopted by the executive. Claiming to be using a method based on the prescriptions of the 1987 Constitution concerning the formation of the permanent electoral council, President Aristide proceeded in the following way to select the nine members of the aforementioned council:

The president of the Republic designated three members.

Three members were chosen by the Supreme Court, the majority of whose judges had just been unilaterally and directly nominated by President Aristide without the constraints imposed by the Constitution.

Three members—among whom, paradoxically, was a prominent Lavalas militant in 1991—were designated by the Senate.

Therefore, seven of the nine members of this new version of the electoral council, created at the beginning of 1995, belonged body and soul to the ruling party. Thus, within this council, where all important decisions are decided by the votes of the members, President Aristide had deliberately engineered a more-than-comfortable majority to attain his own ends.

However, in any democratic system, the holding of genuine, free, honest and credible elections constitutes a reliable means of guaranteeing the stability of the State. This stability yields domestic peace and safety. When, in an ostensibly democratic environment, a regime seizes control of the electoral system, it creates and maintains a climate of tension among the political forces and, consequently, undermines the safety of the population. Moreover, when political institutions lack legitimacy, arbitrariness reigns, attended by its train of consequences—social strains, political confrontations, administrative corruption, political persecutions, discord and many other factors—thus generating an unhealthy environment that is conducive to the reprehensible activities of delinquents and gangsters.

Let us recapitulate. Concerning elections in Haiti, what have we observed since 1995?

The legislative, municipal and local elections of June 25,

1995 took place against a backdrop of exclusion and manipulation. The results were disputed by the independent and opposition parties, so numerous and blatant were the irregularities. The presidential elections held in December 1995 were boycotted by the majority of the political parties, as a consequence of the contempt of the authorities for their claims relating to the results of the June 25 ballots. Because of this boycott, only 15% of the population had taken part in the poll. Then, the elections of April 6, 1997 were organized, at which the participation rate reached barely 5%. With regard to this last poll, the second round, required by law, was never held.

In spite of these disappointing results, the policy of maintaining the CEP under the full control of the executive did not change. This manipulation of the electoral system contributed greatly to increased insecurity in the country. Professor Leslie Manigat, speaking about the Haitian situation in 1998, represents the electoral issue as a component of what he calls "the Gordian knot at the level of the political crisis":

> On the political level, the electoral crisis evident since the fraudulent elections of June 1995 worsened during those of April 1997, whose disputed results remained outstanding without any possibility of proceeding to a second turn nineteen months later! This blocking of the electoral system, in the context of the boycott of the elections by the opposition and the independent political parties, becomes complicated by electoral abstentions expressed by a popular participation rate of 25% in the second turn of the 1995 parliamentary and legislative elections, 15% for the December 1995 presidential elections and less than 5% for the April 1997 senatorial and local elections. This is also a component

of the Gordian knot at the level of the political crisis. (*Les Cahiers du CHUDAC* [*The Notebooks of CHUDAC*], nos 14–15, October–December 1998, p. 39.)

The failure of the April 6, 1997 elections constituted a major factor in the aggravation of the situation of instability and insecurity in Haiti. In January 1999, with the majority of elected officials in the parliament having finally reached the term of their mandate without properly constitutional elections having being held, President Préval profited from this *fait accompli* by deciding to dissolve the parliament, plunging the country even more deeply into crisis.

This is the context in which the formation of the last electoral council, charged with the mission of organizing new elections for the legislative, municipal and local offices, was announced. Has this latest version of the CEP renounced the notion of manipulating the electoral system as practiced by the executive? Far from it!

In 1999, in the new provisional council, the government took six seats and conceded to a coalition of five political parties named *Espace de Concertation* [Consultation Forum] the opportunity of designating the three other members. The other sectors of the political community were kept away! Instead of seeking a consensus to form a truly credible council, President Préval was satisfied with the consent of five political parties among more than 50 evolving legitimately in the national political arena. With six members against three, the executive has the lion's share of influence within this council, where a decision requires a simple majority of votes.

Thus, it is hardly surprising that the elections of May 21, 2000 were a fiasco. The pre-election climate, dominated by a spirit of exacerbated intolerance, was one of the most violent since 1995. During an electoral campaign that was difficult for all the political parties—except the incumbent *Fanmi Lavalas*—more than fifteen people (candidates, members and sympathizers of political parties) had been assassinated, among them Légitime Athis and his wife for the *Mouvement Patriotique pour le Sauvetage National* (Patriotic Movement for National Salvage, MPSN), Ducertain Arnaud for the *Parti Démocrate Chrétien Haïtien* (Haitian Christian Democrat Party, PDCH), Branor Sanon for the *Parti Louvri Baryè* (Open the Gate Party, PLB), Ferdinand Dorvil for the *Organisation du Peuple en Lutte* (Organization of the People in Struggle, OPL), to mention only these names. We can also mention the arson, in broad daylight, of the Headquarters of the *Espace de Concertation*, which, after having major disagreements with the government, has become one of the main opposition groups.

However, despite this sustained climate of violence, the opposition decided to confront the situation, by asking the citizens to perform their civic duty and turn out to cast their votes. On the day of the poll, those who were of voting age did indeed turn out. The opposition parties rubbed their hands gleefully, never suspecting that something quite unprecedented was about to happen once the polling booths had closed and electoral observers had left their posts.

According to reports from the political parties and from journalists, for the first time in the history of the police force in

Haiti, ballot boxes were seized by police officers and official records from the polling stations were falsified by members of the police force. In the morning following the elections, people were astonished to see the streets of Port-au-Prince strewn with marked ballot papers.

To illustrate the blatant domination of the CEP by the executive: the president of the electoral council, M. Léon Manus, an octogenarian, had to flee into exile in the United States "to escape the pressures" that he said he suffered from the executive, and "the death threats" that he received because of his refusal to validate incorrect and fraudulent results.

Following these elections of May 21, 2000, the *Espace de Concertation*, the privileged partner of the government in the implementation of these elections, disgusted by the fraudulence of the poll, called for the resignation of its three members from the CEP. Two of them complied with the order that they received.

Nevertheless, in spite of the denunciation of the many irregularities, the resignation of the two representatives of *Espace de Concertation* and the forced exile of the CEP president M. Léon Manus, President René Préval announced, without embarrassment, that presidential elections would soon be held. Prior to making the announcement, he had already proceeded unilaterally to remodel the CEP by naming three new persons to fill the vacant seats.

The nine members of the electoral council—a constitutionally independent institution—are thus named today by the head of the executive branch of power, M. René Préval, and by him alone, establishing a dangerous precedent. However, M. Préval has never concealed his devotion to a political organization—to *Fanmi Lavalas*, in fact, the party of former president Jean-Bertrand Aristide, candidate for the presidency at the announced elections. This is self-explanatory.

As we have discussed in this chapter, the political decisions made by the executive branch of power in the management of the country—the spirit of revenge, the intolerance, the control of judicial and law-enforcement agencies and the manipulation of the electoral system—could only lead to a climate of tension in the country. This situation created, and still maintains, an atmosphere of intimidation, threats, murderous terrorist attacks and criminal activity in Haiti.

However, besides these pertinent causes, there are other major factors that act as catalysts, starting or stimulating the activities of delinquency, and inevitably contributing to the aggravation of the phenomenon of insecurity in Haiti. We shall study these factors in the next chapter.

CHAPTER III

CATALYSTS OF INSECURITY

At the end of the second millennium, five years after the return to constitutional order in Haiti (thanks to the *Uphold Democracy* operation), Haitians found themselves still exposed to a climate of insecurity that had taken them by surprise. Our terrified intellectuals and scholars have in vain sought the roots, the causes of this overwhelming evil. They have even described the situation as "state terrorism".

Since the State is the sole custodian of the legal means for deterring crimes and offenses, surely it is the responsibility of the State to address the problem of public safety? Surely its impotence in this matter represents a threat to its legitimacy? Surely citizens, for their part, have the right to expect the State to guarantee their safety, thus enabling them to go about their usual business?

Justifiably alarmed by the laxity of the authorities concerning this disconcerting situation, Jean L. Prophète expresses the opinion of a large majority of citizens when he says:

> The climate of insecurity [in Haiti] is an undeniable fact. Neither the will nor the capacity to put an end to it exists. On the contrary, it is maintained in the interest of some hidden power like a far-from-subtle form of state terrorism designed to intimidate—even simply to eliminate—unsubmissive and rebellious people. Thus, the phenomenon of insecurity arises, and is defined in the case of Haiti, as much by the aggressive and fatal nature of the random acts of armed robbery and terrorism, and by their daily multiplication, frequency and regularity, as by the impunity of which the culprits seem to be assured. All the more distressing is the absence of a state institution or an effective constraining governmental force likely to suppress these acts and bring the criminals to court. (Jean L. Prophète, *Inventaire de Fin de Siècle* [*Inventory of the End of the Century*], pp. 22–23.)

At a single stroke, Prophète has identified the catalysts of the climate of insecurity in Haiti: the inability of the authorities to put an end to it, the impunity of which culprits seem to be assured, the frequency and regularity of the assaults and deaths that are not dealt with, and finally, the absence of a political will to counter the phenomenon. Concerning the latter point, we shall analyze the attitude of the foreign forces stationed in Haiti towards this issue during the period covered by our study, to point out their particular responsibility.

A. The Ineffectiveness of Public Services

This point cannot be studied without first considering a related question: Whence comes this phenomenon of insecurity, which currently has a stranglehold on the Haitian people? To answer this fundamental question, we simply put before the reader some ideas on the issue expressed by M. Dominique Joseph:

> For more than two weeks, an increase in the number of acts of slaughter, gangsterism and kidnapping has been recorded. It is in this atmosphere of fear that the nation is fighting and leaving a trail of misery, disappointment, concern, and anguish. Thus, from the city to the countryside, the feeling of fear, which seems to retard the daily routine, is accentuated. Civilians as well as police are anxious....

> By analyzing the situation, one can tell that this insecurity has structural causes and causes arising from the conjuncture. As structural causes, we could mention, among other things, economic misery, unemployment, demographic pressure, etc. At the level of the economic climate, the causes arise from inappropriate political decisions and actions, and from exceptional situations.

> One can also find other reasons for the insecurity that prevails throughout the country:

> 1) We produce almost nothing. Our resources are more and more limited, compared to the rate of population growth. This situation inevitably creates a struggle for life, which takes the form of a stampede for a commodity that is in short supply.

> 2) We note with sadness the collapse of our system of defense and security, the crumbling of our moral values, and institutional and social instability. This produces the impression that no principle, no law, no hierarchical order controls the behavior of individuals. It seems that there exists a moral and legal vacuum, which makes each one of us vulnerable and fragile.

> 3) It also raises the question whether the current insecurity arises from the division and dissatisfaction observed in the various political sectors, division which would cause indifference and form

an environment favorable to any misfortune. (*Le Nouvelliste*, June 5–6, 1996, p. 10.)

Concerning the major cause of insecurity, the ruling party continually accuses former soldiers of the demobilized army. Moreover, although the police force, the press and even the state media have never reported a single case involving a former soldier, this opinion has seemed logical to many since the Head of State himself has not missed a single opportunity to make this accusation. They always justify their opinion by saying that disarmament was not complete on the arrival of the multinational force of occupation in 1994.

This simplistic and unjust way to approach the problem does nothing but worsen the phenomenon. What has in fact happened with regard to the disarmament of former members of the army?

We learn in a report from authorized sources published by *Agence France Presse* [the French Press Agency] that "20,224 weapons were confiscated by the GIs after the landing of September 1994, including 15,985 from the stocks of the army and 4,239 recovered by repurchase". (*Le Nouvelliste*, March 28–29, 1995, p. 2.)

The number of weapons recalled during a repurchase program six months later was even higher. Mr. Michel Renner of the Worldwatch Institute in Washington, DC made the following report concerning the results of this program organized by the US Army in Haiti at the time:

Until March 1995, more than 33,000 weapons had been returned at a total cost of 1.9 million dollars. Weapons in good condition were given to the police force. The rest were melted down. (L'Etat de la Planète 1998, Tableau 8.3, p. 215 [*Editions Economia, 1998. - in Le Nouvelliste* of 11 –15 April 2001, p. 14].)

Thus nearly 50,000 weapons have been recalled. This result can be appreciated by considering the under-equipped body of 7,000 soldiers that was the FAD'H, an institution that kept in its files a receipt and a record for each weapon or item of equipment that it entrusted to its members.

However, while there is a remote possibility that certain former members of the army still hold weapons, it is appropriate to inform the public of an established fact that has always been concealed and only now emerges: Lavalas militants, perhaps thousands of them, still have weapons in their possession. On this subject, the assertions of the former deputy of Cayes, M. Gabriel Fortuné, are more than edifying. Let us listen to them:

Paul Denis was arrested because it was said that he had weapons; but the weapons that Paul Denis possessed, if the reports were true, would have been "weapons of resistance". **All Lavalas militants have in their possession "weapons of resistance"**—and it is these "weapons of resistance" that made Aristide's return to power possible. It is by using these "weapons of resistance" that we destroyed Camp-Perrin. It is by using these "weapons of resistance" that we won in Fort Platon. It is with these "weapons of resistance" that we won in Chantal, that we won in Morency. It is these "weapons of resistance" that destroyed the Haitian Army so that the PNH [National Police Force of Haiti] could be created.

Consequently, following the arrest of Paul Denis, since **I know that every person belonging to the Lavalas movement still has in his possession a "weapon of resistance"**, I ask President

Préval to issue a decree saying that he no longer authorizes "weapons of resistance", so that everyone may go and remit his "weapon of resistance" to the police. (*Radio Vision 2000* news report, May 26, 2000.)

We know that in the chapter "The Armed Forces" in the Constitution, Article 268.1 proclaims that "every citizen has the right to armed self-defense, within the bounds of his domicile, but has no right to carry arms without express well-founded authorization from the chief of police". However, the Constitution by no means grants to citizens the right to hold weapons of war. On the contrary, Article 268.3 prescribes the opposite:

Article 268.3—The Armed Forces have a monopoly on the manufacture, import, export, use and possession of weapons of war and their ammunition, as well as war material.

It is clear that the provisions of the Constitution have been cavalierly trampled under foot in Haiti for some time. However, in all honesty, and without risking discontent of the worst kind, can one transfer the prerogatives of the Armed Forces of Haiti to militant political groups?

This dissenting ex-member of the Haitian parliament, a "Lavalassian" dissident, made these statements at the time of the arrest of M. Paul Denis, another former "Lavalassian", an unsuccessful candidate for the senate in the disputed elections of May 21, 2000. These revelations, coming from the credible voice of a former deputy of the legislative body, make one think of the damage that could be caused by these weapons, which are not registered anywhere and are in the possession of people who perhaps have not received adequate training in handling them properly. The alarming aspect of this greatly disconcerting situation is that these public assertions, so serious that they must be revealed, had no effect on the authorities, who did not pursue the issue. Nobody knows who is authorized to carry heavy weapons in Haiti today. An article published at the beginning of August 2000 is quite explicit on this point of view. Here is an extract:

"On Friday, August 4, at around 11 o'clock in the morning, in the absence of the president [of the senate], a group of candidates from the *Fanmi Lavalas* party in the last elections broke into the institution accompanied by a group of civilians heavily armed with one small caliber machine-gun, two AK47 assault rifles, two T65 assault rifles, four UZI sub-machine-guns, several 9mm pistols, .38 revolvers and grenades."

This is not the scenario of a Hollywood western, it is a detailed report of the visit to the senate of the elected senators during the disputed elections of May 21, made by Senator Edgard Leblanc Junior, president of what remains of the senate of the Republic. (*Le Nouvelliste*, August 4– 6, 2000, p. 1.)

To top everything else, despite the head of the current government's having accused the former soldiers of the demobilized army of being the ones with weapons in their possession, despite a former deputy's affirming that some Lavalas militants still have in their possession weapons that he identifies as "weapons of resistance" and despite the president of the senate's denouncing the fact that members of the ruling political party have heavy weapons in their possession—despite all this a prominent member of the Lavalas movement, Father

Paul Déjean, recently a minister in the current government, makes accusations at an even higher level. Under the title "Minister Paul Déjean thinks that Aristide is an obstacle to democracy", *Le Nouvelliste* has reported:

> The interview granted by Minister Paul Déjean to the journalist Roger Edmond of *Radio Kombit Flamboyant* of Montreal ... has, since that time, been at the center of political news in Port-au-Prince.
>
> Paul Déjean, a former priest, is known to have been one of the closest friends of former president Aristide since well before the latter decided to become involved in politics; and it is for this reason, according to Déjean, that he feels that he has a duty to talk to him today in these strong terms.
>
> "I am the friend of Plato, but I am an even greater friend of the truth," says Déjean, who declares plainly that the former president, "driven by a disproportionate ambition" to gain power, is the person principally responsible for the current political situation of tension, insecurity, crime and disorder. Paul Déjean thinks that Jean-Bertrand Aristide is creating confusion and concern for the express purpose of demonstrating that only he can bring the country back to stability and peace. M. Déjean declares that M. Aristide is currently the biggest obstacle to democracy in Haiti, a democracy that the former president, he says, had a part in restoring to the country.
>
> These are serious declarations, coming from Paul Déjean,

a well-known Lavalas partisan and above suspicion, who does not hesitate to warn Haitians against a recurrence of 1957....

M. Paul Déjean directly accuses former president Jean-Bertrand Aristide of distributing money and weapons to destabilize the country and to create the climate of insecurity with which everyone is familiar. (*Le Nouvelliste*, May 27, 1997, pp. 1–2.) Thus, faced with the extent of the plague of insecurity, the government, politicians, citizens, former partisans of the present regime and others, seized by panic, distressed and disconcerted, all lash out at political leaders, at former heads of state, at former members of the military, at Lavalas militants, at Macoutes, at members of the police force, at the government itself, and even at simple bandits, accusing them of being instigators or sponsors of the many crimes that are committed every day throughout the country. For ourselves, far from following the trend of launching trenchant accusations at random, we would rather say with Jean-Claude Fignolé:

Delinquency, fraud, organized crime, violence—if they have political, economic, social, or even moral causes—mainly find their sustenance (one is tempted to say, their justification) in societies where the State is weak because of the disorganization of its institutions. Then, more and more, day by day, assaults, robberies and assassinations leave the category of the rarity to enter that of the news item. (*Le Nouvelliste*, December 30, 1996-January 2, 1997, p. 7.)

In other words, instead of seeking scapegoats to explain the phenomenon or to clear one's own conscience, it would be advisable to make the State stronger, to organize its penal institutions better and to reinforce the structure of its police force so that investigations succeed, so that the rate of detection of crimes increases and so that more criminals are detected, arrested, brought to trial, judged and sentenced.

There is no doubt that the work of the police, faced with new challenges in recent times, has been made much more difficult and has greatly increased, especially with the resurgence of drug trafficking in Haiti. According to US narcotics agencies, Haiti, with its weakened institutions, has recently become an ideal depot for the routing of cocaine and other harmful substances to the United States. During the period 1995–2000, the quantity of drugs forwarded through Haiti reached a level higher than that during the period of the military *coup d'état*, according to the foreign press.

In an editorial under the title "Drugs Threaten Haiti--and U.S.", the *Miami Herald* said:

Drugs are the greatest threat to the establishment of democracy in Haiti, and the administration must do more to blunt [their] influence.

This poor country is awash in drug money. In a recent two-week period, two small planes with Colombian flags painted on their tails crashed outside the capital. Corruption has infected the justice, customs and port authorities. More than 50 police officers have been dismissed from the fledgling police force for drug trafficking. Said a U.S. Drug Enforcement Administration agent familiar with the agency's operations: "We have a bad situation there. It's a time bomb.'"

Narco-traffickers find it incredibly easy to cozy up to Haitians at all levels of society. And Haiti lacks sufficient political stability to fend off the traffickers' embrace.

....

Washington must take appropriate action before Haiti's weak democratic institutions and infrastructure crumble before the powerful drug lords. Sure, there is enough frustration to go around, especially after using 20,000 American troops to return former president Jean-Bertrand Aristide to power, but the United States cannot back down. (*The Miami Herald*, January 24, 2000, www.herald.com, Editorials.)

This alarming increase in drug trafficking has inevitably been accompanied by a series of criminal acts—assassinations, vendettas, kidnappings, etc.

Another significant factor that further worsens the state of insecurity in the country and complicates the task of the police force is the new practice of emptying the US prisons of delinquents and common criminals of Haitian origin and sending them back to Haiti. This practice totally disrupts the Haitian law-enforcement system, which has no provision for handling such cases. These criminals and delinquents are all the more dangerous for Haitian society because they have acquired sophisticated techniques with which the recently established law-enforcement agencies in Haiti are completely unfamiliar.

Thus, it is easy to understand the difficulties confronted by the police in their efforts to apprehend those responsible for the crimes that are now being committed at frighteningly frequent intervals, crimes that are carried out with heavy weapons that circulate illegally within the country. The Haitian police force, structured as it presently is, cannot face gangsters who are equipped with heavy weapons. To counter this kind of delinquency effectively, a unit specializing in anti-terrorist tactics is needed, a degree of specialization that does not exist in a regular police force.

The FAD'H was dismantled savagely and without any forethought. However, it constituted a barrier that restrained antisocial behavior at a national level. In addition, the abrupt and unexpected removal of this institution created a dangerous vacuum so far as the security of the population is concerned. The absence of any police force in the rural areas and in the majority of the cities and villages of the Republic has created concern among the whole population. At the time when this decision was made, the secretary general of the United Nations acknowledged explicitly that the demolition of the FAD'H was one of the major causes of insecurity in the country.

Indeed, referring to the report submitted by M. Boutros Boutros-Ghali to the Security Council of the United Nations at the beginning of 1995, *Haiti Progrès* commented:

At the security level, M. Boutros-Ghali indicates that there was some notable progress and attempts to show that the current insecurity and criminal activity "are not politically motivated". They are related rather to "a vacuum, as regards the security, rising from the disintegration of the army and the dissolution of the corps of section chiefs", thus "the clear increase in the delinquency and criminal activity in the whole country".... Although it tends to certify that there was considerable progress, the report of the UN secretary-general makes particular mention of the interesting fact that—in its own words—"threats to the future stability of Haiti" are clearly indicated. *(Haiti Progrès*, January 25–31, 1995, p. 1.)

Thus, the then secretary-general of the United Nations, M. Boutros-Ghali, saw in the dismissal of the army "threats to the future stability of Haiti". He recognizes that the resurgence of criminal activity in Haiti is associated with the absence of the army, which left "a vacuum, as regards the security" of the country. However, it was necessary to make the patient take the medicine, even though he might suffer from it. In the words of Maximilien Robespierre: "May the colonies perish rather than a principle!"

Was it wise to ratify or even endorse the ill-considered dismantling of the military when it was obvious that the immediate consequence of such a measure would be to expose the Haitian people to the claws of gangsters and assassins? Can democracy be founded in a country where political instability, chronic insecurity and organized crime flourish? When one considers that an election constitutes the basis for the establishment of true democracy in a country, and that the institution of electoral consultation in Haiti was bound to intensify the competition among rival groups, should not the maintenance of a climate of peace and tranquility take top priority in any program drafted by the nation's decision makers?

Since the month of January 1995, which marks the dismantling of the institution that provided national security,

Haiti has been suffering from the stress caused by the sudden major change in its political structure. Haitian families have found themselves deprived of protection for a significant period of time. When the dismantling of the army took effect, the members of the new police force, who had just been recruited, were not yet ready for the transfer of responsibility. Completely inexperienced, the new force needed a period of adaptation before it could fill the vacuum left by the dismantling of the institution that had replaced the old indigenous army and which, despite all the reproaches that can be heaped on it, had for 80 years courageously fulfilled its mission of protecting Haitian families from the actions of criminals and gangsters.

It should be recognized that at the beginning, the PNH had a major handicap: it was forced to start from scratch. The files of the former police force, the FAD'H, which could have been used as a reference source in investigations, were missing. The files of the Second Bureau of the army's general headquarters, concerning weapons and their owners, were no longer available. For a time the registration of new weapons was not properly organized; consequently, many weapons currently in circulation—for example those referred to as "weapons of resistance"—are not registered.

Moreover, the preparation and maintenance of formal dossiers on all Haitians is no longer required by the public service. The systematic recording and classification of citizens' fingerprints was eliminated from the system by which Haitians are identified. Thus, officers of the PNH, the new institution charged with the mission of policing both the cities and the rural areas, found themselves completely unarmed when they arrived on the scene to face their principal mission of preventing crimes and apprehending criminals

Finally, why has the rural community been left without a police force? For the first time in the two centuries since the time of Toussaint Louverture (1801), there is no official agency to provide protection for the peasants. Alas! They have been left to their own devices.

This great upheaval was initiated in the name of change. What kind of change? Let us heed Alvin Toffler, who said so precisely:

> Whether the changes are perceived as good or bad, the increased speed of events and the reduction of the reaction time produce their own effect.... Individuals, organizations and even nations may crack under the burden of too massive or too sudden a change, to the extent of becoming disorientated and consequently unable to react with intelligent decisions; in brief, to suffer from "future shock." (*Power Shift*, p. 12.)

The weakness of the PNH, in conjunction with the incapacity of the courts to fulfill their role, has facilitated another phenomenon that worsens the climate of insecurity in the country: the reign of impunity.

B. The Reign of Impunity

In Haiti, it has long been the case that criminals generally are neither identified nor apprehended when they commit their crimes, whether in the capital city or in the countryside.

Anonymity, and therefore impunity, prevails. This is attested by the large number of cases that remain unsolved in the files of the penal systems or have never been acknowledged. Moreover, many crimes can be explained neither by robberies nor by personal conflicts. Consequently, there is often a tendency to classify them as being of a political nature or as resulting from the settlement of accounts in connection with drug trafficking, an explanation that refers to what is now a significant source of delinquent activity in Haiti.

This kind of impunity, in all its variety and ugliness, developed in Haiti from the introduction of the principle of *dechoukaj* ["uprooting"], which gained respectability in Haiti after the fall of the Duvalier regime on February 7, 1986. Assassinations, lynchings, destruction of property, etc. were committed openly in the wake of this popular uprising. The plundering of the homes of private individuals by vandals, and the stoning, mutilation and decapitation of human beings by their torturers were accepted as routine, everyday occurrences. These crimes went unpunished simply because the victims, including members of the civil militia, politicians and even former civil servants, were supposed to be partisans of the deposed regime.

Naturally, in this atmosphere of intense fervor, a great number of peaceful citizens were also victimized by compatriots who took advantage of the political situation to vent personal feelings of hatred. These criminals were not arrested after the commission, but their premeditated crimes were publicly overlooked under cover of the euphoria that followed the victory of the opposition.

Faced with the surge of popular passion, the government of the time—in fact the National Council of Government, already suspected of being at cross purposes with the movement that had risen up against the deposed regime, and wanting to avoid being perceived as such—had not initiated any public action against the authors of these crimes, or brought them before the courts. Haiti was going through a period of "democratic debauchery".

The crowd, manipulated by politicians of every profession, had become master of the streets, of domestic peace. Assassins and plunderers took advantage of the political situation to commit the most abominable crimes with complete impunity. This followed an erosion of the authority of the State worsened by a process of destabilization within the law-enforcement system, a recent development in the legal history of Haiti.

After 1986, the courts could not function normally. Those in charge of justice did not feel that it would be safe to challenge and punish assassins who claimed responsibility for the fall of the deposed regime and who even threatened the judges, several of whom had their homes ransacked. Many citizens did not dare to submit complaints against the *déchouqueurs* ("uprooters") of their homes, or the assassins of their close relations. Those who did, saw their complaints simply ignored. This situation led some citizens to dispense their own justice.

This incapacitation of the law-enforcement system lasted for the entire transition period until the advent of the legitimate government on February 7, 1991. At that time, far from improving, another pernicious phenomenon was about to be grafted into the existing situation: the subordination of the law-enforcement system to the interests of the ruling party, which became evident during the lawsuit against those who participated in the failed *coup d'état* of Dr. Roger Lafontant. The executive publicly intervened to influence the verdict of the court regarding this case. At the request of President Aristide, the court handed down a sentence greater than that authorized by the law for such a crime.

The *coup d'état* of September 30, 1991 led to an intensification in the phenomenon of impunity in Haiti. A situation of belligerence prevailed in the country after this forcible takeover, including savage persecution of citizens who did not accept the *fait accompli*, retaliation by Lavalas militants against the military and armed attacks on military installations. Consequently, crime proliferated on both sides, with the law-enforcement system being powerless to intervene. Even spectacular public assassinations were not followed by lawsuits, or even investigations.

A spark of hope was ignited in October 1994, after the return of Haiti to constitutional order, but unfortunately it quickly burned out. Impunity has continued to reign in all its vulgar splendor. The investigations in progress were slow to present findings that might have calmed the apprehensions of society regarding this vital issue. Whether it is a question of murder, drug trafficking or common-law crime, criminals are very seldom detected, apprehended and judged. They are never arrested when the crimes are classified as political. Eventually, the press and often even the PNH spokesperson began to denounce the existence of gangs of criminals sponsored by officers of the new police force.

In such a climate, delinquents and criminals, perceiving no threat of arrest, are encouraged to engage wholeheartedly in thuggery, persuaded that it will be easy for them to escape without trace after their crimes. They become ever more daring, more arrogant and more aggressive.

Furthermore, and most seriously, in many cases in Haiti it happens that the law-enforcement agencies are prohibited from intervening in situations where the aggression or crime involves certain citizens—namely, those who have been publicly identified by the ruling party as opponents of the regime. A recent case is that of retired colonel M. Roger Cazeau.

In mid-June 2000, a persistent rumor arose concerning a report that his body had been discovered at Titanyen, with a bullet wound in the head and his hands tied behind his back. *Radio Focus* of New York reported this crime on June 14, 2000 by broadcasting the concerns of the Cazeau family, who had not heard from the former colonel for several days. According to reliable sources, Colonel Cazeau was effectively assassinated, but the murder left the law-enforcement system of the country unmoved. Fear also paralyzed his parents, who apparently did not explore any avenues for exposing this heinous crime.

M. Roger Cazeau was far from being an insignificant figure in Haitian society. He was a career officer who spent 27 years in the army. He was an instructor at the military academy for many years, after which he became commandant of the Haitian

Air Force and finally assistant chief-of-staff G-2 at the army general headquarters. After his retirement in 1983, he was not heard from until 1998, when he suddenly emerged as the defender of former soldiers of the dismantled Haitian Army. These soldiers were claiming payment of allowances to which they were legally entitled from the government, and the retired colonel could be seen publicly and ceaselessly taking the initiative on their behalf before the US embassy in Port-au-Prince.

As a consequence of this activity, M. Cazeau was under constraint and had to avoid circulating freely after the issuing of a warrant for his arrest for "plotting against the interior security of the State", a very familiar charge in Haiti at this time.

Since the publication of the news of his dreadful death by *Radio Focus*, no one could find any trace of this patriot, except an allusion to his disappearance by the *Haiti Observateur* in its edition of September 27–October 4, 2000 (p. 9) affirming that "Colonel Cazeau was savagely tortured before being assassinated" and that "his corpse, mutilated and abandoned at Titanyen had been stolen by the 'security forces' after his parents requested an official report from the authorities". Nevertheless, the suspicious death of Colonel Roger Cazeau, possibly related to his most recent initiatives on behalf of demobilized soldiers, remained unsolved.

The police demonstrated the same behavior after Urélan Jeudilien, a former sergeant and the official spokesperson of the same demobilized soldiers, was assassinated by being shot in front of the building of the Chamber of Commerce of Haiti on May 27, 1999. Again, the law-enforcement agencies did not intervene in this case. In both cases, the victims were not given funerals and their bodies were not given to their families, as though they deserved neither a proper burial nor even a death certificate. This is the hard truth in "democratic" Haiti. In both cases, no investigation was even commenced—and it was the same with the assassinations of Colonel Dumarsais Romulus, Major Michel-Ange Hermann, General Max Mayard, Pastor Antoine Leroy, M. Jacques Florival, etc., who were all cut down during the same period of time. In all these cases, the criminals responsible continue to enjoy complete impunity.

Thus, when a police force does not open genuine investigations into numerous cases of assassination, even though the crimes are spectacular and committed in broad daylight, it is not surprising that criminal impudence is encouraged. This is why it is so important to draw attention to another factor that strongly encourages assassins and murderers to commit crimes, which in turn fosters the climate of insecurity in Haiti: the frequency of crimes that are committed in a spectacular manner and in broad daylight, but remain unpunished.

C. Spectacular Unsolved Crimes

Another significant factor that kindles the climate of insecurity in Haiti is the large number of crimes that have been committed in a spectacular manner but remain unsolved years after the event. The Commission of Truth and Justice, analyzing the circumstances of the murder of M. Antoine Izméry in 1994 under the putschist regime, reached this relevant conclusion that we reproduce here to encourage readers to reflect seriously on the enormity of the situation:

> The fact that the incident took place in broad daylight, as one can read in the report, is proof of the mood of total impunity in which the assassins operated, and of the existence of a system of repression that functions in a pitiless manner to realize its objectives.... These are the factors that differentiate the assassination of Antoine Izméry from a simple homicide and place this crime within the framework of a systematic policy of selective elimination of political adversaries, for the advantage of an illegal regime and for the purpose of terrorizing the whole population. (*Rapport de la Commission Nationale de Vérité et de Justice* [*Report of the National Commission of Truth and Justice*], www.haiti.org/truth/chapit5.htm#b14.)

This statement from the National Commission of Truth and Justice leads us to ask: How many cases of assassination that occurred after 1995 correspond to the criteria highlighted—that is, having taken place "in broad daylight"? The answer is: many. During the period covered by our study, numerous assassinations of prominent personalities in Haitian society were committed in a spectacular manner, in broad daylight, and often in public and very crowded places, without the murderers being identified, arrested and indicted for their crimes. We have selected twelve cases to illustrate this sad reality.

1. *Mireille Bertin (March 28, 1995)*
Mireille Durocher Bertin, aged 35, was a lawyer, the founder

of a political party, the Movement for National Integration (MIN), the owner and director of the magazine *La Vigie* (*The Watchtower*), an attorney for international affairs and attorney-counselor for commercial enterprises, and professor of business law at the National Institute for Administration, Management and International Studies (INAGHEI), a state university school. During the period 1991–1994, Mme Bertin was a resolute opponent of the return of M. Jean-Bertrand Aristide to power. After a conference that she held in Cap-Haitian on the Haitian crisis, she expressed herself about the recent US invasion of Haiti thus:

> On September 19, 1994, the ideals of grandeur and freedom expressed at the time of this conference were brutally shaken by a "peaceful" invasion of thousands of armed men, imposed under the pretext of being an "American military mission". This time, a turbulent Haiti provided the world with the unprecedented spectacle of a passive, resigned people, mentally crushed by a long and inexorable campaign of subversion, applauding the demonstration of force by the liberating occupiers....
>
> Indeed the Haitian case constitutes a precedent: jurisprudence preceding law. A new international law has been born, to which the former written rules will have to be adapted from now on, with reservations, however. Because, if all countries are, in theory, equal before the international authorities, force will now ensure that, in practice, some are more equal than others.
>
> However, it is too early to speak about the success of the *Uphold Democracy* operation. Though it enabled widespread bloodshed to be avoided, only the medium- and long-term effects on the general situation of the country and the improvement in the prospects of its population will justify a conclusion about the success of the

exercise. Only the future will declare the result. To win the war is one thing; but to manage the victory is another thing, and a much more complicated one. (*La Crise Haïtienne dans le Droit International Public* [*The Haitian Crisis in Public International Law*], pp 21–22.)

Mireille Durocher Bertin was right. In 2000, the failure of the exercise is universally acknowledged; but Mireille had to pay a high price for her opinion. On March 28, 1995, at around 3 pm, she was returning from a professional appointment in the vicinity of the international airport, accompanied by a client, Eugène Baillergeau Jr, a pilot, when her vehicle was attacked by heavily-armed men in Martin Luther King Avenue in Port-au-Prince. Both passengers of the car were riddled with bullets. Patrice Dalencour gives this report of the event:

> On Tuesday March 28, in a completely "safe and sound environment", consternation spread throughout the country, over the airwaves, with the horrible news: someone had dared to do it! Someone had just assassinated Mireille Durocher Bertin, in broad daylight, in the middle of downtown [Port-au-Prince], along with her passenger, a client of her law firm, in whose company she was traveling—Oh! crude irony—to "Democracy" Camp.
>
> Thirty bullets fired point-blank silenced this young woman who always fought with her face uncovered and with no weapons other than her competence, the force of her convictions and her courage. Bullets in response to ideas. They have killed our "watchtower" so that she stops providing political weather forecasts. However, do they not know that the silence that follows the din of their bursts of gunfire sounds louder than any other warning? From the world beyond, Mireille shouts to us: "They want to get us one after the other"!

Mireille Durocher Bertin died, assassinated by a cowardly commando with total impunity. No belated announcement will erase this fact or disguise its significance by veiling its impact. ("Le Hideux Rictus de leur Démocratie" ["The Hideous Grin of their Democracy"], *Le Nouvelliste*, March 29, 1995, p. 6.)

In what context did this assassination take place? What prior events can explain this unprecedented murder? Under the headline "The Assassination This Afternoon of Mme Mireille Durocher Bertin", *Le Nouvelliste* wrote:

Unknown assassins murdered the lawyer Mireille Durocher Bertin, leader of a political opposition movement, this afternoon around 3: 45 in Martin Luther King Avenue.

According to witnesses, armed men traveling in a taxi opened fire on Mme Bertin's car, forcing her to stop. Stepping out onto the road, they discharged their submachine guns at the lawyer, who was accompanied by one of her clients, Eugène Baillergeau Jr while returning from Democracy Camp "to settle some business", according to her husband Jean Bertin. Riddled with bullets, the two occupants of the car died immediately.

Wearing a beige blouse and black trousers, Mme Bertin was holding firmly in her hands a batch of files that probably related to her occupation as a lawyer.

Two hours after the assassination, the bodies of the two victims were still lying inside the car. Close relations of Mme Bertin, among them her husband, affirm that for about a month she had been subjected to harsh, anonymously telephoned threats.

Reacting to the murder, the president of the Order of Lawyers, M. Rigaud Duplan, stated that "things cannot continue like this any more". "It is impossible—the government must take measures," declared M. Duplan, who did not hide his indignation.

In an immediate comment, the spokesman of the American Embassy in Haiti, Stanley Shrager, did not rule out the possibility that the assassination of Mme Bertin could have had a "political motive". "One cannot solve the problems of the country by violence," he said.

Last week, Mme Mireille Durocher Bertin, who had supported the military *coup d'état* against Aristide in September 1991, founded an opposition political party, the Movement for National Integration.

Openly anti-Aristide, she was at the forefront of nearly every public demonstration against the return of the latter, and against foreign intervention in Haiti. She had had a dispute with the American Embassy, which she denounced for its interference in the internal affairs of the country. Mme Bertin, who had made a significant contribution to the establishment of the *de facto* government of Emile Jonassaint on May 11, 1994, had also, by petitioning the members of Parliament, initiated steps to instigate the trial of President Jean-Bertrand Aristide before the High Court of Justice for "violation of the Constitution".

After her unexpected and unexplained departure from the Jonassaint administration, she had kept a low profile until her assassination this Tuesday, March 28, 1995. (*Le Nouvelliste*, March 28, 1995, p. 1.)

The voices of some women, among them that of Mme Odette Roy Fombrun, rose to pay homage to Mme Bertin and "to denounce this violence, which certainly [was] not occurring randomly", but was "aimed at committed people, at prominent people whose life was taken in revenge or as a warning to others". An anxious Mme Fombrun "sincerely hope[d] that this barbarous assassination opens the eyes of the blind and unthinking persons" who should "understand that, in the end, by assassinating peace they assassinate the nation and their own chance for a harmonious development of the country that would bring a better quality of life to them". (*Le Nouvelliste*, April 4, 1995, p. 9.)

This double crime stirred the capital and provoked widespread censure. The political parties and civil society said that they were shocked by the brutality of the act carried out in broad daylight against a woman, the mother of four children, widely acknowledged to be a victim of her political opinions.

The assassination by gunfire of this young politician in these circumstances set a dangerous precedent in the annals of crime in Haiti. It seemed so outrageous to the whole nation that President Aristide, through a formal and personal request, asked the president of the United States, Bill Clinton, to send a team from the Federal Bureau of Investigation (FBI) to Haiti to investigate the case. This special inquiry, the results of which have never been published, did not lead to the identification and arrest of the assassins.

2. *Michel Gonzalès (May 22, 1995)*

Less than two months after the scandalous murder of Mireille Durocher Bertin, Michel Gonzalès, a well-known businessman, was also killed in broad daylight in Port-au-Prince, in the Tabarre district. For many years, M. Gonzalès was the manager of Air Haiti, the first Haitian airline to provide international transport. On May 22, 1995, at around 3 pm, he was mown down, the victim of an attack not far from his home. Near the gate of his residence, four individuals on motorcycles approached his car and opened fire in his direction. Fatally wounded, M. Gonzalès died immediately under the horrified eyes of his daughter who was with him but fortunately was spared.

Commenting on this assassination, under the headline "Assassination of the Director of Haiti Air Cargo", *Le Nouvelliste* reported:

> Bullets killed the general manager of the airline company Haiti Air Cargo [sic], M. Michel Gonzalès, on Monday May 22, 1995 at Tabarre, not far from the residence of President Aristide. M. Gonzalès, aged 61, was at the wheel of his vehicle when four armed individuals riding on two motorcycles shot him. M. Gonzalès was hit in the head. The three other occupants of the car were spared. As yet there is no known motive for this murder. M. Gonzales, a next-door neighbor of President Aristide, worked at Air France. In a press release, the office of the presidency indicated that this act falls within the sphere of the general insecurity, to which the head of a family has fallen victim. (*Le Nouvelliste*, May 23, 1995, p. 1.)

In this closely monitored zone, the attackers were able to leave the scene of the incident without cause for concern. After the commission of this despicable murder, the weekly magazine *Haïti en Marche* presented a description of the general state of security in Haiti, which deserves our attention:

> In fact, the death squads continue their activities with total impunity, except that victims are carefully targeted. Following the orders of persons unknown, they go out, strike—hitting their targets every time—and return to their bases without a worry. They are killers operating totally in cold blood, professionals whose hands do not

tremble—the experts have observed—whom nothing disconcerts, not even seeing in Michel Gonzalès's car his daughter, due to have a baby in a few weeks, or the businessman assassinated at Delmas, whose three daughters were also killed without pity.

In short, there currently exists in Haiti an underworld, a *milieu* as the saying goes, an underworld incredibly well organized and equipped with all the means for carrying out its criminal work: weapons, finances, information and hideouts; strategists, intelligence officers and command centers—a Mafia that lacks nothing, including a guarantee of escaping justice. To be neither seen nor known. I go, I withdraw and I return. Is this not a danger, the greatest danger, to a young democracy? It is even more so in a country that has no institution worthy of the name of security and justice. (*Haïti en Marche*, May 31– June 6, 1995, p. 1.)

This crime, which disturbed consciences and stirred up consternation in the business sector, remains unpunished, and the culprits are still at large.

3. Max Mayard (October 3, 1995)

On October 3, 1995, at 1 pm, Max Mayard, a general of the demobilized army, went to the Téléco [telecommunications company] office in Delmas. Armed men traveling in a cross-country vehicle savagely attacked him and riddled him with bullets. He died immediately from his many wounds.

Their crime committed, the assassins quietly withdrew from the place. At that hour, however, the traffic on the highway was very heavy.

General Mayard, the only son of his mother, a woman of modest means, was known as one of the most moderate officers

---

of the former Haitian Army. He was named deputy commander-in-chief shortly after the return of Haiti to constitutional order, but occupied this position for only a short time. Since retiring at the end of 1994, this distinguished officer had been living a quiet life.

This unspeakable crime, classified by public opinion as an act of revenge against the military institution, was never solved. Under the headline "The Assassination of Max Mayard Remains a Mystery", *Haiti en Marche* wrote:

> One week after the event, the assassination in broad daylight of ex-General Max Mayard, aged 46, remains a total mystery. The talk around the capital is that it is impossible to link this murder, like those that preceded it, to either politics or drugs. According to *Le Nouvelliste*, Max Mayard, General Raoul Cédras' classmate and one of his allies in the *coup d'état* of September 30, 1991, was relatively moderate in comparison with the other authors of the bloody coup....

> On Tuesday 3 October, between noon and 2 pm, in front of the Téléco office in Delmas 41, some unmasked men of imposing appearance immobilized the ex-general's car by riddling its tires with bullets, and mowed down Henri Max Mayard with several bursts of gunfire, one of the men then giving him a final blow with five bullets in his chest while the victim was already lying on the ground.

> At least 20 ex-soldiers and businessmen have been summarily executed in the same manner since a multinational force entered Haiti to reinstate President Aristide on October 15, 1994. Distinguishing features of these crimes are their execution by professional killers, in broad daylight, without any concern for being seen by witnesses, and the disappearance of the perpetrators

after the crime, no one recognizing them or knowing who they are.

"For the moment, these crimes are inexplicable and the only common factor is that they were committed by professionals," said Eric Falt, spokesman for the United Nations. "Whether or not they are political acts remains to be proven"....

Again according to Eric Falt, "there is a great difference between the ONU mandate of maintaining a climate of security, and the reduction of crime, or even preventing commando-style operations, which are very difficult to prevent in such a country". (*Haïti en Marche*, October 11-17, 1995, p. 16.)

The assassins will not be found. In Haiti today, even though crimes take place in the middle of the day and bandits operate unmasked in the most crowded places, criminals are very seldom identified. Nevertheless, the Minister for Justice ordered that an investigation be opened in this case—but that was as far as it went. To date, the results of the investigation are not known, and the persons who committed this dreadful crime still roam the streets with total impunity.

4. *Hubert Feuillé (November 7, 1995)*

It is 2 pm on November 7, 1995 in Turgeau. The news strikes Port-au-Prince like a thunderstorm. A group of armed men in a car has just killed Hubert Feuillé, a deputy of the legislative body. He was mown down summarily, riddled with bullets. This murder, as spectacular as that of Mireille Durocher Bertin, took place barely a month after that of General Max Mayard. Port-au-Prince really has once more become 'Port-aux-Crimes', a name given to this capital after the murder of the founder Jean-Jacques Dessalines in 1806.

M. Gabriel Fortuné, a deputy of the legislative body who accompanied Deputy Feuillé, was miraculously spared during the attack. Nevertheless, he received wounds sufficiently serious to require his traveling abroad to obtain adequate care.

The assassination of Deputy Feuillé provoked general disapproval, and also the particular anger of the president of the Republic, who was a cousin of the victim. This time, a particular sector was targeted—namely, adversaries of the government. They would be the only ones to have weapons in their possession, since not all military personnel were disarmed after the invasion of the American forces. A scapegoat was selected, retired Lieutenant General Prosper Avril, former president of Haiti, whom the government charged with responsibility for this ignominious act. Reprisals were made against the former general and president during the night of 7–8 November. With scandalous contempt for the provisions of the Constitution, his home was raided at 2 am and, because he was not found there, members of his family, including his daughter, son-in-law and brother, were illegally arrested that same night at their home and jailed.

The following Saturday, the day of the funeral, there were riots in Port-au-Prince and in some provincial towns. Following President Aristide's emotional speech at the Port-au-Prince cathedral, crowds poured out into the streets, built barricades at many crossroads and set fire to houses. These violent demonstrators, following orders from higher authorities to carry out searches throughout the country to disarm so-called adversaries of the government, naturally took advantage of the situation to arm themselves by stealing weapons that belonged to citizens.

The folly of the reprisals also broke out in the city of Cayes. The cruelty of the Lavalas crowds was terrible. Concerning this subject, according to the press, "Tuesday's assassination was responsible for the events of Wednesday in Cayes, violent demonstrations that provoked the killing of one man—a supposed neo-Duvalierist, who was beaten to death—and the burning or ransacking of 18 houses". (*Le Nouvelliste*, November 13, 1995, p. 17.)

No compensation was paid to the victims by the government. Many innocent people paid for the actions of the culprits who even now continue to roam the streets with total impunity.

There is no doubt that the murder of M. Feuillé was of a political nature. M. Gabriel Fortuné, another deputy and a survivor of the attack, who said he had time to identify the attackers, declared two months later, during an interview granted to *Haïti en Marche*, that the killers came from the National Palace. At this interview, he declared:

It is very unfortunate that there was not really an investigation. The criminals and their accomplices are still roaming the streets with total impunity.... I said it before and I say it again, the attack of November 7, 1995 was authorized. The privileged young predators of the Palace are still holding the real power. Therefore, I wait [for an investigation]. Everything seems to indicate that the Minister of Justice, René Magloire, received an order not to indict the perpetrators of the attack.

I point out that one of the causes of the attack against me was that

> I had formally asked for an investigation about the 90,000 scholarships totaling 400 million gourdes offered by President Aristide to needy families.... This money has been diverted.
>
> I take the opportunity to thank the men from the Palace for having offered me such a great gift on November 7 in broad daylight at Turgeau. (*Haiti en Marche*, January 3, 1996, p. 7.)

Despite all this, if there was an investigation, it led to nothing tangible. As far as the public record is concerned, Deputy Fortuné has never been asked to testify before any authority. Once again, the killers have profited from the fullest impunity.

5. *Antoine Leroy (August 20, 1996)*

In mid-August 1996, during the annual congress of the Mobilization for National Development (MDN) party that was organized in the city of Cap-Haitian, Professor Hubert De Ronceray, president of this party, announced the opening of the MDN to all demobilized former soldiers. He intended to convert these citizens to the principles of democracy, a worthwhile advance in every country of the world. However, the MDN was immediately perceived by the government as plotting its demise. A few days after this convention, a raid was carried out on the headquarters of the party in Port-au-Prince, with the police force arbitrarily arresting several partisans who were there at the time, among them some former soldiers.

A staff member of this political party, M. Jacques Florival, was also arrested. M. Antoine Leroy, the vice-president of the party, then went to M. Florival's home to obtain information from his relatives. A group of armed men arrived and carried out the summary execution of Pastor Antoine Leroy. The *Haiti Observateur* reports that, according to witnesses, "the killers then brought back Jacques Florival, who was also mown down in cold blood in the very courtyard of his home." (*Haïti Observateur*, August 21–28, 1996, p. 14.)

This double murder took place at around 4 pm, under the horrified eyes of passers-by. The individuals who committed this abominable act were traveling in a cross-country vehicle. After their crimes, they even had the audacity to take away the bodies, which were later found outside the entrance to the mortuary of the State University of Haiti Hospital. The political community was shocked. By considering the methods used to carry out these spectacular crimes, some political groups, like the FNCD, did not hesitate to make serious accusations against the government concerning these events.

This is what was reported in the press:

This Friday, the *Front National pour le Changement et la Démocratie* (National Front for Change and Democracy, FNCD) openly accused the government of being at the center of the assassination last Tuesday of two members of the *Mobilisation pour le Développement National* (Mobilization for National Development, MDN) party (Antoine Leroy and Jacques Florival) and of several police officers killed during the past few months.

Refusing to provide evidence, Evans Paul, ousted former candidate for the City Hall of Port-au-Prince, and Turnep Delpé, disgruntled former candidate for the senate of the Republic, explain that they will give evidence only if President René Préval agrees to prove his assertions that the former soldiers were at the center of acts of insecurity that have occurred in the country. (*Le Nouvelliste*,

August 22, 1996, p. 1.)

To date, neither the MDN party, the political parties nor the civil society has been informed of the existence of any investigation concerning the murders of Leroy and Florival. The criminals have never needed to worry.

6. *Micheline Coulanges (December 22, 1997)*

Micheline Lemaire Coulanges is a businesswoman and an entrepreneur. She was attacked in broad daylight by young bandits who wanted to steal her handbag. She was hit in the abdomen by two bullets. The crime took place at around 5 pm, in front of her store, in a place where an active crowd circulates. Mme Coulanges, aged 44, was married and the mother of three children.

The commercial sector was deeply upset; M. Jean Gerard Pierre dedicated to her a poem that shows the disastrous dimension of the committed crime. Here is the text in prose:

> You fell, you also among so many others, under the assassin's bullets of these "sons of nothingness" at Tiremasse Street, on this Monday, December 22, leaving behind father, mother, brothers, sisters, uncles, aunts, cousins, husband, children, grandchildren, friends, all of whom cherish you, adore you, admire you....

> The news of your death reached every part of the world by Internet. Everyone weeps for you—shocked, indignant, upset, revolted by the manner that you ended your life's journey as an active woman! Everyone has questioned themselves, blasé, depressed, resigned, laid low by the reaction of those in charge of security and of those within society! Everyone is indignant, ashamed, terrified with a fear that paralyzes and confounds all the citizens together....

All of us, in our spirits, valiant women and men, challenge ourselves to say No! and to prevent this slow genocide that threatens us all.

How long will our society remain hostage to the malicious, foolish, criminal, irresponsible and unconscious ones? How long will the citizens accept being paralyzed and obstructed by this laxity without a name? Is it not the moment for Haitian society to recover its former solidarity, its former valor? Today, united together around you, can we not already say that Micheline is one of the last in the series of these shameful crimes that are due to our very passivity? And can we not say to you, Micheline, that you may go in peace since your blood will have contributed to restoring the climate of security and peace that formerly characterized our society?

May your death, at last, bring us the equanimity that we need to continue the struggle, in memory of you!

May the message of your death bring consolation to your family, parents and friends in the hope of your resurrection through the memory that they will keep of you, and in active combat for the revival of your country which you love! (*Le Nouvelliste*, January 12, 1998, p. 10.)

The most direct initiative was that of the deceased woman's children. Considering the extent of the situation of insecurity in the country, they decided to send an "open letter to the governmental authorities, the international community and the Haitians". This letter, dated January 23, 1998 and signed by her three children, Sabine, Olivier and Michaël, grasps, in all its acuity, the poignant reality that Haiti is facing. Here is the content of this letter:

Dear Sirs,

We have just buried our mother, Micheline Lemaire Coulanges. She was only 44 years old, and we still needed her. Coming from work, last 22 December, her body was devastated by two bullets fired point-blank, in broad daylight.

The assassins were two teenagers who apparently wanted her handbag. But these young people, we are persuaded, are not the only or the true culprits. They are victims of a very sick society ... sick from a lack of love ... from a sickness that entices the weakest into the way of darkness. Gangsters are recruited from all walks of life and, so far as the majority are concerned, are manipulated by criminal minds and hands that seem to profit from an incomprehensible impunity.... One month has passed. Not a single police officer has come to inquire, even only as a formality, into the circumstances of her death.

Our society is dying. We certainly have a role to play, a share of responsibility. But if you of the International Community have been here for almost three years now, it is well, because you think that we do not yet have the means to guarantee the democratic transition that will give us access to a more lawful and more human society. And you in charge of the government and of institutions charged with the mission of defending us and protecting us, what are you doing to end this situation, to avoid this tumbling into the abyss?

We ask you, in the name of our mother who loved her country, in the name of every family—every level of society combined—who, like us, grieve for the victims of this "insecurity", to take the measures necessary to give us a chance to live in our country. The list of our deaths is already far too long. Why wait until it lengthens more before trying to control the gangs that operate in broad daylight, ... to restrict the entry of drugs into the country, which exacerbates latent violence ... to end the uncontrolled repatriation of inveterate criminals to this country in crisis, still unable to offer minimal protection to its citizens, ... to supervise the prisons in order to prevent the escapes that currently occur?

Admittedly, the anger and pain of the first moments drove us to want to avenge ourselves, even blindly. But revenge is a vicious circle. Micheline, our mother, did not teach us violence. Today, a feeling of impotence torments us ... If only we could make you understand that this situation cannot continue. Too many people, who cannot or would not write to you, are suffering. Patience has its limits.

We are dismayed by what the future holds for us. You will have noted that our compatriots have again started to flee this country. Again, the poorest desperately run the risk of the sea. The wealthy plan to emigrate. Will all the investments that have already been made, guarantors of peace, have been for nought? Have you missed a chance of helping a people to free themselves from fear and despair? And you, our leaders, will your passage to power have meant only the aggravation of an already intolerable situation? What satisfaction are you able to draw from this failure?

We are certain that all those who have expressed their support to us in this tragedy, all those who have experienced the same pain, all those who fear for the lives of their loved ones, await only one sign to come and join you in barring the path of the criminals who destroy our country. Can we have the consolation of knowing that the death of our mother has served to prevent the continued shedding of innocent blood? (*Le Nouvelliste*, January 28, 1998, p. 6.)

As can be seen, this document exposes the problem of insecurity in all its dimensions: the persistence of crime, the extent of juvenile delinquency, the laxity of the governmental authorities, the indifference of the foreign forces stationed in the country, etc. Nevertheless, its publication did not motivate the location of the young assassins of Micheline Lemaire Coulanges, who still roam the streets without being apprehended and placed in a reformatory for rehabilitation.

7. *Jean Pierre-Louis (August 3, 1998)*

Jean Pierre-Louis, a catholic priest, was the parish priest of Mount-Carmel Church at Bizoton, Port-au-Prince. On August 3, 1998, while he was going to his social center, armed gangsters traveling on a motorcycle attacked him in broad daylight on Chili Avenue and shot him with two bullets. The archbishop's palace in Port-au-Prince, dismayed and indignant, sent to the press the following note, which was published immediately:

> The archbishop's palace in Port-au-Prince announces with regret and consternation the sad news of the death of Father Jean Pierre-Louis, aged 54, mown down in cold blood with two bullets by two armed individuals, on Monday, August 3, 1998 on Chili Avenue.
>
> Father Jean Pierre-Louis, known as "Ti-Jan", is well-known in every place and social stratum. Ordained priest on July 28, 1969 at Trois-Rivières, Canada, he came back to this country, where he exercised a pastoral ministry as the vicar of Sainte-Anne Church, at the Cathedral, then as priest at Léogane, Savannette and Mont-Carmel at Bizoton.
>
> Following a personal vocation, he presented the testimony of a life marked by evangelism, poverty and a genuine concern for the poor. With perseverance, he participated in the fight for law and justice. His radical engagement related to the introduction of democracy in Haiti and a true change in the living conditions of the population, with a particular emphasis on the miserable situation of the peasants. All the cries of the poor and the deprived found an echo in his apostolic heart. This is why he spoke out so strongly,

claiming justice for the exploited and respect for the rights of all citizens.

Is it not absurd that Father Ti-Jan, who so strongly expressed a concern for the welfare and security of his brothers, himself fell, a victim to violence?

Father Ti-Jan, you kept until the end your faithfulness to the service of your God and your human brothers—peace to your heart! May the God of life make your dreams come true, while granting Haiti grace in abundance, so that the unrestrained and futile violence, of which so many innocent and defenseless ones are too often victims, finally ceases! May a new way of existence be established, in which the poor and the deprived live in dignity and respect!

May all believers, in the name of human and Christian solidarity be linked in heartfelt prayer for all those who bewail this brutal abduction! (*Le Nouvelliste*, August 4, 1998, pp. 1, 5.)

Father Jean Pierre-Louis, adored by his parishioners, had a moving funeral; but his murderers remain untraceable and unpunished. The investigation concerning his assassination seems to be still in progress.

8. *Jimmy Lalanne (February 27, 1999)*

Jimmy Lalanne is a physician. On February 27, 1999, he was peacefully working in his office located in Chemin des Dalles, in Port-au-Prince, when a killer calmly invaded his private clinic and cut him down in the presence of shocked patients.

The medical community, terribly shaken, issued a letter of protest signed by all the organizations representing health professionals, describing well the atmosphere in which citizens are currently obliged to live in Haiti.

Health professionals, especially alarmed by the spiral of violence and crime, which continue to strike blindly at every sector of the nation, express their deep indignation, protest vigorously and condemn the villainous assassination of Dr. Jimmy Lalanne while he was practicing his profession in the private clinic at the Central Polyclinic of Chemin des Dalles, on the morning of Saturday, February 27, 1999, following public threats.

The list of physicians killed, either while practicing their profession, while on their way to work or while simply going about their family activities, continues to lengthen, without JUSTICE even once being rendered to their families. We submit as proof the cases of Drs Lowensky Sévère, Wilfrid Figaro, Maryse Plaisimond, Fritz Jocelyn and Anne-Marie Guirand (to cite only a few). Not once was a culprit identified and presented before the proper judges.

Is it necessary that fear should reign among Haitian citizens and professionals to the point of paralyzing every initiative of progress and development? Will the country be allowed to transform itself into a genuine jungle and force Haitian professionals to leave the country in search of security under more lenient skies?

Once again, faced with this crime that brutally ended the life of a young orthopedist known for his skill, his sense of ethics and duty, his tact and discretion, a crime that revolts the conscience of all, the *Association Medical Haïtienne* [Haitian Medical Association] (AMH), the *Sociétés Spécialisées* [Societies of Specialists], the *Association Nationale des Infirmières Licenciées d'Haïti* [Haitian National Association of Registered Nurses] (ANILH) and all Haitian health professionals express their anger and demand that justice be served. It is not enough to shout from the rooftops that Haiti is living under the rule of law. It becomes imperative that the right to life be guaranteed for all by public acts that put an end to impunity and restore the confidence of families (*Le Nouvelliste*,

March 1, 1999, pp. 1, 4.)

As a sign of protest against this unprecedented murder, the medical profession organized an important march to demand the identification and arrest of the killer, and to say "No!" to the increasing insecurity that is the cause of mourning all around the country. However, while the march was extraordinarily successful, the murderer of Dr Jimmy Lalanne, untraceable, continuous to enjoy impunity after his crime.

9. *Yvon Toussaint (March 1, 1999)*

Yvon Toussaint, a physician and senator of the Republic, was mown down by several bullets on March 1, 1999, in Delmas 31, by a hired killer denounced by the leaders of the political party *Organisation du Peuple en Lutte* (Organization of the People in Struggle, OPL), to which Toussaint belonged. This appalling crime, classified as a political assassination by the leadership of the OPL, took place in a district that is densely populated and frequented by hundreds of students.

The political parties and the civil society were upset, and expressed their deep indignation following this crime. This is how the press reported the event:

A clear resurgence of violence was noted in Port-au-Prince, where six people, including a doctor, were killed by bullets during the weekend, while on Monday morning, a senator was murdered with a bullet to the head by an unknown killer. Jean Yvon Toussaint, aged 47, a physician trained in Belgium and senator of the Central Administrative Region, belonged to the party *Organization du Peuple en Lutte* [Organization of the People in Struggle] (OPL), one of the foundation parties of *Espace de Concertation*

[Consultation Forum], which draws together some of the opposition.

Senator Toussaint was killed in Xaragua Street in Delmas 31 by individuals who, according to witnesses, escaped while he was checking a flat tire that had been pointed out to him by those who were about to kill him with a bullet to the head.

Dr. Toussaint, who was an influential member of OPL, had in 1995 been elected first senator of the Center Department; his mandate was to end after two years. He occupied the post of *questeur* [treasurer of the Senate] at the Senate. He was from Mirebalais, married and the father of several children. OPL expressed this opinion in a press release:

"During the past two weeks, cascades of assassinations have bereaved Haitian families—ordinary citizens and professionals—before finally leading to the despicable crime against the *questeur* of the Senate, Dr. Yvon Toussaint of the OPL, who had recently been involved in a dispute with the Ministry of Finance about the salaries of his colleagues," states the note.

"Faced with the odious assassination of the senator of the Central Administrative Region, OPL issues a most vigorous protest and, noting that it is impossible to continue to negotiate in such a climate, has decided to cease all discussion with President Préval until some light has been thrown on the assassination of Senator Toussaint," concludes the note. (*Le Nouvelliste*, March 1, 1999, p. 1.)

A state funeral was organized for Senator Yvon Toussaint, but so far his alleged assassins have not been apprehended, in spite of public denunciations made by staff members of his political party, the OPL.

10. *Roland Décatrel (August 31, 1999)*

Roland Décatrel, a businessman whose premises are in Rue Pavée in Port-au-Prince, was killed at around 9 am on August 31, 1998. A bullet hit him in the head in front of his store. It seems that M. Décatrel was in the firing line of a group of gangsters who were attacking money-changers to rob them.

The commercial sector was struck ruthlessly once more. Journalist Aubelin Jolicoeur provided a description of the event. Here are some extracts from his account of the facts:

In a noisy shower of bullets, armed gangsters who had just committed a crime on the corner of Montalais Street and Pavée Street, during their escape made a target of Roland Décatrel, who had just opened his electrical appliance store at 164 Pavée Street, and mowed him down with two bullets, to the horror of those nearby. It was Tuesday, August 31, around 9 am. Thus, Roland Décatrel, who was full of life when his wife Marie José last saw him earlier, had been subjected to the whim of fate.

No human being's death should leave us indifferent, because death is our common fate and therefore makes us brothers and sisters. We meet death knowing full well that the arrival of this companion is inescapable. When it comes so mindlessly as in the case of Roland, even if it seems unlikely that death awaits us there and then, one cannot help being appalled. Roland had too much life, too much will, too much joy of living and happiness with his loved ones, to have any premonition of death—and yet the reaper came brutally to remove him from the love of his wife, from the affection of his children Lena and Roland, his grandchildren, his brothers and sisters, his mother-in-law, from the friendship of his many friends....

Haitian society, which has not ceased counting its deaths since

the army—which was its safeguard—was abolished, walked in single file, on Friday, 3 September, past the mortal remains of Roland Décatrel, laid on a bed covered with flowers in the funeral room of the church of Saint Pierre of Pétion-Ville under the care of Pax Villa, to mark its solidarity with the adversity of the inconsolable Mme Marie José Décatrel, her children Roland Jr and Lena Martinez, and the other members of the family. (*Le Nouvelliste*, September 6, 1999, pp. 1, 18.)

The investigation into the brutal death of M. Roland Décatrel continues. The police have not yet arrested the bandits who committed this odious act. They still roam the streets.

11. Jean Dominique (April 3, 2000)

Jean Dominique, an agronomist, is a pre-eminent journalist, a responsible opinion leader and the owner of one of the most remarkable radio stations in Port-au-Prince: Radio Haïti Inter. On the morning of April 3, M. Dominique was on his way to work in Delmas as usual, when, on arriving in the courtyard of the broadcasting station, he and an employee of the station, M. Jean-Claude Louissaint, were mown down by several bullets. The latter died at once. Jean Dominique himself died a short time later at the Haitian Community Hospital.

This crime, perpetrated at around 7 am, sent Port-au-Prince into turmoil. Journalists, the political parties, the civil society and the government unanimously condemned this double assassination. This crime has caused the biggest stir in Haiti since the assassination of Mireille Durocher Bertin. The Haitian Chamber of Commerce and Industry issued the following statement:

The Haitian Chamber of Commerce and Industry learned with consternation of the assassination of the eminent journalist Jean Léopold Dominique, and protests vigorously against this form of violence that aims at muzzling the right of expression, an indispensable element of the democratic process.

The Haitian Chamber of Commerce and Industry will not cease challenging the authorities, who have the responsibility of putting justice in motion to repress any act perpetrated against society, to punish the culprits and to prevent the crimes that pour grief on Haitian families.

Today, journalist Jean L. Dominique fell. Tomorrow it will be another professional who will pay with his life for having exercised his rights in society.

It is time for these useless murders to cease! It is time for families to live in peace and in security! (*Le Nouvelliste*, April 4, 2000, p. 14.)

On the initiative of seven women's organizations, thousands of women rushed into the streets of the capital to denounce this assassination. Jean Dominique was entitled to a national funeral celebrated at the Sylvio Cator stadium, which had a large public attendance. The government declared three days of national mourning in order to express adequately the extent of the disaster, with the national flag being flown at half-mast on all public buildings throughout the national territory. The trade and industrial sectors also closed down on the day of the funeral.

As in the case of Deputy Hubert Feuillé's murder, a scapegoat was identified. This time, M. Evans Paul, the leader of the Democratic Unity Confederation (KID) political party, was publicly accused. The headquarters of his political party, located at Bois Verna, were set on fire by the *chimères* in reprisal, with total impunity.

In the period since the return to constitutional order in Haiti, the unambiguous reaction of the Civil International Mission of Support in Haiti (MICAH) to this crime represents a novel and encouraging response. The firmness with which the UN mission reacted undoubtedly marked a turning point in the behavior of the international community with respect to the phenomenon of insecurity in Haiti. Witness the press release that MICAH made public in the circumstances:

> The murder of M. Jean Dominique, director of *Radio Haiti Inter*, and of a guard of this radio station, is an odious and repugnant act. It comes, alas, to be added to a list, already too long, of similar acts that have in recent times stained life in Haiti with blood, and constitutes a serious attack on the freedom of expression and opinion without which there would not be a true democratic debate in an open and plural political space, with respect for the rights of human beings.

> This crime, just like the many other acts of violence that have preceded it, adds in a dangerous and alarming way to the obstacles of all kinds which have been set up to weaken democracy in Haiti and further disturbs the climate of peace, security and dialogue necessary for the organization of free, transparent and credible elections, without intimidation or harassment, and devoid of any spirit of intolerance.

> The Civil International Mission of Support in Haiti (MICAH) condemns most strongly this assassination and all recourse to violence, which can only cause a regression of democracy in Haiti and endanger its gains, obtained at the price of immense sacrifices by the Haitian people.

The Civil International Mission of Support in Haiti hopes sincerely that adequate measures will be taken to stop, once and for all, this spiral of violence, and to defend freedom of expression—of the press in particular—and urges that every effort be made immediately to identify and punish the person responsible for this crime. (*Le Nouvelliste*, April 4, 2000, p. 14.)

Alas! Despite the avalanche of support and protest, the murderers of Jean Léopold Dominique and Jean-Claude Louissaint, and their sponsors, have to date not been found and made to pay for their crimes.

12. *Ary Bordes (May 6, 2000)*

Despite the huge uproar that followed the assassination of journalist Jean L. Dominique, and despite the strong reaction of the international community, the criminals refused to remain idle. Exactly one month after the brutal murder of the director of Radio Haiti Inter, on the morning of May 3, 2000, a Catholic priest was killed in Port-au-Prince in obscure circumstances, by three individuals on a motor cycle. His name was Father Lagneau Belot, priest-parishioner of Thomassique, a town located in the Central Administrative Region. Three days later, Haitian society had not recovered from this severe blow that had been dealt to the Catholic Church, when another murder was committed. This time, it affected a member of the medical profession, Dr Ary Bordes.

Ary Bordes, a physician and former minister of public health, was the founder and first president of the Haitian Association of Public Health (ASPHA). A former president of the Haitian Medical Association, M. Bordes was the author of many works on the history of medicine, public health and family planning in Haiti. He conducted a considerable amount of research in the field of medicine.

Dr Bordes had just taken delivery of his car from the garage and was returning home, when bandits attacked him in Martin Luther King Avenue, in broad daylight—at 1 pm to be precise. His vehicle was blocked in a heavy traffic, and the killer, emerging from a car traveling in the opposite direction, crossed the roadway and shot a bullet into the head of Dr Bordes, who died a few hours later at the Canapé Vert Hospital.

In 1996, following a tour of South Africa, Dr Bordes expressed this opinion in comparing Haiti with the native soil of Nelson Mandela:

> A country of contrasts, like ours, its resources put aside; a country with a history of struggle, like ours, for the freedom of blacks, but which, in the end, managed not to sink into violence. I left there with keen admiration for Nelson Mandela, wishing that his experience would succeed and survive, wishing also that we would take notice of it and that it would serve us as a lesson and a guide in the search for our stability. (*Le Nouvelliste*, January 4, 1996, p. 8.)

The experience of Mandela did not serve Haiti as the lesson that Dr Ary Bordes had wished it would—and today, he is himself a victim of the violence of which he warned Haitians in his 1996 article. Moreover, his assassination occurred one year after the successful march held on March 4, 1999 by more than one thousand physicians and health professionals to protest against the assassination of Dr Jimmy Lalanne. All clothed in white and with cries of "Never, never again", the participants in that demonstration brandished signs bearing the slogans: "Yes to justice, No to violence, No to impunity".

Today, not only has the assassin of Dr Lalanne not been jailed, but also another member of the medical profession has been mown down in the same climate of violence that the marchers denounced one year earlier.

The murder of Dr Bordes thus caused much agitation within Haitian medical circles and threw the whole of Haitian society into panic. At the beginning of May 2000, *Le Nouvelliste* again expressed its opinion about the Haitian situation, in a leading article published two days after the murder of this eminent doctor:

> Blind violence, institutional crisis, a financial situation close to bankruptcy, disintegration of the socio-political situation: such is the situation that prevails two weeks before the holding of the projected elections.

> Gangsters own the streets, people's consciences and especially impunity. The impotence of the civil society and of the State to manage the chaos are more than plain. So one folds one's arms; and, in the most tragic depression, the question returns: Who will be next?

> Over the last weekend, it was our collaborator Ary Bordes who paid the price. The news, if one starts to analyze its trend, is of rather an obituary nature. The truth is that nobody is exempt from it.

> Perhaps it is time to overcome the fear, this fear that prevents us from identifying the bull in order to take it by the horns. Perhaps, it is necessary rather to shout—come what may!—with a loud voice the great theme of a visionary sermon: Do not be afraid! (*Le*

Nouvelliste, May 8, 2000, p. 1.)

The feeling of panic throughout the society is masterfully expressed in the following note of the Haitian Medical Association:

Once more, as already too many times, the blind, gratuitous and unpunished violence has struck again. This deadly wave that long ago became an institution has once more mown down one of the most eminent personalities of the medical community, Dr Ary Bordes, on Saturday, May 6, 2000. At a moment when this figurehead of our community valiantly faced the pangs of a terrible disease and made himself the apostle of its prevention and of its procedure by means of his testimony, the irresponsible imagination—the insane indifference, even—of those responsible for crime abruptly stopped this example and this medical reference in his tracks.

We of the Haitian Medical Association, simple citizens, professionals practicing medicine in circumstances at the limit of what is acceptable, are tired of suffering powerlessly this surge of violence, and protest vigorously against this *fait accompli* according to which crime is the only way of solving problems, whatever their nature.

Beyond this protest, we revolt against this passivity, this docile resignation that limits itself to simple condemnation of this violent death row in which each of us waits as death passes by.

The assassination of Dr. Ary Bordes, a symbol of medicine in Haiti, must challenge the conscience of all. We ask all sectors of the civil society, either in Haiti or abroad, to join with us in a common riposte to this torrent of insolent violence so that everything may be implemented to ensure the well-being and security of all citizens. (*Le Nouvelliste*, May 8, 2000, pp. 1, 4.)

Dr Bordes had a funeral worthy of his stature as a respected citizen. During the ceremony, the president of the Haitian Medical Association, Dr Claude Surena, read out a Declaration by the association that was signed by 1,726 members. Here is an extract:

> For some time, our society has been the target of revolting terrorist acts. There is never a day when the press does not report odious crimes committed by gangsters against peaceful citizens. This is "an evil which spreads terror", and worse, it tends to trivialize crime itself, this terrible new evil that tends to become a custom, a way of life, in our society. Distress and fear can be seen on every face. Insecurity envelops us and strangles us in our homes and places of work. We lose every strand of solidarity, which, in another time, enabled us to resist and to survive the worst calamities.... Insecurity, whatever its origins and transformations, is bound up with our daily life.
>
> All Haitians, whatever their social or economic conditions, religious beliefs or political convictions, feel like hunted animals.... The list of victims lengthens and becomes weightier with every second that passes. The blind massacre of innocent lives, sending many families into mourning, plunges Haitian society into a terror that recalls that of "the period of the bayonets". (*Association Médicale Haïtienne—Hommage au Docteur Ary Bordes* [Haitian Medical Association—Tribute to Doctor Ary Bordes], p. 30.)

Finally, the moving speech made at the funeral by the niece of the deceased, Mme Evelyne Bordes David, reminded everyone of the last instructions left by this honest and wise man, just a few days before being savagely assassinated: "It is necessary for us to relearn to love this country." Mme David then asked for assistance "to keep a glimmer of hope" so that the death of Dr Bordes should not be in vain, and so that Haiti might finally abandon the spiral of violence and of unrestrained and unpunished assassination.

We shall stop with these twelve cases of summary and spectacular executions. We could have added other cases—such as that of the mayor of the town of Chansolme in the North-West Administrative Division, Mme Erla Jean-François, who was killed on the morning of May 30, 1996 in Port-au-Prince; or that of the businessman M. Serge Brierre, who was mown down in the middle of the commercial district in Port-au-Prince, at 10 am on November 8, 1999—but the list would be too long.

From the report of these crimes, all committed in broad daylight by professional killers acting openly, we shall not venture to conclude, as did the National Commission of Truth and Justice, by referring to "the existence of a systematic policy of selective elimination of political adversaries ... in order to terrorize the whole population". We shall limit ourselves to stressing one central point: the incapacity of the authorities to discover, apprehend and bring to trial the criminals and gangsters responsible for any of these murders, even though the crimes were perpetrated in broad daylight and in a spectacular manner.

As a consequence of this established fact, not only are the delinquents encouraged to strike out more boldly on the path of committing other odious crimes, but also the citizens are no longer willing to trust the country's security institutions. Indeed, if criminals who operate openly and in broad daylight cannot be detected, how can members of society feel protected against delinquents operating at night or in deserted places?

The situation is serious and disconcerting. It should not only challenge the conscience of all Haitians, but also alert the international community, which expended so much energy in restoring constitutional order to Haiti in 1994. Unfortunately, instead of providing the follow-up that this effort deserves, the international community, through its many missions and military units based in Haiti, has adopted from the very beginning the attitude of a spectator, a morally culpable form of behavior with regard to the problem of insecurity. It chose to adopt a policy of *laissez-faire*.

D. The Laissez-Faire Attitude of the UN Forces

A factor no less significant for our study is the attitude of indifference adopted by the United Nations personnel present in Haiti with respect to the deterioration of the political climate. Right in front of the eyes of the UN missions in Haiti, political leaders are having attacks made on their life (Mireille Durocher Bertin of the MIN, Antoine Leroy of the MDN) and being forced into exile (Carl Denis of the *Organisation pour la Démocratie en Haïti*, Organization for Democracy in Haiti, OPDH). Some are choosing to leave the country voluntarily after receiving death threats (Duly Brutus of the *Parti National Progressiste Révolutionnaire Haïtien*, National Progressive Revolutionary Party, PANPRA; Déjean Bélizaire of the *Mouvement National Patriotique du 28 Novembre*, National Patriotic Movement of

November 28, MNP 28), and others are dying in prison after deliberately prolonged pre-trial custody (Claude Raymond of *Parti du Rassemblement pour l'Entente Nationale*, Party of the Assembly for National Harmony, PREN). Journalists are being forced into exile (Daly Valet of Vision 2000); popular radio programs are being suspended because of political threats, etc.

The UN missions and forces present in Haiti have plainly adopted an attitude of indifference towards the problem of insecurity in the country. Were not these forces, dispatched to and stationed in Haiti, charged with the official mission of establishing and maintaining in the country "a secure and stable environment"?

The indifference displayed by the international community in 1995 at the time of the shocking assassination of the lawyer and politician Mireille Durocher Bertin seems to have been perceived by criminals and their sponsors as a kind of approval. At the time of this scandalous murder—the first case of spectacular political crime since the return to constitutional order in September 1994—many Haitians wondered, perplexed, how such an event could occur on the soil of the Republic of Haiti in the presence of the troops of the Multinational Force, which, in theory, has a mandate to enhance democracy and security in Haiti.

The impression made by this horrible drama consolidated the idea that in Haiti there exist, on the one hand, untouchable people who are able to defy the laws with impunity and, on the other hand, marginalized individuals who are kept at bay and who have no rights or protection. This perception encouraged delinquents of all kinds to act arrogantly and even openly when committing their misdeeds. Following this assassination, the faucet of summary executions was thus opened wide in Port-au-Prince where most of the international forces were stationed.

Barely a month after this odious act, the press rang an alarm bell:

During the past week, the people lynched several robbers. Summary execution is tending to become a daily practice in the capital, note the observers. (*Le Nouvelliste*, April 25–26, 1995, p. 6.)

However, two days after the scandalous murder of Mme Bertin, which was perceived by the Haitian public as an act of revenge against her because of her ideas, President Bill Clinton arrived in Haiti and, in his speech, asked all Haitians to reconcile themselves in order to facilitate the development of their country. He had designed for the Haitian people a promising future, which, he said, would undoubtedly follow the decision to restore President Jean-Bertrand Aristide to office by force of arms. Here are the words of this historic message:

For several centuries, the Haitian people knew only blood-baths and terror. Your opportunities were stolen and you were deprived of your fundamental rights. Your children grew up amid violence. From *Cité Soleil* to the farthest village of the country, you accepted many sacrifices in your search for freedom. **Now you are at the dawn of a new and hope-filled period.** Now you have a chance to fulfill the dreams of those who freed your nation nearly 200 years ago.

The tasks to come will not be easy. Democracy does not run

naturally like a river, prosperity does not grow straight out of the ground, and justice does not blossom in the space of a night! To obtain them, you must work hard, you must have patience, **and you must advance together, with tolerance, liberality and co-operation.** I believe that you can do it and, as President Aristide said, the challenge is great, but your will to succeed is even greater.

Your democracy will be maintained and reinforced by free elections and respect for the rights and the duties prescribed by your Constitution. Your government, the United Nations, and **the United States will do all in their capacity to guarantee free, honest and secure elections**, initially in June and then in December. We know from experience that if the elections are free, honest and secure, you will take part in them. It is what democracy requires from you and we know that you will do it.

Your nation has been stripped of many of its natural resources; but the most significant of its resources—you the people—have survived with dignity and hope. As the proverb says, "to hope is to live". Now you have the chance to unite yourselves in order to cultivate your rice plantations, to harvest corn and millet, and to build schools and private clinics, which will provide a better future for your children. **We, your neighbors, your allies and your friends, will support your efforts for the creation of jobs, for foreign investment, and for the rebuilding and the repair of your devastated country.**

In a few months, the paving of 1,000 kilometers of roads will be begun; and later **during this year, I will send the volunteers of the Peace Corps to help you plant millions of trees.** During the construction of the roads and the forestation, **thousands of Haitians will find jobs.** While you begin this work, I will request your fellow-citizens who fled the terror to return to help you rebuild your country, which is also theirs.

Economic progress requires much patience, but we will be at your sides, while you put yourselves seriously to work, which will sometimes be strenuous. *Men anpil, chay pa lou.* [Many hands make light work.] While you are building democracy and heading towards prosperity, there will be moments of great frustration; but today, Haiti has more friends than ever, and once again, I request each citizen of this nation to gather in this spirit of unity that President Aristide has so eloquently encouraged. I cannot do better than to repeat his own words: '**Say No! to revenge, No! to vengeance, Yes! to reconciliation**".

Justice will not always be immediate; sometimes it will not seem equitable—but **the rule of law must prevail. The police force and the courts will have to be strengthened quickly.** The citizens should not make justice for themselves. Each one of you must choose, as many among you have already chosen, to build instead of to destroy. (Translated from French from *Le Nouvelliste*, April 3, 1995, p. 14.)

This message contains the outline of a program for Haiti's development. We have highlighted parts of it to draw attention to the main points, which, if they were heeded by the Haitian decision-makers, would undoubtedly have saved the country from the catastrophic situation of latent insecurity, institutionalized intolerance, exacerbated violence and utter misery. Very recently, American journalist Paisley Dodds made the following statements about the Haitian situation, a sad description of the aftermath of *Uphold Democracy*:

In the peak years of the United Nations' presence in Haiti, hotel verandas were packed with diplomats, white UN all-terrain vehicles lined the crumbling streets and impoverished Haitians imagined things might finally be getting better.

But as the United Nations prepared to fold up its latest mission today, the cast of thousands dwindled to fewer than 200. At Hotel Oloffson, the gingerbread house made famous in Graham Greene's novel "The Comedians," the wicker chairs stand empty and forlorn.

Those who hoped the mission's one-year mandate would be extended are disappointed, believing they never had enough time to make an impact.

Years after the US military intervention and the deployment of UN peacekeepers in 1994, the UN International Civilian Support Mission in Haiti was supposed to promote human rights, reform the judiciary and build an effective police force.

Instead, one year after the mission opened, many would write off the nation of 8 million as one more country where a well-intentioned UN operation ran afoul of impossible conditions on the ground.

"I am still waiting for things to get better," said Gladys Metellus, 45, who sells charcoal here in Haiti's capital, Port-au-Prince. "I don't know what the United Nations has done, but I still struggle to survive."

Economic growth plummeted to 1% last year, down from 4.5% the year US troops arrived. The gourde, Haiti's currency, has lost more than half its value, while the minimum daily wage has stayed the same for six years and is now worth just $1.45 a day. Steady population growth has worn down an already-tattered infrastructure.

The problem soon became apparent. As the mission unfolded, the Haitian Government was preoccupied with parliamentary and presidential elections, which ultimately soured Haiti's relationship with the international community.

Foreign governments suspected irregularities in the May parliamentary balloting that gave the party of Jean-Bertrand Aristide a majority. They demand a recount. Mr Aristide, whose ouster as president in 1991 led to the US intervention, was elected to another term, virtually unopposed, six months later.

Then there was the money. The United States, which has poured $2.3 billion in aid into Haiti since 1994, held up the UN mission's $24 million budget, of which it provides nearly $14 million....

And the lawlessness. In August the UN transport chief, a Barbadian, was dragged from his car by a mob and shot to death. In November, UN Secretary General Kofi Annan recommended closing the mission.

"A combination of rampant crime, violent street protests and incidents of violence targeted at the international community could severely limit the ability of the mission to fulfill its mandate", he wrote. (*The Washington Times*, February 6, 2001, p. A12.)

What happened? How could Haitians have missed their appointment with modernity, development and progress after this investment of $2.3 billion by US taxpayers and such a commitment to Haiti from the leader of the richest and most generous nation in the world?

If it is obvious that the Haitian rulers did not do the right thing after 1994 to create a suitable political environment for realizing the key ideas of President Clinton's message and for launching the country down the path of durable development, it is equally undeniable that the international community has, for its part, made the fatal error of not insisting, through constant and firm pressure right from the start, on the application of the main ideas presented in the US president's speech: reconciliation, free and honest elections, the rule of law, tolerance, respect for the rights of all Haitians, etc.

Instead of requiring that the authorities behave in a way that was compatible with these plans to create and maintain the environment necessary for the execution of this program, and far from making their presence felt within the framework of the fight against the violation of human rights and all the forms of insecurity that poison the social climate, the international forces and missions in Haiti adopted a policy of *laissez-faire*. They were satisfied with just noting, observing and sometimes reporting, without intervening in the Haitian situation. Not only did they not participate in the fight against insecurity, but neither did they say a word concerning the many violations of human rights tolerated by the Haitian authorities, all of which has contributed to instability. Right in front of their eyes, arbitrary arrests were made and the penitentiary was filled with political prisoners, while throughout the country the number of political murders was increasing in an alarming way.

Furthermore, when the crowd, in the pay of the ruling power, rushed violently into the streets and made exactions of all kinds against citizens and private properties, the foreign forces billeted in the country never intervened.

This assertion is corroborated in an article titled "Port-au-Prince Under Burning Barricades" about the popular demonstrations, which took place right after the funeral of Deputy Hubert Feuillé in November 1995:

On Saturday, demonstrators favoring President Jean-Bertrand Aristide set up barricades before setting fire to them at the principal corners of Port-au-Prince, at the time of a ceremony in memory of a deputy who was assassinated at the beginning of last week. After the ceremony, several groups representing a small percentage of the population set fire to barricades all across the city, shouting hostile slogans against all those who intend to stand as candidates at the presidential elections on December 17....

The Haitian police and the international forces deployed in the capital and in the other parts of Haiti let demonstrators proceed.... In the downtown area of Port-au-Prince, the demonstrators set fire to a hotel, Le Voyageur, owned, according to them, by a partisan of the military regime. In several districts, young people also proceeded to make wild and random searches of cars in the traffic, some in an aggressive way, according to witnesses....

On Sunday, further demonstrations demanding disarmament occurred sporadically in Port-au-Prince. These demonstrations were marked by the burning of tires in several districts of the capital.... The members of the United Nations Mission in Haiti (MINUHA—6,000 soldiers including 2,500 Americans and 900 international police officers) were satisfied on Saturday and Sunday to help the national police control the traffic while letting the demonstrators proceed. (*Le Nouvelliste*, November 13, 1995, pp. 1, 17.)

This attitude did not change during the period 1995–2000. Four years after the above report, a prelate, Monsignor Guire Poulard, bishop of Jacmel, expressed a very negative opinion about the behavior of the UN forces in Haiti towards the phenomenon of insecurity. *Le Nouvelliste* wrote on this subject:

Mgr Guire Poulard, bishop of the diocese of Jacmel, declared this morning into the microphones of journalists that a resurgence of criminal activity, murders and assassinations in broad daylight is noticeable each time the mandate of the UN soldiers approaches its end. According to the bishop of Jacmel, the UN soldiers did not help the PNH [the national police force] to combat acts of violence and to establish a climate of safety and social peace in the country. "The presence of the UN soldiers is purely symbolic", commented the bishop. (*Le Nouvelliste*, November 29, 1999, p. 5.)

Furthermore, the spectacular assassinations were never firmly condemned by representatives of the various missions in Haiti. Rare denunciations of the reprehensible practices of government officials are often softened by a comparison between the present situation and that which existed under the government of the military putschists. International envoys have been happy to mention in their reports that there are far fewer cases of human rights violations and victims of insecurity in Haiti now than there were between 1991 and 1994. Such remarks transform almost any reproach into a report favorable to the current regime.

Such was the behavior displayed by the UN forces in the face of the grave and alarming phenomenon of insecurity in Haiti. Having imposed upon the nation the return of the Lavalas government, they expect Haitians to manage by themselves the re-establishment of security in their country. It was not part of their role to intervene, the spokesperson of the UN forces affirmed peremptorily.

Many Haitians, confused by this deliberate policy, could not understand how the insecurity could reach such an unprecedented level in Haiti while security forces stronger than the dismantled army were distributed across the national territory, backed by all the support and prestige of the United States of America. What, then, was the purpose of their presence in the country?

While the climate of insecurity reduced Haitians to despair, this question was considered by the representatives of the international community in Haiti to be a trivial one. A few days before the assassination of Mireille Durocher Bertin, an article by journalist Daly Valet titled "Insecurity Underestimated by Diplomats" gave a clear idea of the opinion held by official envoys in Haiti on the subject:

"It is obvious ... that the Multinational Force does not ensure the security of the population. In addition to an approach to the problem that is not compatible with the realities of Haitian society, the effectiveness of the co-operating international police officers drowns lamentably in their passivity and their refusal to engage." These are the words in which, here at *Le Nouvelliste*, we commented on this "blazing of insecurity through the country" in our edition of Friday 10 to Sunday 12 March 1995.

Since then, the situation has hardly improved. It takes on more and more alarming proportions, and voices continue to rise to denounce this intolerable established fact. Senator Eudrice Raymond of FNCD goes so far as to question the presence in the country of the members of the Multinational Force, which, according to him, does not seem to be of any use to the population so far as insecurity is concerned. To avoid anarchy, he proposes a re-negotiation of the agreement allowing the deployment of foreign police and military elements in the country.

"They must be really ungrateful to say that the situation has not changed in the country since the arrival of the Multinational Force," M. Eric Falt, spokesman for the United Nations in Haiti, responded last Thursday, March 16. Pointing out that before September 19 a climate of political violence had spread over the whole country with the disappearance of political militants, M. Falt made it clear that "some people profit from the vacuum of security to commit common law crimes." However, he added, 'this insecurity is considerably lower than that of other countries."

With the passage of time, and as one takes pleasure in saying that "the environment is secure and stable", this thesis of the United Nations has became the refrain of the official foreign diplomats in Haiti. "Concerning the crimes committed in broad daylight throughout Haiti, there are plenty of them in every country, beginning with mine and all the neighboring countries. **Haiti is again becoming a normal country**," the French ambassador to Haiti, Philippe Seltz, declared to *Le Nouvelliste*.

According to him, since the return to constitutional order, Haitians have been rid of the lead scarf that the putschist regime constituted. "Since the departure of the people who represented the *de facto* regime, there has been a considerable reduction of political tension.... A senior and responsible person in the government said recently: 'Perhaps a crime is discovered here or there, from time to time, but one no longer finds ten corpses in the streets of Port-au-Prince every day', as was the case—and as I myself witnessed—during the three years of the *coup d'état*. From the point of view of the French authorities, the situation is radically different from the preceding situation, and overall much better," said M. Seltz, who recognizes that it is true to say that total security has not been ensured.

"But it is the same in my country," he added, before saying that if they were going to change from the Multinational Force to the MINUHA on March 31 this year, then it means that the United Nations and the Security Council have agreed that there is effectively in Haiti an 'environment', a 'stable and secure' climate, permitting a change from one phase to the other. The French ambassador categorizes the crimes perpetrated almost everywhere throughout the country in terms of social gangsterism, thus classifying them under the label of 'common law crimes'.

At the American embassy, the arguments are not much different. "The lack of security is a crime problem," affirmed spokesman Stanley Shrager. "Under the military regime," he said, "political violence was directed against the partisans of President Aristide." "Now, what we have is crime, a local problem that does not threaten the future of the State of Haiti as a democratic country, in the same way that the crime that is constantly rising in the United States does not threaten the future of the United States as a democracy," he pointed out. To overcome the problem, he recommends the setting-up of a 'well-organized and 'non-political' force. (*Le Nouvelliste*, March 20, 1995, p. 3.)

This is the opinion of diplomats concerning crime in Haiti, where the crime rate was almost insignificant before 1986.

Are not general insecurity and unbridled crime as harmful to a population as political repression? Moreover, is M. Seltz unaware that the "ten corpses [found] in the streets of Port-au-Prince ... during the three years of the *coup d'état*", to which he refers, came straight from the mortuary of the Hospital of the State University of Haiti (HUEH), and that their distribution over the streets of Port-au-Prince was the result of political maneuvering intended primarily to tarnish the image of the military leaders of that time? Here are the words of Mr. Lynn

Garrison, witness of a remarkable episode that occurred in the streets of Port-au-Prince during the putschist regime:

> Street value of a corpse, to be used in Lavalas human rights incidents, plummeted to $60 Haitian. In a rush to use up inventory, before it spoiled, Aristide's people sometimes created unintentionally bizarre situations. Each morning Lavalas hustlers would tour the hotels at breakfast time with the cry "I have got the body!" Foreign photographers would jump up from their bacon and eggs, gulp a last mouthful of coffee and dash off to record the most recent example of military brutality.
>
> This was a growth industry. Lavalas fixers made a lot of money from eager foreigners. In one of these incidents, journalists were touted on a new body that had been found in Cite Soleil. Photographers arrived to see a frost-covered corpse full of new bullet holes. There was no blood. That might come later in the day when the thawing process was completed. I often needed a forensic specialist to tell us when the bodies had died and when they had been shot. These events would rarely coincide. (*Voodoo Politics: The Clinton/Gore Destruction of Haiti*, p. 360.)

Finally, to hear this foreign diplomat declare, despite the proliferation of assassinations in the country, that "Haiti is again becoming a normal country" just because "there are plenty of crimes committed during broad daylight in every country", must we believe that the French people are like the Haitians, looking on helplessly day after day as spectacular crimes go unsolved?

It is a serious error on the part of these diplomats to use the historical period of control by the military putschists as their criterion in their assessment of the extent of insecurity in Haiti. We think that the quality of life in Haiti before 1991—that is, before the extremely confused period of the putschist regime, marked by a severe total embargo—rather constitutes a natural standard for comparison.

It is true that, regardless of how an analyst defines the word "violence", the assessment of the level of insecurity in a society is measured by comparison either with other countries during the same period, or with an earlier period in the same country. However, our thesis affirming that security in Haiti has severely deteriorated and that this situation should urgently be corrected contradicts the notion that earlier periods were much worse and that for this reason one can minimize consideration of the violence that occurs in the country today. We reject this notion vigorously, because the period chosen as a reference to support this opinion represents one of the most disturbed periods in Haitian history.

Nevertheless, the scandalous murder perpetrated against journalist Jean L. Dominique on April 3, 2000 seems to have opened the eyes of the members of the United Nations in Haiti. After the perpetration of this murder, a complete change was noticeable in MICAH, representing the UN mission in Haiti, who released to the press a firm and unambiguous condemnation of the crime. Remaining silent about the climate of insecurity in Haiti was—fortunately—no longer an option for the international community.

The UN mission again reacted firmly to the assassinations of some candidates from the opposition that were related to the elections of May 2000. The same attitude was observed following the flawed elections and the series of violent public acts that accompanied them. People were very pleased to see MICAH sending a commission to Petit-Goâve to inquire objectively into exactions made by partisans of the ruling party against members of the opposition. Haitians thus began to perceive a change in the right direction. They greeted with much satisfaction the behavior of the United States, Canada, France, Japan, the European Union, Chile and Argentina in denouncing the acts of insecurity and the electoral fraud that characterized the elections of May 21, 2000, and they welcomed the threats to impose sanctions as a means of motivating the regime to adopt suitable corrective measures.

We ardently hope that, for the good of the country, the diplomats delegated by the international community to Haiti will maintain this policy.

In this chapter, we have tried to highlight some catalysts of the situation of insecurity that is strangling the Haitian nation. The weakness of police and judicial institutions, the reign of impunity in which spectacular crimes remain unsolved, the *laissez-faire* attitude of international mentors, and many other factors combine to worsen the phenomenon, which exacts a heavy toll. We shall now present a survey of the environment in which the crimes were committed, for each year of the period 1995–2000.

We remind readers that this survey will represent a non-exhaustive inventory of victims of insecurity collated from information that has been gleaned from Haitian newspapers.

Mrs. Mireille Durocher Bertin
Lawyer, journalist, founder of a political party
Assassinated by gunfire in broad daylight on March 28, 1995.

M. Michel Gonzalès
Businessman, President of Air Haiti Cargo
Assassinated by gunfire in broad daylight on May 22, 1995.

General Max Mayard
Officer of the Haitian Army
Assassinated by gunfire in broad daylight on October 3, 1995

M. Hubert Feuillé
Deputy at the Haitian Legislative body
Assassinated by gunfire in broad daylight on November 7, 1995

Révérend Antoine Leroy
Pastor, Staff member of a political party of the Opposition
Assassinate by gunfire in broad daylight on August 20, 1996

Mrs Micheline Lemaire Coulanges
Businesswoman and Entrepreneur
Assassinated by gunfire in broad daylight on December 22, 1997

Reverend Father Jean Pierre-Louis
Parish priest of Mont-Carmel Church at Bizoton, Port-au-Prince
Assassinated by gunfire in broad daylight on August 3, 1998

Dr. Jimmy Lalanne
Physician
Assassinated in his office in broad daylight on February 27, 1999

M. Roland Décratrel
Businesman and Entrepreneur
Assassinated by gunfire in broad daylight on August 31, 1999

M. Jean Léopold Dominique
Agronomist, journalist, owner of Radio Haïti Inter
Assassinated by gunfire in broad daylight on April 3, 2000

Dr. Ary Bordes
Physician, former Haitian Minister of Public Health
Assassinated by gunfire in broad daylight on May 6, 2000

Dr. Yvon Toussaint
Physician, Senator at the Haitian Senate
Assassinated by gunfire in broad daylight on March 1st, 1999

CHAPTER IV

THE TOLL

After three years of arduous and thorough research, the National Commission of Truth and Justice, which was mandated in 1995 to inquire into the atrocities committed under the putschist regime between 1991 and 1994, had counted "333 forced disappearances and 576 summary executions". (*Rapport de la Commission Nationale de Vérité et de Justice* [*Report of the National Commission of Truth and Justice*], Chapter V, "General Presentation of Cases", www.haiti.org/truth/chapit5.htm#b1.)

What about the number of people killed by shooting or other causes of violent non-accidental death in Haiti, between 1995 and 2000—that is, after the return to constitutional order?

The toll appears to have been heavy—very heavy. The results obtained from our research are alarming, because although the data were gleaned here and there from Haitian newspapers, the number of summary or non-judicial executions listed after 1995 far exceeds the figure of 576 reported by the Commission during the three years of the putschist regime. However, after the landing of the multinational force, law and order was monitored and enforced in the presence of the many UN military and civil missions stationed in Haiti in association with the *Uphold Democracy* operation. The last mission would not leave Haiti until February 7, 2001.

To understand properly the comparison between the two periods, it is advisable to consider a statement of the National Commission of Truth and Justice, interpreting "a statistical study made of the records of the Hospital of the State University of Haiti (HUEH) for the ten years preceding our study (1985–1994)":

> The experience of other countries that have known dark periods of repression indicates that certain dictatorial regimes left behind more files concerning their crimes than they would have believed. In the case of Haiti, the records of the hospital were a providential source of information.

> Statistical analysis of these files shows how, during the reference period [that of the *coup d'état*], the number of political assassinations increased appreciably, compared to previous years. On the statistical level, the difference is highly significant and shows that the average number of victims has more than doubled—increasing from an average of 10 deaths per month during the previous years to approximately 24 deaths per month. Moreover, this period has the highest number of assassinations (576 summary executions) of the last ten years, during which there were a certain number of non-democratic regimes. (*Rapport de la Commission Nationale de Vérité et de Justice* [*Report of the National Commission of Truth and Justice*] www.haiti.org/truth/chapit5.htm#b1.)

The Commission thus affirms that the average number of violent deaths per month increased from ten during the years preceding 1991, to twenty-four during the period of the *coup d'état*, ending in 1994. How has the situation changed since then?

A simple glance at the HUEH statistics would show that these figures are being greatly exceeded at the present time, and that the number of violent, non-accidental deaths recorded per month in this hospital clearly continued to rise after 1994. Beginning with the murder of lawyer Mireille Durocher Bertin in March 1995, including those of pastor Antoine Leroy, deputy Hubert Feuillé, senator Yvon Toussaint, physician Jimmy Lalanne, journalist Jean L. Dominique, doctor Ary Bordes, etc., and continuing to that of former deputy Thénor Rood Guerrier in December 2000, there are many Haitians in both the capital and the provinces who have paid with their lives for the current democratic experiment with its prevailing situation of insecurity.

Faced with these paradoxical findings, we present in this chapter a non-exhaustive account of the victims of insecurity over the last six years. We will do this while reporting on the general situation in the country during each year of the period under consideration.

Section 1 – 1995

For Haitians, 1995 was a year of hope, a year during which the country was supposed to start profiting from the financial and economic recovery that would naturally accompany the restored stability. As a precondition of this, Haiti needed to hold fair and credible elections for the renewal of its national democratic institutions: Parliament, city halls, and Communal Sections Administrative Councils (CASECs).

Therefore, from the start, there was an urgent need for the government to create a calm political environment to encourage political parties to participate in the electoral contests, the only democratic means of ensuring the continuity of the State—a legitimate State capable of managing well both local resources and the promised international assistance.

The political community, for its part, nourished the hope that things had really changed and that it would finally be provided with honest, credible and transparent elections. Moreover, the presence in Haiti of the multinational force inspired confidence regarding the security and integrity of the polls.

However, about mid-January, President Aristide's declarations announcing the dismantling of the army, tinged as they were with a thinly-veiled desire for revenge, worried the more skeptical minds. Moreover, the circulation of hit lists throughout Port-au-Prince caused concern among many Haitians close to the fallen putschist regime, who, predicting a witch-hunt by the restored power, went in exile.

In mid-February, the electoral law for legislative and local elections was promulgated. The elections were scheduled for June 25, 1995. However, the political parties' keenness to participate in the poll was blunted fifteen days later when the government ordered a series of arrests for "plotting against the interior safety of the State". This unexpected act of the ruling party was interpreted as a move to intimidate potential opposition candidates.

Such an initiative provoked serious doubts about the true intentions of the government—all the more so as the executive, at the time of these arrests, had made some drastic changes in the legal system, clearly indicating its intention of dominating the next electoral competitions: the executive branch of power was putting the state law-enforcement and judicial system at its own exclusive service.

Under the title "Arrests in Port-au-Prince", *Agence Haïtienne de Presse* (the Haitian Press Agency, AHP) confirmed these disturbing acts of the government:

Several arrests were made in Port-au-Prince over the past weekend, against the backdrop of a "plot against the interior safety of the State", AHP learned from a generally well-informed source. In conjunction with this, according to the same source, the services of M. Kesner Michel Thermezi, as government prosecutor before the Civil Court for the first jurisdiction of Port-au-Prince, were terminated. The duties of that office will be taken over temporarily by the substitute Jean Auguste Brutus. AHP also learned that M. Hénock Voltaire was dismissed on Friday, February 24 from his position of senior judge of the same court, and was replaced *ad interim* by Judge Bien-Aimé Jean. (*Le Nouvelliste*, March 2, 1995,

p. 1.)

Thus, in conjunction with the arrests that were made at a frightening pace, changes were made simultaneously at the *parquet* [public prosecutor's office] of the Civil Court and at the Court of First Instance. Nobody could be mistaken about the government's true intentions.

As expected, the new judicial team went promptly into action. On March 6, the local media informed the nation of the issuing of a multitude of warrants against about thirty citizens. This caused the atmosphere in Port-au-Prince and in the countryside to become overheated. As a consequence, there was an unexpected increase in insecurity.

The following newspaper article gives a more precise idea of the atmosphere that prevailed in Haiti during March 1995:

Blazing of Insecurity throughout the Country

The inadequacy of the resources of the Haitian police, the ineptitude, the resignation even, of the foreign forces, together with the obvious flare-up of organized crime, form today the backdrop for a dramatic situation where the civilian population is practically left to its own devices, undefended, at the mercy of ever more organized crime.

One wonders, perplexed and uneasy, what police officers can do without weapons, with only a simple stick, against organized gangs of robbers and killers equipped with firearms, machetes and knives. We have learned that the police stations have only ridiculous revolvers and such unreliable vehicles that they cannot respond to all the requests that they receive. It is obvious that the motivation and the will to ensure security exist, but this is not enough when the means to do it are so obviously lacking.

It is also evident that the multinational force does not ensure the safety of the population. In addition to an approach to the problem that is incompatible with the reality of Haitian society and customs, the effectiveness of the international team of police officers is lamentably limited by their passivity and their refusal to get involved. Many cases are reported where victims are arrested while their attackers are able to leave the scene with insolence and audacity.

Living today in Port-au-Prince is a real nightmare. There are gangsters on every street corner. Assassinations, assaults, robberies and also looting plague the downtown area and the commercial area on a more and more alarming daily basis. To go downtown for any activity —such as a purchase, a sale or a banking transaction— becomes more and more a perilous adventure. In the public markets the spectacle is frightening: routine holdups, people unnecessarily wounded with knives, tradesmen regularly deprived of their daily takings, warehouses ransacked, stores broken into, vehicles stolen or having their windshield removed, shoppers stripped of their wallets, jewels and even clothing.

All this very often occurs in the presence of unarmed police officers, who are impotent against the gangsters' fire-power. Nightfall never fails to heighten the pervasive unease. Yesterday evening, for example, vehicles cruised the streets, and their occupants opened fire on everything that moved. People are robbed in taxis caught in traffic jams. Cases of house-breaking have increased alarmingly. The city is left defenseless, even deprived of a fire service, among other things.

To go out when an emergency arises at night is a real drama. People die in their homes simply because they cannot be taken to hospital or because someone cannot go out and get urgently needed medicine for them.

The situation is no less dramatic on the highways. In the same way, in the provincial towns and in the countryside, cases of assassination and acts of revenge have become alarming. Yesterday evening, a truck on the road from Cap-Haitian to Port-au-Prince was attacked in the area of Gonaïves; the driver, the conductor and one passenger were killed. In the Cabri zone, armed gangsters killed three passengers on board a bus coming from Mirebalais. Recently, three trucks coming from Port-de-Paix were attacked and their passengers robbed of their last pennies. The scenario on the road to the city of Hinche is the same. In Limbé, two people were wounded with bullets. People were wounded in Gonaïves also.

The formation of vigilante brigades has as yet provided neither the hoped-for improvement in this state of affairs nor the desired support to the efforts of the temporary police force. The latter will have to be equipped to deal with this situation, which goes from one drama to the next within a population that is liable to lose faith in its efficacy. To prevent that happening, it is vital that the police force obtain resources and equipment adequate for their task, to enable them to play their part and fulfill their mission, which is to protect lives and property. One supposes that they have the will, but they also require the means. (*Le Nouvelliste*, March 10–12, 1995, pp. 1, 15.)

Such was the state of insecurity in Haiti three months before the holding of the electoral contest scheduled for June 1995. Notwithstanding this reality, the departure of the multinational force of occupation was announced for the end of March, suggesting that the mission of this military contingent concerning the establishment of a "secure and stable environment" in Haiti had been achieved. In the same strain, *Agence France Press* (the

French Press Agency, AFP), in a statement dated March 28, 1995, informed the whole world: "Haiti has been politically stabilized in spite of serious problems of insecurity".

On that same day, however, a young woman, the head of a political party and an opponent of the Lavalas regime, Mrs Mireille Durocher Bertin, was murdered in broad daylight in the streets of Port-au-Prince. Ironically, as fate would have it, the statement that the country "has been politically stabilized" was published in the same issue as the report of this horrible and revolting assassination. *Le Nouvelliste* reports:

> The human rights organizations Human Rights Watch and the National Coalition for Haitian Refugees express concern "about the danger that a precarious security in Haiti poses at a time when the UN blue helmets are on the point of taking charge".
>
> These organizations estimate that "when the multinational force, currently under US direction, hands over its command to the UN blue helmets on Friday, the 'climate of peace and security' required by Resolution 940 of the UN Security Council will not be present. On the contrary, the UN forces will have to face an increasing political tension and a great lack of security, which has been worsened by the creation of a temporary police force drawn from the Haitian army"....
>
> In fact, one is indeed forced to admit that insecurity is defined these days in terms of escalating terror. Not a day goes by without people being killed in their homes, in the streets, whether in broad daylight or at night; without houses or stores being robbed—and the assassination this afternoon of Mrs Mireille Durocher Bertin intensifies an already extremely worrying situation, especially because of Mme Bertin's personality and political activity.

There is no doubt that the execution of Mrs Mireille Durocher Bertin will cause a big stir in the political community and in public opinion, especially because Mme Bertin had just formed a political party of opposition, the Movement for National Integration (MIN.) At a moment when we are assured to the contrary, are we not experiencing new chapters of violence in Haiti? (*Le Nouvelliste*, March 28–29, 1995, p. 1.)

The editor had seen clearly. "New chapters of violence" did indeed open in Haiti. Following the assassination of Mireille Durocher Bertin, the insecurity continued its devastation throughout the year, often punctuated with spectacular murders—for example, businessman Michel Gonzalès (May 22), general Max Mayard (October 3) and deputy Hubert Feuillé (November 7).

We refer the reader to the non-exhaustive list of the victims of 1995 (Appendix 1) to obtain an idea of the damage caused by insecurity during the year. Our research discovered 272 cases of summary execution by shooting, lynching, knifing, necklacing, stoning, etc.

After exploring the list, it will be noted that 1995 was a year of many murders committed in various forms against peaceful citizens, and many summary executions of presumed gangsters who were killed without having had the opportunity of standing trial in court.

Nevertheless, presidential elections were held at the end of the year, enabling prediction of a certain reduction of insecurity. The prospect of new leadership in Haiti caused the reappearance of hope for an effective change in the right direction.

However, following the many problems that emerged on the political scene during the year—a hardening of the opposition parties' attitude, a boycott of the presidential race, etc.—the advent of President René Préval, who was elected with a small electoral participation rate (15–20%), suggested the application of a policy of co-operation and national reconciliation. Only such a policy, announced since the re-establishment of constitutional order in 1994, could contribute to a solution of the problem of insecurity in Haiti.

Was Haiti to enjoy such a solution?

What was the forecast for the political climate in 1996?

Section 2 – 1996

Already during the first days of January 1996, Port-au-Prince's environment was darkened by several events that were recorded in various points of the city and that were associated with the prevailing insecurity. The more striking cases occurred at Cité Soleil, a populous zone recently transformed into a hotbed of violence where cases of killing, lynching and arson of private properties have multiplied in an alarming way.

A group of bandits, members of an organization called the "Red Army", sowed terror in this over-populated slum. Where did these bandits get their weapons? Who gave them so much power? These questions were never asked, but in any case police seemed impotent to deal with the bandits. To try to restore peace to this community in turmoil, President Aristide himself went personally to Cité Soleil to promote "reconciliation between the members of the so called 'Red Army' and the police officers" of this locality. (*Haïti Observateur*, January 24–31, 1996, p. 2.)

Nevertheless, this disconcerting situation, as alarming as it was, did not prevent the successful transfer of power from the outgoing president, Jean-Bertrand Aristide, to the newly elected president, René Préval, on February 7, 1996. The inaugural ceremony, greeted by the international community as unique in the annals of Haitian history (so they said), proceeded smoothly without incident.

February 7, 1996 was quite a successful day. The speech

delivered by the new president during his inauguration was well received. The fundamental changes necessary to initiate recovery in Haiti were considered: restoration of the authority of the State, reinforcement of unity among Haitians, a reduction in the cost of living, an increase in national production, etc. The topic dominating this speech was the restoration of a climate of security in Haiti.

Indeed, the restoration of the authority of the State would *ipso facto* mean the elimination of insecurity, because it would entail the end of the reign of the ravagers, a barrier to the rampant violence in the streets, the neutralization of the armed bands defying the police, and, above all, an end to the total impunity that was being enjoyed by criminals. The political community, the business sector and the civil society, satisfied, waited for President Préval to get on with the job.

On February 29, 1996, the newly appointed director of the police force, M. Pierre Denizé, appeared before the Senate, an obligatory formality of official investiture. On that occasion, he promised faithfully to work towards re-establishing the "authority of the State" that had been advocated by the president. His primary objective, he affirmed, would be to fight insecurity, the "evil that spreads terror" throughout the country.

On March 4, the new prime minister, M. Rosny Smarth, formally presented his government's general policy to Parliament. The second point was centered on the "immediate implementation of measures to guarantee a climate of safety and of justice" in Haiti. Under the heading "Safety and Justice", the prime minister stipulated in unambiguous terms the measures that he was going to implement to rehabilitate the eroded authority of the State. Here is the wording:

A guarantee of justice and public security is the indispensable condition for peace, and economic and social progress in Haiti. To this end, the government proposes:

To set up in the immediate future a national plan of security capable of guaranteeing the security of lives and of property, and also an effective control by the State over its borders and territorial waters. This plan will include the following aspects:

to reinforce, discipline and train the national police force;

to ensure a better coverage of the territory by the national police force;

to integrate all bodies of intervention and public safety into the national police force;

to constitute the Office of Protection of the Citizen;

to institute reform of the legal system, and

to make justice accessible to all.

The combined effect of these measures will be to facilitate an end to the reign of impunity and to establish the rule of law. *(Le Nouvelliste*, March 5, 1996, p. 19.)

The new government thus seemed to be well under way with its project of fighting insecurity.

However, as early as the day after the ratification of this policy, bandits of the aforementioned "Red Army" reappeared in Cité Soleil, killing, burning and ransacking. Arrogantly, with weapons in their hands, they even went to attack the police station in the community. The press reported:

> The district of Cité Soleil became the scene of confrontations between armed civilians—members of a so-called "Red Army"—and officers of the National Police Force stationed there.

> This Wednesday morning, at around 8–9 o'clock, a group of heavily armed bandits opened fire on the police station of Cité Soleil, which they finally took over from police officers armed only with .38 caliber revolvers and .45 caliber pistols. Media sources report that five people died during the attack. A police officer wounded by being struck with bottles was admitted to the Canapé Vert Hospital.

> According to testimonies collected on the spot by a reporter from *Le Nouvelliste*, the attack on the police station was planned the previous evening after the discovery of four bodies, including three in Cité Soleil. The fourth body, found on the Batimat road, was that of a leader in the "Red Army", whose execution was attributed to the police. (*Le Nouvelliste*, March 6, 1996, p. 1.)

In response to such serious incidents, the new police chief reacted firmly. Before long, there was no more talk about a "Red Army". However, this success was not enough to put an end to the insane journey of the train of insecurity around Haiti. Events took a more alarming turn on May 28, 1996, when a minor, little Boris Pautensky, was kidnapped from his school at Pétion-Ville.

This spectacular kidnapping stirred up the capital and the surrounding areas. For the first time, there was a massive mobilization in a police operation. According to *Le Nouvelliste*, "nearly 400 Haitian police officers, including many from the presidential guard, supported by two helicopters and 300 soldiers of the United Nations Mission in Haiti (MINUHA), were searching for the kidnappers of little Boris"—but it was all in vain.

Naturally, the Lavalas leaders took advantage of the incident to try to tarnish the images of their political adversaries. We were very surprised to hear, on Port-au-Prince radio, the political authorities identifying us, in contempt of our status as former president of Haiti, as one who could have committed such a cheap and degrading deed. Nevertheless, the police paid no visit to our residence where we calmly remained.

Little Boris would never be found. In fact, when professional investigators realize that a case has become a political issue, they simply abandon it in order not "to interfere in things too sensitive for them". Thus, perpetrators are granted opportunities to evade apprehension, benefitting from the advantageous position that the attitude of the authorities confers on them. In fact, the government virtually exonerates perpetrators of their crimes when it officially diverts all attention onto someone else.

The phenomenon of insecurity intensified on August 18, 1996 during the simultaneous bizarre attacks on the central police headquarters at Champ de Mars, the National Palace and the building of the legislative body. The government promptly used these strange events as a backdrop against which they launched an extensive operation of repression against the Mobilization for National Development (MDN) political party and its leader, Professor Hubert De Ronceray.

The next day, a raid was carried out on the headquarters of the MDN, where some former soldiers who had recently become affiliated with the party were arrested. As mentioned in the previous chapter, this heavy-handed action by the police led to the assassination on the afternoon of August 20, 1996, two days later, of Pastor Antoine Leroy and M. Jacques Florival, two MDN staff members.

Following these spectacular murders and the increase in insecurity within the country at that time, the Episcopal Conference of Haiti uttered through the press a cry of alarm: "Bloodshed must stop!"

Here is a fragment of the reflections of the Catholic bishops on the general situation:

> For some time, there has been an acceleration of the deterioration of the quality of life in Haiti. We are the saddened witnesses of a situation where despair seems to be treading on the hope that had begun to germinate in people's hearts.

> The sky darkens in our dear Haiti. The sound of heavy weapons disturbs the silence of the night and the peace of our spirits, just when the whole population had finally become convinced of the need for peace and harmony if we were to begin to make progress.

> The insecurity spreads. Everyone feels concerned and threatened. This largely explains the climate of fear, alarm and anguish in which we live. It also worsens the situation of unmerited misery for the urban and rural masses, deprived of the necessary economic means to satisfy the most elementary needs of human existence: the need for food, health care, clothing, shelter, employment, and education for children.

> This is an occasion to recall what constitutes the very basis of life in society:

> Respect for human dignity. As we often sing, "Everyone has a

special story. Humans are formed in the image of God". It is thus necessary to respect the personhood, the rights and the life of everyone.

The primacy of human persons over institutions and organizations.

Respect for unity in diversity.

In the name of the God of life:

Bloodshed must stop in this country! Weapons must be silenced!

Insecurity must be overcome so that an atmosphere of confidence reassures those who are prepared to approve investments that generate employment!

Violence must disappear, because democracy cannot be organized and the country cannot be made to produce and progress unless everything is put into operation to create a climate of security and peace!

Human life must be protected and respected!

May the God of hope continue to accompany the Haitian people in their walk towards life, and strengthen them in their search for truth and peace!" (*Le Nouvelliste*, August 23–25, 1996, pp. 1, 22.)

In spite of this intervention by moral authorities, the situation of insecurity did not begin to decrease during a year that ended with the same apprehension among families. The cry uttered by eminent intellectual, journalist and mother Anaïse Chavenet, a victim of bandits in her home on Christmas Eve, is revealing. She wrote:

The *zenglendos* [bandits] invaded my residence at Lison, in "Plaine du Cul-de-sac" on the night of 23–24 December—and, being under the foolish and naive illusion that we were living in a protected

State, or even an organized State, I did not have any means of defense.

Seeing the trauma suffered by the occupants of the house, the desolation of my parents, the shock of close relations and the indifference of the so-called "law and order" agencies, I realize that each case of insecurity is a personal and a collective drama that extends beyond the brief confines of the news articles to which they are generally relegated.

My conviction from now on is clear: in the unrecognizable Haiti at the end of the century, where *zenglendos* are given free rein and where the law of retaliation is the only one that is still applied, it falls to each citizen to ensure his or her own defense. (*Le Nouvelliste*, December 30, 1996–January 2, 1997, p. 3.)

Far from improving, the situation worsened during 1996. The number of victims exceeded that of 1995. The number of reported cases rose from 272 to an even higher and more appalling 285 (see Appendix 2).

What would the situation be in 1997?

Section 3 – 1997

The year 1997 began without any sign of an improvement in the situation. On the contrary, everyday life was constantly marked by street demonstrations organized by the politically very powerful popular organizations (OP) close to the ruling party, which paradoxically claimed the resignation of the government of Prime Minister Rosny Smarth. These OPs blamed the Smarth government for the application of a "neo-liberal" economic policy. They were against the privatization of public enterprise that the government advocated.

Worsened by a teachers' strike that paralyzed the normal functioning of schools, the atmosphere of violence in the streets indicated clearly that things were continuing to deteriorate.

Here is the diagnosis of the general situation at the beginning of January:

Insecurity—whether one acknowledges it or not—is rampant in Haitian society. Not a day passes without individuals, families and districts being victims. Many choose—out of fear, dislike, discretion, policy or other reasons—to hide their disappointment. *Kase fèy kouvri sa* [Hiding the facts]. Thus was born the perception that cases of insecurity are sporadic.

But it happens, from time to time, that certain specific events awake us from our torpor and prick our consciences. Such a case is that of the young Haitian, 35 year-old data-processing specialist George Colbert Jr, who was assassinated on Friday, January 3 at his residence in Fragneauville, on the outskirts of Delmas 75, known in Port-au-Prince as *Trou Lanmò* [Death's Hole].

According to several reports, George Colbert was just returning from a movie theater and a visit to his mother in the company of his 4 or 5 year-old son, when he was ambushed in his courtyard by armed individuals who blew his brains out in front of his son and also his wife who was running to meet them. (*Le Nouvelliste*, January 10–12, 1997, p. 1.)

The year 1997 thus started very badly. At the beginning of this year dedicated to the holding of important elections all around the country, a resurgence of violence soon occurred. In the capital—more precisely, in Cité Soleil—confrontations between armed gangs started again and caused several deaths, many of them by shooting. According to the news, the number of victims reached nearly 20.

Surprisingly, the authorities showed no concern about the source of the weapons possessed by the gangsters. The young police force thus had to face a major challenge: to fight hidden forces, which often were better equipped than they were. At the end of February, there was an escalation of criminal acts. The toll for one week was heavy: thirty-two murders including three police officers.

At the beginning of March, the month preceding the elections scheduled for April 6, 1997, the situation of insecurity throughout the country was still worrying. Businessmen expressed their concerns through the medium of the Center for Free Enterprise and Democracy:

The Center for Free Enterprise and Democracy (CLED), dismayed by the accelerated deterioration of public safety during these two last weeks, condemns the cowardly assassinations and all other criminal acts perpetrated in Port-au-Prince and its surroundings, and in some of our provincial towns.

CLED deplores the fact that the government, although involved in the early stages of the establishment of a climate of social peace favorable to investment, employment and production, has until now elected not to condemn publicly the first outbreak of this genuine terror, and has delayed in taking the necessary measures to guarantee for the population the exercise of its elementary constitutional rights.

CLED is also amazed by the timidity of the Haitian national police, which, apart from calling for calm, never informs the population of any measure of coercion against the individuals who have sown mourning and distress in the community.

Must one conclude that the disorders at Cité Soleil were satisfactorily controlled and the risk of their resurgence eliminated, or that no trail was left behind in any of the recent cases of crime?

Moreover, CLED wonders about the reasons for the remarkable discretion of the MANUH forces in our security panorama, and wants to know to what task these forces are devoted. The rule of law, which we all dream of and endeavor to build, cannot arise amid chaos, contempt and a lack of respect for life. It is the duty of the government to fulfill its responsibilities! (*Le Nouvelliste*, March 6, 1997, pp. 1–2.)

One week later, the Mission of the United Nations in Haiti (MANUH) affirmed that ensuring the security of Haitians was not part of its mandate. Confirming this position, *Agence France Presse* reported:

On Wednesday, the spokesperson for the Mission of the United Nations in Haiti (MANUH), Patricia Tomé, said that she was worried by the intensification of violence in Port-au-Prince, specifying however that the international mission could not take any initiative because of its mandate and its limited means (1500 military personnel and 240 civil police officers.) "MANUH is not the multinational force that landed in 1994 to restore the constitutional government, nor even MINUHA which took charge in March 1995", said Mrs. Tomé....

She stressed that MANUH is there to provide technical support for the people in charge of security, to provide assistance with the improvement of the police force and to contribute to a secure and stable environment in the country. "It seems that people expect too much from the MANUH", she said regretfully. (*Le Nouvelliste*, March 12, 1997, p. 3.)

The day before this affirmation, a senator, M. Méhu Garçon, was the target of bandits. He received a bullet in the nape of the neck, which almost killed him. His driver was less lucky—he died on the spot.

The following day, the presidency and the UN/OAS International Civilian Mission in Haiti (MICIVIH) expressed their concern at the flood of violence around the country. *Agence France Presse* wrote:

The presidency of the Republic highly condemned Thursday's "wave of blind violence", which, in fifteen days, has been responsible for 37 deaths by shooting including six police officers in Port-au-Prince.

In an official statement signed by President René Préval's cabinet director François Severin, the presidency indicates that it "condemns this violence regardless of where it comes from and what its motivation may be: delinquency, economic and political destabilization, electoral conflicts, etc." "Any troublemaker will be punished in accordance with the law", adds the official statement, which "calls upon the people's sense of civic responsibility ... to collaborate with the national police in the fight against insecurity and to protect itself while showing respect for law and order".

For its part, the UN/OAS International Civilian Mission in Haiti (MICIVIH), whose mission is to see that human rights are respected in the country, on Thursday "deplored vigorously this wave of violence", underlining in an official statement that the police force is endeavoring to dam it up "with responsiveness". (*Le Nouvelliste*, March 13, 1997, p. 1.)

Unfortunately, besides these condemnations, the effectiveness of the announced measures was not apparent. In spite of President Préval's call upon "the people's sense of civic responsibility", violent demonstrations intensified in the streets. Moreover, another factor heightened the insecurity: the summoning of Prime Minister Rosny Smarth before Parliament. This initiative contributed to the further weakening of the government, which already had difficulties finding the authority necessary to maintain peace in the streets and in homes.

Insecurity, political pressure, intolerance, orchestrated violence, confusion, weakening of the authority of the State, justified mistrust of the political parties: such was the environment in which the elections of April 6, 1997 were held. The very low rate of electoral participation—estimated at around 5–10 %—was a consequence of this.

In the month following the election, the Organization of the People in Struggle (OPL) party, the main opposition political group that took the opportunity of participating in the contest, demanded the annulment of the results.

During this period of dispute concerning the elections, another serious factor was added to the causes of insecurity. A crisis in the education system that had lasted for more than a year came to a head with the revolt of the students of Lycée Alexandre Pétion, a public high school in Port-au-Prince. To top everything, while they were in contact with the police force, students received serious wounds, eliciting concern and complaints from their parents. On another front, teachers from the public system took to the streets of Port-au-Prince demanding payment by the authorities of a substantial wage increase that was several months overdue. On May 15, 1997, the tension characterizing the situation was described thus:

> The chronicle of foreseeable misdeeds is written more and more in terms of violence and bloodshed within the high schools. This Thursday, there was almost a riot at Lycée Pétion: vehicles set alight or damaged, burning barricades, forceful intervention by the police, tear gas, bursts of gunfire, rock-throwing (the situation could be described as a Haitian counterpart of the Intifada). The Court of Peace of the Eastern section (in Pétion Street) was burnt; fire-fighters could not intervene. Bullets seriously wounded two high-school students and two passers-by. There was very heavy property damage. (*Le Nouvelliste*, May 15, 1997, p. 1.)

Following this uprising by the high-school students, serious charges were laid against the police. Under the heading: "Why this Bloody Repression?" *Haiti-Progrès* reported:

> According to an assessment made by the Commission for Justice

and Peace of the Archdiocese of Port-au-Prince, "seven high-school students in uniform fell under the gunfire of killers from the national police. Their bodies were hidden in bags and taken to an unknown destination. Several other high-school students were wounded by being beaten with sticks or rifle-butts, and by bullets, without any mercy being shown to passers-by and residents of the Bel-Air district, "who were not spared". (*Haïti Progrès*, May 25–27, 1997, p. 1.)

This environment of uncertainty, disorder, violent demonstration, mistrust of the national police force, and assassination of humble citizens and police officers, was maintained all year long with rare breaks. The situation became even worse later on with the trauma caused to the population by the shipwreck of the Fierté Gonâvienne in September 1997, when hundreds of Haitians drowned during the crossing from Gonâve Island to the town of Montrouis on the main land.

Finally, the atmosphere of insecurity was worsened by the political situation at the end of the year. Following the explosion of a homemade bomb on November 10, 1997 near the Hospital of the State University of Haiti, a plot against state security was "discovered" implicating M. Léon Jeune, former candidate for the presidency in the December 1995 elections. M. Jeune was apprehended on November 16, 1997, "on the charge of destabilizing the government by sowing disorder inside the country". He was then put in jail for several days. In addition, "the police authorities had linked the current resurgence of organized crime and drug trafficking to this plot that, they said, aimed at the assassination of President René Préval" (*Le*

Nouvelliste, November 19, 1997, p. 1.)

It was a dangerous insinuation. However, in spite of the gravity of the charge laid on him, M. Léon Jeune was released less than one month later, on December 11, 1997.

So far as insecurity is concerned, the year 1997 knew no respite. The number of victims, however, dropped slightly, reaching 239 cases (Appendix 3).

The prevailing situation at the end of 1997 was well outlined by the Center for Free Enterprise and Democracy (CLED):

The Center for Free Enterprise and Democracy (CLED) observes with much concern that insecurity spreads throughout the whole country and becomes more systematic each day. Assassinations, robberies, drug trafficking, organized invasions and damage to private property all multiply.

This concern is transformed into anxiety when it is the local "authorities" who organize, as vulgar "*déchouqueurs*", invasions of land, especially that belonging to private owners. It is astonishing that people who fought for the return to constitutional order convert themselves into real gangsters, violating, with impunity, the laws of our country and ridiculing the Constitution on which they founded their political claims.

To this serious threat, the response of the authorities is only indifference, tolerance and even, sometimes, friendliness.

It is time for that to cease. It is time that the authority of the State be restored. It is time that the persons in charge in our country show courage and firmness in order to make the people respect the law. It is time that the troublemakers, the criminals, whoever they are, answer for their actions before the court. CLED remains convinced that the leaders of our country will understand the urgency of this call and will finally assume responsibility so that Haiti is ruled as a State where the law maintains respect. (*Le Nouvelliste*, December 17, 1997, p. 1.)

The year 1997 thus ended on a note of apprehension concerning the future of Haiti.

Would the authority of the State for which everyone yearns be finally restored in 1998?

Section 4 – 1998

The year 1998 began with skepticism. Traumatized by the heavy toll of the previous year, Haitians did not know to which saint to dedicate themselves any more. They were losing confidence in the capacity of the police force to maintain order and to restore security in the country. Crimes continued to be committed without the perpetrators being arrested.

For example, the assassination of Mme Maryse Débrosse, a businesswoman, at the end of January, in broad daylight serves to confirm this painful reality. M. Roselor Jusma, who even insinuated that this crime could have had a political motivation, expressed the mistrust of the population. He wrote:

> I transmit an SOS to the civil society in general, to the governmental authorities, to the international organizations and to the organizations that defend human rights particularly, to help the Haitian people turn off this faucet of blood that haunts our spirits and every day generates orphans, leaves people stranded and further destroys the social fabric and the nation itself....
>
> Maryse, for not having known how to keep quiet and *laissez-faire* [leave things alone], being guided by your sense of duty and of honesty, you have suffered the punishment of the hearts of the elite. (*Le Nouvelliste*, February 9, 1998, p. 16.)

For another example, when mayors claimed the right to organize a police force within their respective communities, a serious conflict ensued between them and the governmental authorities. The latter sent the city halls a warning through the media, reminding them that "constitutional prerogatives with regard to maintenance of law and order throughout the territory fell within the particular domain of the National Police Force of Haiti (PNH) and that no other armed body of any kind could therefore exist within the national territory." (*Le Nouvelliste*, February 4–5, 1998, p. 1.)

The situation worsened in February 1998 when the secretary of state for public safety this time launched an ultimatum to the three city halls in the metropolitan area, demanding "that they return the heavy weapons that are held by their security services". If not, according to the note, then the penalty would be "an attack by the police force". The atmosphere was highly charged. Some highlights from an article published on the subject will provide readers with a better understanding of the explosive situation prevailing at the time:

> The secretary of state for public safety, Robert Manuel, sent an ultimatum to three city halls in the metropolitan area of the capital, to deposit with police authorities all heavy weapons that are being held by their security services. In the event of the city halls not complying with the injunction before the expiration period, which is Friday, at 17:00 hours local time, an operation aiming at the recovery of these weapons would be considered....

> In this letter dated February 3 addressed to the mayor of the capital, Joseph Emmanuel Charlemagne, and to those of the neighboring communities of Delmas and Croix-des-Bouquets, of which IPS obtained a copy, the secretary of state for public safety indicates that the possession of automatic weapons is against the law. Moreover, he reminds everyone that the constitutional prerogatives with regard to maintenance of law and order throughout the territory falls within the reserved domain of the National Police Force of

Haiti (PNH) and that consequently no other armed body can exist on the National territory....

According to information obtained by IPS, a forcible takeover of the city hall of Port-au-Prince would be very difficult or could end in blood. The reason provided by the informants is that the police cannot accurately assess the arsenal held by the mayor and those loyal to him, men recruited inside the police force or among the demobilized soldiers of the former army. The retention of unauthorized automatic weapons by the municipal authorities and other groups has been for nearly three years a source of concern to those in charge of the Haitian police.

In a letter dated May 27, 1996 addressed to the minister for the interior, the mayor of the capital, Joseph Emmanuel Charlemagne, had indicated that he holds eleven assault rifles and some submachine guns. His project, two years ago, was to set up, parallel to the PNH, a municipal police whose mandate was not clearly defined. This project was abandoned following the refusal of the government to authorize the institution of a parallel armed body.

At the same time, Patrick Norzéus, the mayor of Delmas, had declared that he had run as a candidate in this community "to guarantee the safety of President Aristide", whose private residence is located in this jurisdiction. The name of Norzéus had been mentioned in several conflicts involving armed civilians in the large ghettos of Cité Soleil, located on the edge of the capital. A significant percentage of the population were killed in armed confrontations in this area in 1995.

His assistant Ernst Erilus bragged on several occasions about possessing a significant arsenal including M-1 rifles, Uzi submachine guns of Israeli manufacture and fragmentation grenades. In the presence of journalists invited to a press conference, Erilus held a grenade in his hands as a demonstration of his power. Erilus justified the retention of these heavy weapons by the fact that police officers attached to the security of some leaders are illegally carrying these same types of weapons....

In an exclusive interview with IPS, the mayor of the Haitian capital defied the police. He firmly declared that no operation could be carried out against him.... He asked the police authorities first to recover the weapons held, according to him, by close relations of former president Jean-Bertrand Aristide.... He revealed that some police officers still on active duty had been implicated in political assassinations including that in 1995 of lawyer Mireille Durocher Bertin. (*Le Nouvelliste*, February 4-5, 1998, pp. 1, 5.)

The facts reported in this article eloquently indicate the disorder that exists regarding the control of firearms in Haiti and the great loss of prestige by the national police force. Faced with this reality, a gloomy uneasiness grasped Haitian families. The authority of the State had become so weak that the government felt obliged to threaten state employees to impose its view. However, if the secretary of state for public safety indicated the illegal character of the "retention of automatic weapons by the city halls", he did not say a word about several other people who, with the knowledge of the authorities, hold this type of weapon. This is a double standard.

The negative attitude towards the Haitian police appeared also in the provincial towns. For example, at Mirebalais, a provincial city, events occurred that clearly indicated not only the extent of violence prevailing in the countryside, but also the impotence of the policemen billeted in some communities to enforce the law. *Le Nouvelliste* reported:

Police in Rout at Mirebalais

Violent incidents: two deaths, including the police chief, who was hacked, stoned and burned.

Loiterers standing around in front of the doors of closed houses, empty streets giving the impression of a city in a state of siege, police vehicles patrolling the streets among the remains of tires set alight the day before—this is the image that Mirebalais, a community located 55 kilometers north-west of the capital, presents this Friday.

The inhabitants of the city have not yet recovered from the incidents that cost the lives of two people, of whom one was the police chief of the city. Unarmed police officers were beaten and others had to go into hiding to escape death, faced with the Kadhafi machine guns and M-1 rifles of the attackers.

Of 39 police assigned to the Mirebalais police station, only five were at the station on Friday afternoon. There has been no news of two them. Several police officers were beaten and threatened with necklacing by members of the armed group. Others had to go into hiding to escape death.... "We are not safe here. The situation is difficult here where publicity for a gang is broadcast from the antennas of a local radio station", a police officer declared.

"When gangsters are arrested, they are then freed by the judicial system. One cannot arrest anyone here if it is not the will of the *chimères*. Only they can arrest people", declares another policeman....

During this incident, two vehicles belonging to the police and one belonging to the National Penitentiary Administration (APENA) were burnt. One motorcycle, five revolvers, three 12-gauge rifles … and other police property was taken away. Members of the popular organization *Met lòd nan dezòd* [Put order into the disorder] freed 76 prisoners, among them some condemned to life sentences, the assistant-director of the APENA confirmed on the spot. Only one escaped prisoner was recaptured in the afternoon.

"That was very tough. We experienced yesterday evening a hunt for police officers. People chased them. They came to my home last night. We managed to enter the police station using an alternative entrance and discovered that the body of the police chief had been stoned and mutilated. There are some police officers that we have not yet been able to locate", said an agent. (*Le Nouvelliste*, February 8, 1998, pp. 1, 4.)

The police officers were under siege and were not afraid to admit it. We have already described the phenomenon of the *chimères* in Chapter II. The existence of the PNH in the Center Department was then seriously threatened.

To heal the rifts, the personal intervention of President René Préval was required. He quickly resolved the conflict between the government and the city halls. In addition, special units were dispatched to the Central administrative region to restore the tarnished prestige of the police force there. Were the persons responsible for the slaughters in Mirebalais identified, arrested, brought to court, judged and sentenced? It cannot be affirmed.

However, in the middle of the year, there were signs that some progress had been recorded in the control of insecurity. The rate of acts of aggression had dropped. Thank God for one significant factor that facilitated a clear improvement of the whole scene: the soccer World Cup, which was held in France during the summer of 1998.

The situation was heading towards one of net decrease when

the spectacular assassination of the parish priest of Mount-Carmel Church, Father Jean Pierre-Louis, was perpetrated in Port-au-Prince in August 1998. A renewal of insecurity then appeared again in November, with the horrible assassination of another monk, Brother Hurbon Bernardin, of the Brothers of Christian Instruction, at Vallée de Jacmel.

Towards the end of the year, the number of cases of aggression increased at worrying intervals. Taken unawares by this sudden resurgence of violence, police authorities tried to revive the "vigilante brigades"—groups of citizens organized, and often armed, to ensure safety in their area. The UN/OAS International Civilian Mission in Haiti (MICIVIH) promptly opposed this idea, describing the project as unconstitutional and "dangerous". (*Le Nouvelliste*, December 3, 1998, p. 1.)

In December, the tendency towards aggravation of the problem was eloquently indicated by *Haïti en Marche*, which, under the very suggestive heading "An Overall Criminality", wrote:

The problem of criminal activity in the Haitian capital is severe. It is a major problem because one deals with criminals of various kinds: minors who should be at school and towards whom society, however self-absorbed it may be, should feel responsible; recidivists whose place is in a maximum security prison and of whom the US continues to send us whole batches.

But lastly—believe it or not—it is the very members of the new police force who put the capital into the most turmoil. They are either police officers dismissed from the corps for reprehensible conduct or those still in office ... until the temptation becomes too strong. For example, those who disappeared with the notorious 450 kilos of cocaine, which caused such a stir but of which no one has found the least trace.

The problem is all the more significant as the authorities are obviously overwhelmed, and their denials and attempts at diversion (such as inviting the population to organize vigilante brigades) do nothing but convince more strongly of their impotence." (*Haïti en Marche*, December 9–15, 1998, p. 1.)

Compared to the preceding year, 1998, with 147 listed cases, showed an appreciable fall in the number of victims (Appendix 4). However, taking into account the abrupt resurgence of crimes of blood at the end of the year, many wondered anxiously whether the government would find the right formula and take adequate steps to eliminate the fear that haunts Haitian families. Would 1999 have the virtue of refuting the gloomy forecast of an intensification of the phenomenon of insecurity in the country?

Section 5 – 1999

The year 1999 announced the passage to the third millennium. Bearing hope for the whole of humanity, it found Haitians facing an important deadline: the end of the mandate of all the deputies and of the majority of the senators of the 46th legislature, elected in 1995. When this deadline arrived, the executive, profiting from this *fait accompli*, dissolved Parliament. Thus, confirming the gloomy predictions of the end of the previous year, 1999 began with a serious conflict between the executive and the legislature, a conflict that would soon be manifested in violent demonstrations against Parliament by popular organizations in the pay of the ruling party.

Since 1995, elections had not been held regularly at the times stipulated by the Constitution. Because of the many irregularities denounced by the opposition, and the subsequent intransigence of the government, the elections organized for April 1997 could not be completed, since it was impossible for the CEP to undertake the second round and thus enable the winners to be determined. Finally, the major disagreements about these elections led to the resignation of the prime minister, Rosny Smarth, plunging the country into a serious political crisis.

As the Constitution envisaged it, the legislative chambers should have opened a new parliamentary session on Monday, January 10, 1999. The following day, surprisingly, President René Préval issued a decree dissolving Parliament one year before the constitutional time, according to a provision of the electoral law enacted contrary to the Constitution's prescription of a full four-year term for deputies, starting from their appointment to office (Article 92). The same presidential decree also affected the city halls and CASECs. Citizens called "temporary executive agents" would replace the elected mayors. From that date, the institutional crisis had worsened, because, in addition to the absence of a legal prime minister, Haiti was functioning without elected senators, deputies, mayors and CASECs, and the president was governing by decree.

Senators and deputies refused to accept the presidential decision. Then, on the next day, January 11, 1999, groups of demonstrators invaded the streets and caused serious disturbances to force parliamentarians to leave the legislative building. On that occasion, dozens of cars belonging to peaceful citizens were damaged in violent acts by *chimères*.

This situation, bordering on anarchy, aggravated the climate of insecurity. On Tuesday, January 12, a revealing signal of the extent of the phenomenon was given: President Préval's own sister, Mme Marie-Claude Préval, was involved in an attack in Port-au-Prince that cost her driver his life. Seriously wounded, she herself was miraculously spared.

This attack caused a situation of panic throughout the country. Many Haitians questioned themselves, disconcerted: if the presidential family was not safe from the actions of bandits, who could pretend to be protected? Thus, 1999 began in an atmosphere of fear, even hysteria.

Meanwhile, a manipulated crowd maintained an atmosphere of disorder in Port-au-Prince. On Monday, January 27, owing to the persistence of the parliamentarians who wanted to keep their position in Parliament, the vandals again invaded the streets "to sing in their way the funeral of the 46th legislature". That day, a generalized fear stole over the capital.

Here is how the press described the environment prevailing on that day:

> This demonstration, which belied all predictions, was dubbed "Operation Popular Shield". It was soon transformed into a general strike. All activity underwent a complete slow-down. The population recalled the day of January 11 when many acts of violence were recorded; in particular, demonstrators in the downtown area had broken dozens of windshields.

> Early in the morning, the remains of calcined tires could be seen in various places around the capital. Showers of rocks were thrown in Fronts-Forts Street. The city looked like a ghost town, contrary to its usual appearance on a Friday. The rare motorists who drove through were hurrying to get home. Public transport was three-quarters empty owing to a lack of passengers. The various services around the capital were partly inoperative. It was very difficult to find either a tap-tap or a truck to go to the countryside.

> In the downtown area, the streets were empty not only of merchants but also of the cars that are usually parked there. The stores and commercial banks closed their doors for fear of the climate surrounding "the Popular Shield operation".... Schools, universities and institutes also closed their doors. Students and teachers chose to stay at home for fear of aggression. In fact, the day of January 25 generated a real panic among parents. (*Le Nouvelliste*, January 25–26, 1999, p. 5.)

From the month of January, in this atmosphere of disorder, the capital and several provincial towns were also exposed to a resurgence of criminal activity that brought mourning to families and disturbed the citizen's peace of mind. The population seemed to have been left to its own devices because, in spite of the public character of the perpetrated acts, police very seldom intervened to arrest the criminals.

At the beginning of March, social life was, once again, strongly disturbed by the riots of schoolboys. At the Lycée Alexandre Pétion, the students expressed their anger by rioting because of the many days of class time lost following a two-year-old conflict between the Ministry of National Education and the teachers. An attempt by the police force to control the revolt caused unfortunate misdeeds, which aggravated the situation. The young demonstrators took over the streets by violence, turning Port-au-Prince upside down.

Here is how the day of March 2, 1999 was described in the press:

> Twenty-four hours after the violent scenes of high-school students demanding the resumption of courses in their school, emotion can be read on the face of everyone in Port-au-Prince. A hysterical fear has come upon all those who, for one reason or another, must go out in the streets, particularly in the zone known as Bel-Air.

> Every sector is affected; every institution is paralyzed, or almost paralyzed, by the exacerbation of the crisis between the teachers' trade unions and the Ministry of National Education, Youth and Sports. Thus, all activities have stopped: businesses are idling, the public administration is the same, the private schools operate with reduced staff, while the doors of the national schools and colleges

are almost closed due to the fact that the students are expressing their anger in the streets, breaking car windshields, setting fire to vehicles and throwing rocks at all who pass by. (*Le Nouvelliste*, March 2, 1999, p. 1.)

It was in this overheated psychological climate that, on March 8, an agreement was signed between the government and five political parties—the Democratic Unity Confederation (KID), the National Progressive Revolutionary Party (PANPRA), the National Congress of Democratic Movements (KONAKOM), Generation 2004 and *Ayiti Kapab* [Haiti is Capable]—to enable the organization of elections to fill the vacancies in the Senate and to replenish the legislative chamber, the city halls and the CASECs.

Did this agreement have a calming effect on people? Absolutely not. The insecurity was rather exacerbated. At the beginning of April, over a single weekend, a dozen people including a police officer were assassinated in Port-au-Prince. The situation reached its climax with the murder of a Lavalas political activist, Phillis Michel-Ange, alias "Boa". The killing of this man, attributed to a police officer, was the signal of the release of unprecedented violence that lasted several days, paralyzing the activities in the capital.

The Center for Free Enterprise and Democracy (CLED) intervened:

An activist was killed yesterday evening, Tuesday April 20, 1999, in circumstances that remain to be established. This assassination elicited reactions from the parents and friends of the victim. Unfortunately, these reactions, quite comprehensible at first, degenerated into demonstrations of extreme violence. This uncontrolled violence was characterized by acts of vandalism against vehicles, stores, banks and the displays of street traders. Moreover, confrontations took place between groups of demonstrators and the police force.

Today, it has started again! Tires are burning in the downtown area, rocks are being thrown at vehicles, and financial and business premises, once more taken hostage, are closing their doors. This situation is intolerable! The authorities of our country, guarantors of the safety of lives and of property, must fulfill their responsibility immediately, so that this situation ceases. We challenge the president of the Republic, the prime minister and his government to take energetic measures against the authors and instigators of acts of violence, whoever they may be.

A climate of calm and confidence is necessary so that private local and foreign investments become a reality and so that the country may be put to work. This climate is also essential for organizing free and honest elections. We cannot let small political groups of hooligans and organized criminals spoil the Haitian people's dream of democracy, progress and stability (*Le Nouvelliste*, April 21, 1999, pp. 1, 32.)

This note, in spite of its relevance, did not prevent the situation from worsening. The population was very sensitive. At the beginning of May, following a simple initiative by the mayor of Port-au-Prince to dislodge street merchants from the public highway, the latter protested this decision and demonstrated violently against the municipal officials. In a moment, more than ten cars belonging to private individuals were burnt at the commercial center, and others had their windows broken, their windshields smashed, and all with total impunity.

The following day, the mayhem resumed with greater force. Individuals armed with sticks, machetes and firearms, their faces masked, made their appearance in the commercial zone. The mere sight of their costume invoked fear. Police did not intervene to protect citizens.

The same day, a rumor went around that another fierce Lavalas militant called Frantz Camille had been cut down. This rumor was sufficient to provoke general turmoil in Port-au-Prince:

> Hippolyte market was immediately shut down, barricades were set alight, there were demonstrations of anger, the APN [National Port Authority] was besieged, there were showers of rocks, genuine Intifada, the downtown area was declared hot. The commercial zone was closed. Many vehicles were damaged; three were burnt in Cité Militaire. A short time later, there was a burst of automatic weapon fire at Pacot. (*Le Nouvelliste*, May 6, 1999 p. 1.)

Faced with this alarming situation affecting commercial, industrial, financial and cultural activities, and the visible incapacity of police to maintain order when disturbed by the *chimères*, the business sector decided to mobilize citizens at Champ de Mars on May 28, 1999. "No! to insecurity" was the slogan of the day.

This gathering of tens of thousands of people was the most significant mobilization against insecurity in Haiti. Unfortunately, police suspended the demonstration—paradoxically, "because of insecurity". Indeed, a group of vandals identified as Lavalas militants had thrown showers of rocks and plastic bottles filled with malodorous urine at the participants. The police, always unarmed when facing these groups of protected vandals, decided to put an end to this peaceful meeting. This is Haiti in the age of restored democracy.

On the afternoon of this May 28, the police were on trial: witnesses implicated some police officers in the summary executions of young people at Carrefour-Feuilles, a district of Port-au-Prince. A few days later, as if this scandal were not sufficient, the press announced that officers of the national police were similarly involved in another sordid affair: an investigation of the MICIVIH revealed that police officers were implicated in the matter of a mass grave discovered at Titanyen, and in acts of assassinations and disappearance. *Haïti Progrès* reported:

> Within the framework of the discovery of bones at Titanyen, the UN/OAS International Civilian Mission in Haiti (MICIVIH) has collected enough compromising information on the role of the Haitian police force in cases of disappearance and summary execution. The Mission affirms that "six girls and two young boys were arrested in a house at Croix-des-Missions, on the night of April 16–17, 1999; these people were not found despite a search by their close relations". According to the MICIVIH, "close relations and neighbors of these missing young people identified parts of the clothing found at Titanyen as similar to certain clothing worn by three of these young people". (*Radio Haiti*, July 22, 1999.)

Moreover, the Civil Mission ... was alerted this week to at least sixteen cases of assassinations by shooting and disappearances imputed to a group of armed men described as "vigilante brigades" operating in the zone of Drouillard, surrounding Port-au-Prince, and "supervised by police officers". "We should carry out an inquiry into the first discovery of bodies. According to testimonies, last May, an operation involving 20 men, of whom two were in police uniform, took place at *Bois Neuf*", a member of the MICIVIH indicated. (*Haïti Progrès*, 28 July–3 August 1999, pp. 1, 15.)

The accusations were direct and public. However, the MICIVIH was satisfied merely to denounce these serious and shocking facts. No action was undertaken to correct these misdeeds. Moreover, the results of the investigations were never made public.

The increased mistrust, justified or not, towards elements of the national police made security in the country even more precarious. The uncertainty of the population intensified when the secretary of state for public safety, M. Robert Manuel suddenly resigned, in October 1999—all the more so since his resignation was followed by the assassination, in the streets of Port-au-Prince, of Colonel Jean Lamy, intended, according to rumors, to replace him.

During the month of November alone, three other spectacular crimes were committed. On November 8, the well-known businessman, Serge Brierre, was assassinated at the same time as his driver, mown down in broad daylight and in a commercial zone by the bullets of bandits. On November 17, Port-au-Prince would know the height of indignation at the painful spectacle of the dreadful execution of a nun, Sister Marie Géralde Robert. Armed gangsters cruelly cut down this nun in front of the Institution St-Louis de Bourdon school. Sister Marie Géralde Robert was a nurse and the director of a health center at Côtes-de-fer, in the South-East administrative region. "This crime, like all the others, is the cancerous sign of a sick society", said the Episcopal Conference of Haiti's president, Monsignor Hubert Constant, at the moving funeral of the deceased nun.

Such was the general panorama of 1999, which saw the number of the victims reaching its highest level of 287 (Appendix 5).

During this year, the police force itself was severely attacked by bandits. "According to the office of the general director of the PNH, as can be read in the MICIVIH report for the year, 19 police officers were killed since the beginning of 1999, and 63 have lost their lives in the performance of their duties since the creation of the PNH in 1995." (*Le Nouvelliste*, November 25, 1999, p. 36.)

The year 1999 was thus a catastrophe as far as safety was concerned. Consequently, the economy idled. During that year, the Club Med decided to withdraw from Haiti—for "reasons beyond our control", the people in charge affirmed. According to the employees, this decision was taken in view of many factors: "no customers, bad condition of the roads, insecurity and cancellation of the direct airline service to Europe".

The tourism sector's misfortune reflected the general situation of insecurity in Haiti at the end of 1999. Here is a fragment of an article published in the press about this:

> The climate of insecurity in the country still evokes fear in businessmen in the center of the Haitian capital, in spite of the announced measures and the considerable reduction in criminal

activity as recorded by the national police during the year-end festivities. Several businessmen, interviewed today by *Le Nouvelliste*, expressed their concerns about the phenomenon of insecurity, which was taking various forms, they said, in response to the new measures adopted by the police in the framework of the *Boukle Pòtoprens* [Buckle Port-au-Prince] operation launched at the beginning of the month. (*Le Nouvelliste*, December 27, 1999.)

Would this police plan to "buckle Port-au-Prince" bring peace to the inhabitants of the capital and spread its beneficial impact over the whole country? Would these announced measures produce the desired effects in the year 2000?

Section 6 – 2000

Finally, we are in year 2000, the last period of our study. The third millennium surprised Haiti, still facing the demon of insecurity. At the beginning of January, the community in the town of Jacmel lived through the nightmare of a triple murder perpetrated on two French nationals, the couple Fernand Mullier, and a Haitian who was accompanying them, M. Aspin Obin. This terrible and insane triple murder was unanimously deplored by the Jacmel community, coinciding as it did with acts of vandalism perpetrated against a tourist project implemented by other French citizens at Ile-à-Vaches in the south of Haiti, and the Tourist Association of Haiti (ATH) took advantage of the sad incident to denounce the general situation of insecurity prevailing in the country at the beginning of 2000:

> The Tourist Association of Haiti (ATH) condemns most vigorously the assassination in the vicinity of Jacmel of two French nationals and a Haitian citizen who was accompanying them. It also condemns the recent acts of vandalism, arson and aggression perpetrated against the tourist village of Port-Morgan, at Ile-à-Vaches.
>
> The ATH calls upon the proper authorities to ascertain the circumstances in which these reprehensible acts occurred, to bring the results of the investigations to the attention of the public and to punish the culprits according to the law....
>
> We urge the authorities responsible to take the measures needed to rectify this intolerable situation of insecurity, which, only four years away from the celebration of the bicentenary of our independence and of our existence as a nation, will lead us rather to the forfeiture and destruction of the grand dreams of our

forefathers. (*Le Nouvelliste*, January 14–16, 2000, p. 1, 32.)

Like other vital sectors of the country, tourism was thus badly affected. The Haitian State still did not seem to be able to fight this evil effectively even in the capital, in spite of the implementation of the "Buckle Port-au-Prince" plan that had recently been adopted by the police authorities. In view of the weak results that this plan produced, President René Préval believed that it was his duty to participate personally in its execution. The singular character of the direct involvement of the head of state in police operations highlights the seriousness of the problem. It deserves our attention:

> The president of the Republic, René Préval, decided to go to the rescue of the guardians of public safety, who have been experimenting for some time with a plan for security, aiming at considerably reducing the general criminal activity in the metropolitan area.

> For a few days, the head of state has taken part personally in search operations carried out by national police patrols. On Tuesday evening, President Préval was in Carrefour to lend the support of the presidency to the efforts of the police in its fight against crime.

> "It is my responsibility—as head of State, responsible for guaranteeing the safety of the population—to monitor the application of the security plan and to ensure that the State puts at the disposal of the police force the means necessary for the success of its mission", President Préval declared in an interview with Signal FM. (*Le Nouvelliste*, January 11, 2000, p. 1.)

Unfortunately, this initiative of the supreme authority of the country had only a temporary effect. Moreover, eight days later, the last contingent of US armed forces based in Haiti disengaged. According to the mandate justifying the presence of these troops in the country, their final departure meant that from now on the political and social environment in Haiti was "secure and stable", despite the great concern recently shown by President Préval concerning the matter.

In fact, in addition to the prevailing insecurity, daily reality indicated on the contrary the reign of a climate of violence throughout the whole country, three months before the elections scheduled for April 2000. During the pre-election period, candidates and campaign directors from several political parties were attacked by unidentified groups of partisans. More than fifteen politically motivated murders occurred in several towns of the country, while common crime multiplied. Impunity was institutionalized.

During March, the election skirmishes reached their climax. In Port-au-Prince and several provincial towns there was an atmosphere of panic. The election campaign had been transformed into a true battle where only the party best-armed (in the literal sense) could win. Hordes of supporters and henchmen claiming affiliation with a certain political group invaded the streets and made life difficult for peaceful citizens. According to the press, Monday, March 27 was particularly " hot " in Port-au-Prince. Far from calming down on the following day, the situation worsened.

Under the heading "Elections—New Acts of Violence in Port-au-Prince", *Le Nouvelliste* wrote:

The news is still characterized this Tuesday by very violent demonstrations in the metropolitan area, paralyzing commercial activities and traffic. Indeed, hundreds of enraged, aggressive demonstrators inundated the streets of the capital, setting up burning barricades, throwing rocks at the windshields of private and public vehicles, and forcing drivers to turn back. Under threat of attack, most store owners in the downtown area closed their doors; retailers and window-dressers ran away to escape the fury of demonstrators, especially in Boulevard La Saline, Portail Saint-Joseph, Ramparts Street, Saint Martin, Tiremasse, Macajoux ... where the traffic was very light.

Tap-tap, truck and bus drivers coming from Bon Repos, Croix-des-Bouquets, Arcahaie, Saint-Marc ... dared not enter the downtown area for fear of becoming victims of reprisal. *(Le Nouvelliste,* March 28, 2000, p. 1.)

On the next day, March 29, the environment of violence was further aggravated. *Le Nouvelliste* described the concern and skepticism of the population faced with the generalized disorder that had plagued the country for three consecutive days. Here is a fragment of this article:

Port-au-Prince, Tires Burn ... Life Ebbs

The climate of tension generated by the burning barricades and the showers of rocks and bottles on car windshields reigned until today throughout the metropolitan area. Anti-riot squads and policemen, uniformed and heavily armed, venture onto the streets—but their presence cannot restore order in the capital because there are so few of them.

Members of popular organizations (OP) again stepped on the accelerator of violence this Wednesday and again paralyzed all activity throughout the country. The sectors most affected and most targeted by these OPs are: public transportation, trade, industry and, to a lesser degree, schools....

This Wednesday, in some hazardous zones (Sans Fil, Rue Neuf, La Saline, etc.), unidentified persons disturbed activities with bursts of gunfire and showers of rocks. Traffic in the abovementioned districts was almost non-existent.... Port-au-Prince today gives the impression of a gasping, distraught city. The threatening demonstrators managed to force store owners as well as window-dressers and retailers to stay home....

The violence extended to other cities, particularly Petit-Goâve where, against the backdrop of election campaigns, two members of the opposition were murdered. (*Le Nouvelliste*, March 29, 2000, pp. 1, 5.)

Where did these "unidentified persons" get these weapons? Reading these articles confirms that the measures announced at the beginning of the year, and the personal involvement of President Préval did not produce the expected salutary effects. On the contrary, the historical year marking the end of the second millennium was characterized by a series of spectacular crimes which raised the ire of Haitians and of members of the international community: the assassinations, one after another, of figureheads in Haitian society, like journalist Jean Dominique, director of Radio Haiti Inter (on April 3); Father Lagneau Belot, parish-priest of Thomassique (on May 3); doctor Ary Bordes, eminent member of the Haitian medical corps (on May 6). A climate of anarchy, of collective fear and anguish had settled over the country during the approach to the elections of May 21, 2000.

However, in spite of this worrying pre-election environment

and the assassination of more than fifteen members of the political opposition during the election campaign, the Lavalas *chimères* remained in their dens on election day, as if complying with a strict order. Citizens were able to cast their ballots in perfect safety, to the satisfaction of all the political parties and especially of the international community, which had much at stake regarding the success of the poll. However, it was necessary to await the closing of the polling booths before the unthinkable was discovered: many irregularities and massive frauds were going to sully the results of these elections.

The denunciation of these irregularities by opposition parties created an atmosphere of tension in the country. Indeed, they demanded the simple cancellation of the poll, which they described as an "electoral masquerade". In reaction, towards mid-June, the partisans of the ruling party, *Lafanmi Lavalas*, decided to paralyze national life in order to force the Provisional Electoral Council (CEP) to publish immediately the results of the elections that were being disputed by the other political parties, the OAS and even the president of the CEP.

Paradoxically, the inhabitants of Port-au-Prince were about to live through a strange situation for many days. The weapon of popular uprising, usually used as a threat against those in power, was used this time by those in power to force the opposition parties to submit to their will. The police force—naturally—proved ineffective to counter this special kind of violence sponsored by those in high places. An account of the facts produced by two journalists, Evans Dubois and Claude Gilles, will enable readers to understand clearly what is happening in Haiti today and to gauge the extent of the danger to which the whole of Haitian society is exposed:

Port-au-Prince Paralyzed

Port-au-Prince and surrounding areas awoke this Friday [June 16] amid burning barricades and tires. Early in the morning, members of popular organizations associated with the party of former president Jean-Bertrand Aristide, *Lafanmi Lavalas*, occupied the principal streets of the city. They demand that the Provisional Electoral Council publish the final results of the senatorial, legislative, municipal and local elections of May 21. They also denounce a "plot hatched by a sector of the international community (OAS) aimed at changing the results of this poll won by the party of Aristide, according to interim calculations". They also pointed out that the secretary-general of the United Nations, Kofi Annan, had denounced certain irregularities.

In several districts—Bel-Air, Lalue, Nazon, Carrefour and the commercial center—members of popular organizations set up barricades made of stones, old cars, and dustbins. They even used worn trestles and television sets to block access to the Cathedral Square. Smoke from tires could be seen for kilometers around. The capital had the aspect of a city under insurrection. Occasional passers-by who ventured there hastened to return to their homes. Constant showers of rocks were reported almost everywhere. The *chimères*, not more than a hundred, were armed with rocks and broken bottles. They shouted invectives against the opposition, in particularly against the *Espace de Concertation*, which they accused of having a pact with foreigners and of being used as an instrument of malevolent propaganda aimed at destabilizing the Lavalas party's power. With scowling faces, they went around the streets, singing: "*OEA, lè m grangou mwen pa jwe*" [OAS, I do not joke when I am hungry] to the tune of "*OEA lè m grangou m pa jwe*", the favorite chant of those close to Michel François and Raoul Cédras, the putschists of September 1991.

At Carrefour, rocks were thrown at cars, which had their windshields broken. Burning barricades had been in place since 2 am. At the time of going to press, the situation had not improved. All the secondary roads in the community were cut. Passers-by received showers of stones—one received a split forehead on the bridge at Carrefour. School children who had official examinations for the primary studies certificate experienced difficulties on this day of tension. Police patrols and fire-fighters worked hard. Arrests were made, but those arrested were released a few minutes later, after simple phone calls from high-ranking officials.

There were some bizarre scenes where police officers who wanted to cross the barricades begged members of popular organizations to help them. Moreover, police were absent from the capital. Tires were burning only a few meters from the "anti-gang" squad, and members of the CIMO (Company for Maintaining Order) were going about their business. It was not until 11 am that fire-fighters used a water-tanker to extinguish barricades of burning tires. Pick-up trucks pertaining to a public service could also be seen distributing tires and gasoline.

Gérard Jean-Baptiste, one of the organizers of the movement at Carrefour, declared that he was "satisfied". He estimated that the popular organizations made their voices heard and he announced other, more significant movements in the next days: "A general strike is in preparation. Nobody will be able to go out onto the streets," said another organizer.

Obviously, the stores closed their doors. Only a few private banks functioned until 2 pm. A few merchants who had ventured to open their businesses closed them under showers of rocks and other forms of intimidation. On Grand Rue and other commercial avenues, there was a stampede. The public markets were not operating. It was the same with public transportation, except for the "Service Plus" company.

National highway no. 1 also awoke to burning tires. Members of OP claiming to be from *Lafanmi Lavalas* set up barricades near the town of Arcahaie to demand the immediate publication by the CEP of the final results of the May 21 elections. Press correspondents reported that police officers on the spot did not try until the end of the day to free the road linking the Northern and Western administrative regions.

The mayor of the community of Arcahaie, Pierre Julio Joseph, who was elected under the banner of *Lafanmi Lavalas* at the May 21 elections, indicated that the movement begun in Arcahaie was a herald announcing a vast mobilization throughout the country to force the CEP to publish the final results of the May 21 elections without any modification. (*Le Nouvelliste*, June 16–18, 2000, pp. 1, 5.)

Such was the situation in Haiti in the middle of 2000. As a consequence of these pressures exerted by the government to force the publication of falsified results in favor of the ruling party, M. Leon Manus, the president of the Provisional Electoral Council (CEP), had to go into exile in the United States to escape threats against his life because he refused to endorse the frauds.

In spite of M. Manus's departure, the results of the first round of the elections were published by a new CEP set up unilaterally by President Préval, and the second round announced. Offended, the OAS Mission monitoring the electoral process left Haiti before the date of the second round that took place in its absence, to the great disappointment of the political community and the civil society. The Lavalas party was then able to win without contest all remaining seats in the Chamber of Deputies. Consequently, an improvement in the situation of insecurity in the country remained a pious vow in this environment that the State itself seemed to encourage.

Among the victims of the year 2000, we would like especially to mention the brutal disappearance of a great lady of Haitian society, a victim of this insecurity that spares nobody: Mme Carmen Boisvert Alexandre, assassinated in her residence on July 25, 2000. She was the wife of late physician Benoit Alexandre, colonel of the FAD'H, director of the health service of the army for many years, and later, Haitian ambassador to the Vatican.

A very cultured woman who lived in a historic and very well-maintained house located on a large property at Martissant, Mme Alexandre was 74 years old when she was assassinated by bandits who broke into her home. According to her close relations, her death probably occurred after a long session of torture and abuse by her assassins, judging by the many bruises that were observed on many parts of her body. The funeral home took great care not to expose her face to her family and many friends, who came to accompany her to her last resting place.

In spite of the blatant nature of the crime, after remaining 10 days at the mortuary of the Hospital of the State University of Haiti, the body of Mme Alexandre was given for burial to the family of the victim, who affirm that no autopsy was performed on the body. Thus, in her case there was no investigation. Moreover, apart from the obituary announcement, the press did not publish a report on this horrible assassination.

The following month, Port-au-Prince witnessed, among so many others, yet another senseless assassination. On Monday, August 7, the train of insecurity crushed a member of the United Nations delegation in Haiti, Mr. Garfield Lyle. He was killed by a single bullet in the head while he was traveling in a vehicle belonging to the Mission. Although the United Nations acknowledged the unfortunate character of this crime, it was very rare to observe an incident of this kind in Haiti where diplomats have always enjoyed the greatest respect of the population and are usually protected by the people even during times of internal conflict.

In fact, during August, the alarming situation of insecurity had not changed in the slightest degree. This is what *Haiti Progrès* affirms:

One no longer speaks about an increase of insecurity or about its reduction, because the situation has become a constant feature of life in the capital. The statistical recording of one victim more or one victim less from one day to the next cannot express the tension to which the citizens are daily subjected. Indeed, during past weeks, one cannot count a single day in which two or three people have not fallen under bullets from bandits in the metropolitan area—and those are only partial reports, few cases being reported by the press.

Regarding this trend, August began as the previous month finished—that is, under the sign of insecurity, of which no one sees an end in the current circumstances. The first half of this month saw an uninterrupted succession of criminal acts of which we will mention a few examples.

On Saturday, August 12, the bodies of two individuals were found on national highway no. 2 near the town of L ogane. One showed traces of machete blows and the other the impact of a bullet in the head.

On the same day, the body of a young man of about thirty years of age was discovered at dawn on Richard-Jules Street in Delmas 35.

In the Tele Haiti zone in the Bicentenary [district], a man approximately 50 years old was found dead in his car.

On Friday, August 14 at about midday, former colonel [sic] Gabriel Painson died in hospital from wounds he received a few days earlier during an attack on him in Debussy, where his driver had died. [This report confuses the victim with a former colonel of the same name.]

The agronomist Luc Sainvil of the English NGO Oxfam was wounded on the night of August 11 while trying to flee from bandits who apparently wanted to seize his vehicle. He had come from the Cin Imp rial in Delmas 19.

On the night of August 10 11, Sylvestre Solages, professor of mathematics at Jean-Jacques Dessalines High School, was found dead in Champ-de-Mars Street. According to Judge Lyonel Dragon, the victim was strangled with a rubber cord that was in the trunk of his car.

Several bullets cut down Laurore H rold, a seller of second-hand books, who ran a shop near the tourist bureau at Champ-de-Mars, on Saturday, August 19. His assassin or assassins did not steal anything, and his neighbors, two other merchants, said that they saw nothing but heard three shots and then discovered M. H rold lying in his own blood.

Around 4 pm on the same day, Frederic Moïse, 24 years old, was killed at Lalue, on the corner of the 1st Rue Jérémie. The day before, a 53 year-old man named Willy Thervil, a former soldier in the United States Army who returned to Haiti in 1986, was stripped and murdered by two individuals in his business premises at Carrefour-Shada.

Furthermore, one no longer counts the rapes, assaults, robberies and other crimes that continually occur. In certain provincial towns, the situation is not much different, especially where gangs have free rein to establish their headquarters. At Mirebalais and Plaisance, the residence of the mayor of Ville-Bonheur and the city hall were burglarized; on the morning of August 15, at the public market of Carrefour-Dufort, not far from Léogane, gangsters riddled with bullets two people coming from the capital whom they wanted to punish for encroaching on their territory! Again in the area of Léogane, the body of a young man was found riddled with bullets on the bank of the Rouyonne River. (*Haïti Progrès*, August 28, 2000, cited at www. haitianconnection.com)

In the same month of August 2000, the US State Department issued a warning to US citizens who were eager to visit or invest in Haiti:

The grave political, economic and social crisis that has been buffeting Haiti for more than two years has consequences for general security conditions in the country. In fact, in past months we have noted a clear deterioration of security (a rapid increase in "settling of accounts", armed attacks, petty thievery, break-ins …), which the national police have not been able to control fully. This phenomenon, which is not fully evident in the capital, has also begun to affect visiting and resident foreigners.

It is therefore wise to postpone any visit to Haiti that is not strictly necessary or a case of emergency. Great discretion is recommended to people who, for one reason or another, must travel to Haiti; they should be careful to take precautionary measures. Avoid walking alone in the poorer neighborhoods and shanty-towns, especially around the port and airport of Port-au-Prince, and do not attempt to walk around the city at night because of the darkness. Avoid traveling by car at night on the roads to provincial towns and in the vicinity of the capital.

Do not wear any jewels or valuable objects, do not display cameras or other photographic equipment, and generally avoid arousing envy. Abstain from all behavior that could be interpreted as provocative, arrogant or ostentatious; do not photograph or film people without first obtaining permission; generally avoid photographing extreme poverty-stricken areas. Refuse to transact any business with street traders, especially involving cigarettes and alcohol. Avoid gatherings of curiosity seekers and young loiterers, which can quickly turn into uncontrollable mobs. Decline invitations to unauthorized Voodoo ceremonies; do not venture outside the towns.

Considering the extreme sensitivity of police officers, behave courteously and extremely calmly when dealing with them, and be fully respectful of local laws; in case of difficulty do not hesitate to contact the embassy. In case of armed attack, it would be best not to resist. Considering recent incidents involving foreign luxury boats, you are strongly advised not to anchor in Haitian waters. (http://travel.state.gov/haiti.html, August 16, 2000)

Haitians themselves expressed an identical perception of the situation at that time. On the occasion of the moving funeral of M. Patrice Gousse, who was assassinated in broad daylight at Musseau in Port-au-Prince on September 17, 2000, M. Emmanuel Ménard painted a dark and sad picture of the quality of life in Haiti:

"The deaths cannot be counted anymore", he declared, "the city has been emptied and has become a den of cut-throats". The people are perplexed, and wonder if the assassins are not more numerous than the citizens; and the citizens, impotent, taken as hostages by the assassins who are assisted by the twilight or dawn, have their residences ransacked, their businesses plundered, their inheritances set on fire, their sisters raped, their sons killed. (*Le Matin*, September 30–October 2, 2000, p. 12.)

The environment thus described, far from improving with the passing days, rather worsened more as the end of the year approached. In November 2000, a large number of victims were counted. On several occasions, heavily armed individuals opened fire on police stations and also on groups of peaceful citizens at bus stops and in homes in poor districts, causing deaths and casualties, with total impunity.

These sad events were reported in the press:

Bloody Weekend in Port-au-Prince

A shooting on Friday evening at the crossroads of the Aviation (the intersection of Boulevard Jean-Jacques Dessalines and the Delmas road) characterized life in Port-au-Prince in a bloody way. Six people were killed and a score of others were wounded during the drama. Four of the victims died immediately, and two died at the Hospital of the State University of Haiti. One of the wounded people, Hérold Mésidor, 34, was left paralyzed, his upper and lower limbs no longer functioning.

Witnesses reported that the gangsters operated quite calmly on Friday evening around 6:30, remaining on the spot after the drama to rob and mistreat bus drivers and their passengers.

Traveling in a pick-up truck, the gangsters opened fire on the crowd that had massed at the crossroads of Aviation. According to information reported this Monday by Radio Haiti Inter, confrontations between two armed gangs were the cause of the drama that cost the lives of these six people. According to Radio Haiti Inter, certain members of a brigade set up by the municipal authorities of Port-au-Prince were involved in the confrontations between the armed gangs....

In addition, five gangsters armed with revolvers opened fire on the police station at Soleil 2 [in Cité Soleil] on the evening of Thursday, November 2. Four police officers stationed at Soleil 2 police station said to Radio Haiti Inter that they had already undergone attacks from the gangsters on October 15, 16 and 23. The police officer added that individuals had tried, several times, to set fire to the police station, but that the police had received support from members of the public....

Unidentified armed men also wounded three American journalists in Cité Soleil during the week. In this Monday's *Inter Actualités* magazine, a journalist quoting public transport drivers reported that approximately three people are assassinated every week at Portail Léogane. (*Le Nouvelliste*, November 7, 2000, p. 7.)

We waited for news of an improvement in the situation right up until the moment of concluding our study, but it was in vain. On the contrary, a week later, the phenomenon of insecurity had worsened. *Le Nouvelliste*'s editor described the atmosphere of generalized fear enveloping the Haitian capital thus:

It is not enough to "*naje pou w sòti*" [paraphrasing an expression of President René Préval, meaning "swim in order to be able to escape"]; it is necessary, in these last days, to *pare w pou w kouri* [be ready to flee].

Since the beginning of this week, the insecurity has assumed alarming dimensions: holdups, gun blasts that provoke a *kouri* [fleeing] in certain parts of the downtown area. After 6 pm, the city is empty. Businessmen, small retailers, school children and older students … who run as fast as they can during the day, return quickly to their homes, thanking God that they have not become victims of the growing insecurity.

Insecurity is blind. It affects every sector of the population. Some have fallen for having committed the sin of being at a street corner waiting for a tap-tap [popular transport vehicle in Haiti]. Some have become victims for being at the wheel of a car and thus being objects of envy. Others are targeted because they are owners of businesses that generate jobs in this country corroded by unemployment....

Finally! The list would be too long.... Well may the experts distinguish between organized crime, political violence, delinquency and others; but what concerns us is the way that these various kinds of insecurity combine in an explosive cocktail that harasses the population in a situation of permanent stress....

Insecurity also captures the sea. "Pirates" of another kind attack boats making the run between Port-au-Prince and La Gônave.

It is difficult to choose between *naje pou w sòti* and *pare w pou w kouri*. (*Le Nouvelliste*, November 15, 2000, p. 1.)

As the date of the November 26 elections approached, the climate became even more unhealthy. One week before the contest, explosions caused one death and wounded about fifteen people in Port-au-Prince. "From now on, fear in Port-au-Prince is more than justified. As we approach the November 26 elections, violence has not finished counting its victims, particularly from bombs that are exploding almost everywhere in the capital and its suburbs", wrote *Le Nouvelliste*, four days before the elections. (*Le Nouvelliste*, November 22, 2000, p. 1.)

The situation had not improved by the end of the year, which ended with the tragic death of former deputy, engineer Rood Thénor Guerrier, journalist Gerard Dénauze and manager Reynold Ambroise, all three assassinated at the end of December 2000, in disconcerting circumstances, without their murderers being arrested. On another front, confrontations in Cité Soleil again led to deaths and casualties from shooting in this populous community.

Thus, no significant progress towards an attenuation of the phenomenon of the insecurity in Haiti was recorded between 1995 and 2000. Affirmations of the authority of the State and of the safety of the population never tallied during this period.

At the time of completing the manuscript of this book, the number of victims for the year 2000 had reached 223 (Appendix 6).

Section 7 – Summary and Prospects

We have together just made a long and difficult journey from 1995 to 2000, a journey strewn with human remains. We have listed a total of 1451 cases of violent deaths including summary executions by shooting, knifing, lynching, stoning, strangling, necklacing, etc. (Appendix 7). This assessment, far from being exhaustive, is the result of information gleaned here and there from newspapers in Haiti and abroad.

In concerning ourselves with making available to readers sources that can easily be verified subsequently, we intentionally omitted many cases of crimes that were reported on radio and television but not in the newspapers. For the same reason, we did not use statistical data from official organizations or foreign institutions working in Haiti. We readily acknowledge that the assessment presented here can only be approximate.

Nevertheless, we think that, with its clear references that can be accessed and verified by anyone, our work, although incomplete, will allow the gravity and extent of the phenomenon of insecurity in Haiti to be evaluated adequately. The method that we have used also emphasizes the vitality of the Haitian press. If no remedy has yet overcome the evil, the Haitian journalists cannot be blamed, having effectively provided information for opinion leaders, authorities and potential decision makers—their voice simply was not heard.

Taking into account the sources of the data used (that is, newspapers), many crimes were not indexed because they were not acknowledged by the print media. In addition, many cases surely escaped the attention of this researcher. For example, while we counted 285 and 223 victims for the years 1999 and 2000, respectively, the official report presented by the spokesperson of the police force (PNH) lists 536 and 340 assassinations and attempted murders, respectively, for these years (*Le Nouvelliste*, December 28, 2000, p. 1.) Our assessment therefore has fallen short of the black reality with which the Haitian population is confronted.

However, we believe that it was much more significant for Haitians to consider tangible facts, cases experienced by everyone. Thus, they will be better informed about the extent of the damage and the need for them to engage in deep reflection concerning the insecurity in Haiti. While exploring the list of victims identified by name (Appendix 8), they will come to the realization that the period covered by our study was one of great destruction according to the values of Haitian intellectual, moral, professional and political leaders. Many well-educated minds among our intelligentsia—doctors, engineers, businessmen, politicians, priests and pastors, tradespersons, religious brothers and sisters, agronomists, soldiers, police officers, lawyers and academics—were eliminated by vicious acts of gangsters and by political violence.

The problem is all the more serious since less than about five percent of the perpetrators and sponsors of these crimes were identified, apprehended, brought to trial, judged and sentenced.

Faced with the tide of delinquency of all kinds, the Haitian penal system was swamped. The clearance rate of cases—that is, the number of cases solved compared to the number of cases brought to the attention of the police force—continues to decline. The rate is currently so negligible that many parents and friends of victims lose hope of ever seeing the files of their close relations surface again. Thus, as the days pass, the number of crimes recorded by the police and not yet solved will become so high that no democratic police organization could reasonably reach a solution without a considerable budgetary increase.

In the same way, the courts are very slow in the handling of the cases that are submitted to them. This situation causes a swelling in the number of outstanding cases, which leads the prosecutor's office simply and ineluctably to close a large number of them. To tell the truth, the judicial system is confronted with the same constraints as the police force: a proliferation of punishable acts and a limit to available resources.

However, the legal authorities' laxity, the courts' limitations and the incapacity of the police force and of the prosecutor's office to fulfill their constitutional missions are precisely what feed impunity. Hence, besides the unfortunate political choices of the ruling power, the problems confronted by the authorities of the law-enforcement system—the police force, the attorney's office and the courts—constitute the very mechanism of impunity, which itself encourages the proliferation of crime.

In our study, we have voluntarily remained silent about many flagrant cases of insecurity, such as burglaries, kidnappings, disappearances, attacks on goods and private property, seizure of vehicles, verbal assaults, attempted murders, etc., that also compose the daily life of Haitians today. Besides, an increase in the rate of homicides goes hand in hand with a rise in spectacular robberies and attacks of all kinds. Moreover, when these offenses are not seriously taken into account, the trust of the population in its protective structures is reduced and, consequently, a strong feeling of insecurity overwhelms citizens. Thus, we cannot underestimate their importance.

> Although a resurgence of crime is worrying, this is not merely because some particularly odious and aggressive acts are committed from time to time, but rather because many less serious misdemeanors are committed that eventually lead to more serious crimes. It is more the frequency than the seriousness of criminal acts that makes people fear a decline in moral standards. (Sébastian Roché, *Sociologie Politique de l'Insécurité* [*Political Sociology of Insecurity*], p. 29.)

Therefore, it is the duty of any law-enforcement system to treat all types of offense seriously.

However, by confining our study to the victims whose lives have been snatched away by this galloping insecurity that ravages Haiti, we believe that we have reached the essence of our objective: to prick consciences about the fact that Haiti risks getting bogged down in an irreversible situation if pragmatic solutions, stripped of any spirit of partisanship, are not urgently applied, and if the criminals continue, with total impunity, to defy the national law-enforcement systems.

Under the current conditions of insecurity, foreign investors—reticent, concerned and disillusioned—will systematically refuse to participate in the recovery of the Haitian economy, the most weakened in the Americas. Recently, the Ambassador of Japan to Haiti drew the attention of the Haitians to this crucial point:

> "The devices of intimidation and threat enormously discourage the business sector of Tokyo, which planned to place investments in Haiti. Our colleagues in Tokyo cannot consider new projects in Haiti because we cannot ensure the full execution of the projects in progress", the Japanese diplomat indicated, stressing that the ensuring of security is the first stage in a durable and reliable process of development. "If the security of Japanese technicians cannot be guaranteed, we cannot give them the green light to come to Haiti", he added. (*Le Nouvelliste*, July 19, 2000, p. 1.)

As we have seen, these concerns were also expressed and emphasized in the US State Department warning. When it is considered that the majority of foreign investment in Haiti relies on US investors, do not such descriptions of the dangers to which foreigners are exposed in Haiti today, made by the US government itself, indicate that the country is moving with large steps towards the abyss?

In fact, the return of M. Jean-Bertrand Aristide to the presidency does not augur well for a rapid improvement of security in the country. Two days before his inauguration ceremony, scheduled for February 7, 2001, the US State Department published an even more serious warning to American nationals eager to visit Haiti:

The Department of State warns U.S. citizens against travel to Haiti due to the unstable security situation throughout the country. The Department has authorized the departure of family members of U.S. Government personnel from Haiti. If they have not done so already, U.S. citizens in Haiti should establish and maintain contact with the Embassy and consider their own personal security situations in determining whether to remain in the country.

The security situation in Haiti continues to be volatile and unpredictable. The Presidential inauguration of Jean-Bertrand Aristide, slated for February 7, 2001, has the potential to spark violent demonstrations and individual acts of violence. The Haitian government has failed to contain certain violent and dangerous incidents, including bombings in public areas, politically-motivated killings, indiscriminate gunfire directed at pedestrians in Port-au-Prince, and incidents directed at diplomatic facilities and vehicles.

Crowd behavior is unpredictable, and violence can flare up at any time, so American citizens are warned to avoid political gatherings and demonstrations. Travelers encountering roadblocks, demonstrations, or large crowds should remain calm and depart the area quickly and without confrontation. Assistance from Haitian officials, such as the police, should not be expected during public political events.

In addition to civil and political unrest, violent crime is on the rise throughout the country. The state of law and order is of increasing concern, with reports of armed robberies and break-ins, murders and car hijackings becoming more frequent. The limited response and enforcement capabilities of the Haitian National Police and the judiciary mean there is little relief for victims of crime.

....

SAFETY AND SECURITY: Haiti continues to experience civil and political unrest. Crowd behavior is unpredictable, and violence can flare up at any time. Demonstrations and protests occur periodically throughout the country. American citizens traveling to or residing in Haiti are advised to take common-sense precautions and avoid large gatherings or any other event where crowds may congregate. For current information on safety and security, please contact the U.S. Embassy at the telephone numbers listed below.

SPECIAL CIRCUMSTANCES: Haiti's presidential elections took place on November 26, 2000. The new Haitian president is expected to take office on February 7, 2001. Historically, Haitian elections have been accompanied by increased violence, and the days leading up to the election were marked by demonstrations and bombings. During parliamentary elections in May and July, activists established unofficial, temporary roadblocks throughout the country, at times cutting off major thoroughfares and the airport. Protesters succeeded in paralyzing Port-au-Prince and other major cities in the aftermath of the first round of elections using flaming barricades and bonfires, with U.S. Government buildings serving as the focal points of some of these actions. The Haitian government has failed to contain certain violent and dangerous incidents, including bombings in public areas, politically-motivated killings, indiscriminate gunfire directed at pedestrians in Port-au-Prince, and incidents directed at diplomatic facilities and vehicles. Political events are often held in public areas and some have turned violent; American citizens are advised to avoid such gatherings.

Travelers encountering roadblocks, demonstrations, or large crowds should remain calm and depart the area quickly and without confrontation. Assistance from Haitian officials, such as the police, should not be expected. Particular caution should be taken in the days immediately preceding and following elections and the release of results.

CRIME: There are no "safe areas" in Haiti. Crime, already a problem, is growing. The state of law and order is of increasing concern, with reports of armed robberies and break-ins, murders and car hijackings becoming more frequent. The police are poorly equipped and unable to respond quickly to calls for assistance. While not specifically targeting U.S. citizens, criminals nonetheless killed or maimed several U.S. citizens in 1999 and 2000. Travelers should be particularly alert when leaving the Port-au-Prince airport, as criminals have often targeted arriving passengers for later assaults and robberies. Criminals also surveil bank customers and subsequently attack them; some recent incidents have resulted in the victims' deaths. Holiday periods, especially Christmas and Carnival, see a significant increase in violent crime.

Travelers and residents should exercise caution throughout Haiti. They should keep valuables well hidden, ensure possessions are not left in parked vehicles, favor private transportation, alternate travel routes, and keep doors and windows in homes and vehicles closed and locked. If an armed individual demands the surrender of a vehicle or other valuables, the U.S. Embassy recommends compliance without resistance. Criminals have shot drivers who resisted. The Embassy also recommends against traveling at night, particularly outside Port-au-Prince. The limited response and enforcement capabilities of the Haitian national police and the judiciary frustrate crime victims.

Certain high-crime zones should be avoided when possible, including urban route Nationale #1, the airport road (Boulevard Haile Selassie), the port road (Boulevard La Saline), and Carrefour. Due to high crime, Embassy employees are prohibited from entering Cite Soleil and La Saline and their surrounding environs, and are strongly urged to avoid Delmas 105 between Delmas 95 and Rue Jacob. Under no circumstances should one attempt to take photographs in these areas because this almost inevitably provokes a violent reaction. Neighborhoods in Port-au-Prince once considered to be relatively safe, such as the Delmas Road area and Petionville, have been the scenes of increasing incidents of violent crime.

Use of public transportation, including "tap-taps" (private transportation used for commercial purposes), is not recommended. It is suggested that travelers arriving at the airport be met by someone known to them. Mariners should note that Americans and other foreigners have reported the theft of yachts and sailboats along the Haitian coast over the past year. Some of the thefts were carried out by armed gangs, and one foreigner was killed. Cameras and video cameras should only be used with the permission of the subjects; violent incidents have followed unwelcome photography. (http://travel.state.gov/haiti.html, February 5, 2001).

In short, Haiti's future looks gloomy. The increase in unpunished crimes continues unabated in the year 2001. At the time of delivering this manuscript to the editor, we note with anguish that the social renewal that the Haitian people desire so strongly does not seem to be on the horizon. This year began, like the preceding ones, punctuated by brutal and spectacular murders. Among others, a peaceful family man, Georges Derenoncourt (on February 24), a dynamic businessman, Gérard Cassis (on March 3), a young manager, Jessy Pierre (on March 9) and a technician and US citizen, Claudio Ramirez (on April 3) were mown down in broad daylight—but the perpetrators of these foul crimes were not identified and incarcerated; and still the violent crowds dispense their own justice in the streets.

The questions that arise now are: How can such a situation be rectified and the decay be halted? How can this train of death, which sows mourning among Haitian families, be stopped?

In the next chapter, we will try to answer these questions by humbly contributing to the debate certain reflections likely to help decision makers in the search for appropriate solutions to this vexing problem, which endangers the very existence of the Haitian nation.

Journalist Jean Léopold Dominique
in conversation with the Author (July 1989)

Miss Christine Jeune
Police Officer at the Haitian National Police (PNH)
Assassinated in obscure conditions on March 19, 1995

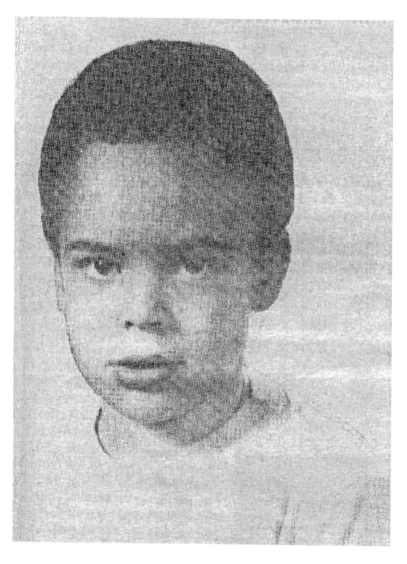

Little Boris Pautensky (6 years old)
Kidnapped at his School on May 28, 1996

Mrs Erla Jean-François
Mayor of the City of Chansolme (in the North-West)
Assassinated by gunfire in broad daylight on May, 30 1996

M. Joseph Rony C. Charles
Banker, Deputy Director at PROMOBANK in Cap Haitian
Assassinated by gunfire in broad daylight on August 5, 1996

M. Louis Emilio Passe
Deputy at the Haitian Legislative Corps
Assassinated by gunfire on October 16, 1997

Colonel Roger Cazeau
Retired Officer of the Haitian Army
Former Commandant of the Haitian Air Force
Assassinated by gunfire on June 14, 1999

Sister Marie Géralde Robert
Nun, Responsible of a Health Center at Côtes-de-Fer (in the South)
Assassinated by gunfire in broad daylight on November 17, 1999

Brother Hurbon Bernardin
Brothers of the Christian Instruction
Assassinated and mutilated at La Vallée de Jacmel
on November 30, 1999

Mrs Carmen Boisvert Alexandre
Scholar, Businesswoman
Tortured and then assassinated on July 25 juillet 2000

M. Patrick Gousse
Manager
Assassinated by gunfire in broad daylight on September 17, 2000

M. Jean-Rood Guerrier
Engineer, former deputy at the Haitian Legislative body
Assassinated by gunfire on December 20, 2000

Colonel Jean Lamy
Counselor at the Haitian National Police
Assassinated by gunfire on Octobre 8, 1999

CHAPTER V

PROPOSALS FOR SOLUTIONS

In the preceding chapters, we have tried to describe the most prominent aspects of the evil of insecurity from which Haitian society has been suffering. We have exposed its disturbing dimensions and also its harmful impact on the development of the country, both socially and economically. However, a work design to open the eye of the society to such a serious situation is incomplete if it remains a simple narration or examination of the facts. Any narration, study or critique of an acute problem must postulate solutions so that the work may bear fruit for both present and future generations. In such a frame of mind, we take this opportunity to outline some proposals for solutions to the problem of insecurity in Haiti.

After six years of the lame functioning of Haitian democracy in the wake of the *Uphold Democracy* Operation, the *Human Development Report 2000* of the United Nations Development Programme (UNDP) paradoxically classifies Haiti among the poorest of the western hemisphere nations, in spite of an investment of more than two billion dollars by the United States and an injection of more than 500 million dollars of foreign aid into the Haitian economy since 1994. This sad result may appear surprising to many—but how could it be otherwise when the need to establish and reinforce security in the country was not considered to be important by the decision makers of the time?

Now that the international community has decided to abandon its *laissez-faire* attitude and to adopt a more active policy of insisting on the strict observance of respect for human rights and the correction of the excesses and abuses against democracy that have been committed in the country, Haiti should take advantage of this new attitude to eliminate completely the phenomenon of insecurity from its society.

We believe that Haitians will succeed if together they apply themselves to the task with ardor, patriotism and altruism to establish four preconditions that constitute, in our humble opinion, the road to success in this undertaking—namely, national reconciliation, independence of the judicial and electoral structures, strengthening the national public force and, finally, a policy of public investment and job creation for the benefit of the people.

Let us examine the details of this rescue plan.

A. National Reconciliation

On July 3, 1993, at the height of the situation generated by the *coup d'état* of September 30, 1991, a solution to the crisis seemed to have been found: the signing of the Governors' Island Agreement. This document, which was considered to be the basis of a new departure for Haiti, ended with these provisions:

> The president of the Republic [Jean-Bertrand Aristide] and the commander-in-chief [Raoul Cédras] agree that these terms constitute a satisfactory solution to the Haitian crisis and the beginning of a process of national reconciliation. They are committed to co-operating fully in the realization of a peaceful transition to a democratic, stable and durable society, in which all Haitians will be able to live in a climate of freedom, justice, security and respect for human rights. (*Le Nouvelliste*, July 5, 1993, p. 2.)

Launched in this way, the first attempt at national reconciliation was begun in 1993 by Prime Minister Robert Malval, who was installed as the head of the government in accordance with the Governors' Island Agreement. As early as his first day in office, on September 3, 1993, M. Malval, in his inaugural speech, invited all Haitians in exile to return to their native land to work towards the development of their country. We were one of the first exiled persons to respond to the call. From the Dominican Republic, we crossed the border the very same day to reoccupy our family home, in Pétion-Ville.

Soon after taking office, M. Malval launched the idea of a national conference of reconciliation, to be held in Miami, Florida. Unfortunately, this laudable initiative failed. To the great disappointment of Haitians, *Le Nouvelliste* announced in its headline on December 15 that the project had been canceled:

The Conference for Reconciliation Canceled

Robert Malval returned this afternoon to Port-au-Prince, advising, with a sob in his voice, that the National Conference, planned recently on his initiative, will not take place.

"I put into it all my courage, all my patriotism, all my democratic dreams, all my good faith, all my integrity, but...", the Prime Minister declared at the international airport, with distress in his voice and containing his sobs with difficulty, barely hiding the personal drama of a man who runs the risk of failing to make his "exit from the scene an exit from the crisis." (*Le Nouvelliste*, December 15, 1993, p. 1.)

This declaration by M. Robert Malval of his inability to accomplish the patriotic meeting, to some extent, sealed his fate and ensured his departure from the position of prime minister. However, hope had not completely evaporated. "This conference will be held after the return of President Aristide", he said during this press interview.

Indeed, as we have seen in Chapter I, upon his return to the country on October 15, 1994, President Aristide included national reconciliation as one of the major topics of his message delivered to the Haitian people and the rest of the world.

Moreover, President Bill Clinton, during his visit to Haiti on March 30, 1995, echoed the same key idea in exhorting the Haitian people to take the salutary route of reconciliation. Mr. Clinton said: "I cannot do better than to repeat President Aristide's words: 'No! to revenge, No! to vengeance, Yes! to reconciliation'". *(Le Nouvelliste*, April 3, 1995, p. 14.)

National reconciliation is a topic that is impossible to avoid. Judging by general opinion, the unification of Haiti's sons and daughters constitutes the key that will open the door to success for any policy that aims to raise the living standard of the Haitian people. Only the application of this life-saving formula will allow, at one stroke, the eradication of the phenomenon of insecurity, the establishment of peace and tranquility among Haitian families, the restoration of the country to normality and the success of economic recovery. Assuredly, we will never cease repeating these famous words of former US president Richard Nixon:

> Lack of national unity makes democracy almost impossible, economic development a remote dream and internal tension a constant reality. (*La Vraie Guerre* [*The Real War*], p. 42.)

What is reconciliation?

The word "reconciliation", which is defined as the action of restoring friendly relations between people in discord (*Larousse*), implies the end of a state of conflict, disagreement, division or dissension existing between individuals or groups of individuals, and the beginning of a state of union, peace, mutual respect and reciprocal consideration. By an act of reconciliation, relations of harmony, understanding and peaceful coexistence are restored among the people who compose a population, who formerly have been considered to be enemies.

This word also implies the idea of a compromise between two protagonists who voluntarily recognize the need to abandon futile conflict and to unite to achieve a common goal: the good of their community.

"Reconciliation" does not mean abandoning one's

ideological convictions—no! This term connotes rather the renunciation of rancor within a framework of agreed rules. It is not the expression of a capitulation by a person or group, but rather the effect of a courageous act performed by two protagonists who decide by mutual agreement to put an end to a climate of discord, hatred and contempt that has existed between them.

Neither should the concept of reconciliation be conceived as a condescending favor granted by one of the parties to the other. One does not ask an opponent to bow in order to become worthy of reconciliation. One of the antagonists must offer a hand to the other, without any ulterior motive or intention to humiliate the other or diminish the other's dignity.

The causes of discord are often imaginary or even ignored by the antagonists. Members of a community hate each other; groups of citizens clash and discredit each other without ever having met as individuals. Sometimes, people who maintain a relentless hatred know each other only through intermediaries who, for some unknown reason, have contrived to place them in opposition. Often, this attitude is the result of unresolved historical misunderstanding.

One of the major obstacles to reconciliation is the widespread belief that it must be preceded by an act of justice. Nothing is more inaccurate. In the implementation of this noble project, the desire to give or receive justice before considering reconciliation must be put aside.

After 1986, as president of the Republic, encouraged by the

success of a national forum that brought together more than 26 political parties and groups around a discussion table in February 1989, we were the first to propose the idea of the need for altruism and charity in facilitating national reconciliation and thus avoiding disaster for the country. Unfortunately, this call was ignored. In the speech that we delivered on Flag and University Day, May 18, 1989, highlighting the importance of forgiveness in the reconciliation process, we said:

> I am convinced that only reconciliation can help us to save this country. It is indeed impossible to erase the sufferings that have been endured, the abuses that have been undergone and the wrongs that have been committed by some against others; but, conscious of the misfortune that hangs over our country, in the light of the experiments of the past, it is urgent for us Haitians to find peace, and only reconciliation can enable this. Former victims and subjects of trauma may say that it is too much to require of them. What, then, would be our destiny today if the divine creator were of the same mind—he who made the great gesture of forgiveness by the sacrifice of his son? Intractable individuals may still stiffen their opposition, but are they ready to accept responsibility for the collapse of our dear country? For, without this national reconciliation, the country will collapse. (*Le Silence Rompu* [*Breaking the Silence*], p. 156.)

Although it may be true that reconciliation is sometimes accompanied by "justice", the former can also precede the latter, as has happened in the Republic of South Africa under the leadership of Mr. Nelson Mandela.

A Haitian scholar, M François Roc, writes on this subject:

> To say that there is no reconciliation without justice appears to me

quite normal, because reconciliation is primarily a political initiative that seeks to give cohesion to a ruptured, splintered and self-destructive society. National reconciliation has meaning only so far as it is a response to this disintegration. As a political gesture, it cannot proceed without acknowledgment of the fact that the victims still carry pains or handicaps.... In this sense, only justice can justify, dare I say, the credibility, even the success of the initiative.... The question remains how to link justice and reconciliation.

For several years, I believed ... that justice should precede reconciliation. This position has the principal defect of treating justice as an end in itself. In other words, to some extent it forgets the crisis, while the devouring crisis continues its devastation....

All this does not mean that victims' right to justice should be denied. Moreover, justice for victims is part of our aspiration to a more just, and thus more coherent, society. Thus, justice and reconciliation can and must go together, necessarily and realistically. Here are some current examples: it is in a reconciled France that, fifty years after the Second World War, those accused of crimes against humanity during the Nazi occupation continue to have a rendezvous with justice.

Nelson Mandela placed South Africa on the path of reconciliation. Even though the ashamed face of the black ghetto-towns still exists, victims and torturers of the apartheid era continue their testimonies. ("Entre la Raison et l'Explosion [Between Reason and Explosion]", *Le Nouvelliste*, March 17, 1998, p. 6.)

The task of reconciling intractable enemies is rarely easy. The victims are on one side, and the alleged offenders on the other. Success in the process of reconciliation requires a serious effort by both parties. The victims must, without denying justice as an ideal to be sought, begin to abandon hatred, revenge and violence, to create and maintain a climate of understanding, tolerance and mutual respect; and the offenders must make a firm commitment to behave in the same way, while expressing regret for their past behavior, confessing their guilt and expressing an attitude of repentance.

Within the political community, the leaders of the parties must commit themselves to acting ethically towards each other, while regarding themselves as adversaries rather than enemies, and accepting ideological pluralism and the principle of political alternation as foundations of the democracy to which the country aspires.

The guiding principle remains: the initiators of reconciliation must humble themselves and offer forgiveness. Often, it can also be a question of reciprocal forgiveness for offenses. Everyone knows that violence begets violence. In South Africa, for example, the black leaders of the African National Congress (ANC) party recognized that they, just like the whites, had committed excesses during their struggle to free their country from apartheid. In this matter, *Agence France Presse* reports:

Johannesburg, December 4 (AFP). On Thursday evening, Winnie Madikizela-Mandela begged for "forgiveness" for all that "awfully took a tragic turn" in the years 1986–89 and led to violence and murder among the entourage of her football club in Soweto. The ex-wife of the South African president, who denied any direct or indirect responsibility for the score of murders that took place among her entourage at that time, said for the first time, however, that she was "deeply sorry".

At the end of a nine-day hearing of the Commission for Truth and Reconciliation (CTR), she was answering the petition of the president of the debates, Archbishop Desmond Tutu, who appealed to her: "Please, please, please ... say 'Sorry'".

Previously, the archbishop had summarized the feeling of the Commission by saying that "one will undoubtedly never know the details" of what occurred at that time, concerning Winnie and the Mandela United Football Club. (*Le Nouvelliste*, December 4, 1997, pp. 1, 13.)

That is it! There is no sacrifice too great when it is a question of establishing harmony and concord among citizens for the good of a common homeland. In a case where both parties have committed excesses, reciprocal forgiveness should be encouraged and obtained, as Archbishop Desmond Tutu managed to do.

To implement the project of national reconciliation, it would be necessary to create a new moral entity capable of serving as an intermediary between the parties being reconciled. For Haiti, this moral intermediary could be a conference composed of wise delegates from the Episcopal Conference of the Catholic Church, the Confederation of Protestant Churches, the World Council of Churches, the Freemasons, the voodoo religion, etc. Is this not a judicious proposal that could be applied in Haiti as it was in South Africa where a Commission of Reconciliation operates effectively as a moral force and an intermediary between the groups and parties involved?

Reconciliation, once achieved, would banish from Haiti the mindless hatred that exists between certain groups of

Haitians—Lavalassians, dissenting Lavalassians, Duvalierists, former Duvalierists, etc.—and between the ruling party and those who shun public affairs because of their ideological belief, doctrinal affiliation or political past. While retaining their differences, the citizens of past regimes and those of the present could agree to sit down around the same table together to identify, analyze and construct solutions to the nation's problems.

Once this problem had been resolved, the country's leadership would be able to undertake, with a greater chance of success, another exciting task: the reforms necessary to enable everyone, without distinction, through credible and genuinely independent legal and electoral structures, to participate, according to their skill and wisdom, in the affairs of State. Indeed, as a corollary of national reconciliation, these reforms would be easier to implement, given the contribution that new technicians, specialists, doctors and scholars would be able to make to the nation under a restored unity.

B. Independence of the Judicial and Electoral Institutions

For approximately eight years, the Haitian political and social panorama has been affected by an endemic evil: rampant injustice. Haitians demand justice. The leaders always promise to deliver justice, announcing that it "will be healthy and impartial"—but can such a wish be fulfilled by means of a legal system that is riddled with politics and corruption, and in which judges are chosen without considering their qualifications, or are chosen from militant members of political groups?

1. Reform of the Judicial System

The deplorable, lamentable, shameful state of the Haitian judicial system is well highlighted by M. Joseph Guyler C. Delva who writes:

> The Haitian judicial system is confronted—everyone recognizes this—with enormous difficulties, specifically of a structural, logistic, intellectual and even political nature, which prevent it from fulfilling its mission to the satisfaction of all. The Haitian judiciary, like many other branches of the State and public institutions in Haiti, has its hidden face, its lower parts made of venality, trading of favors, corruption, etc. (*Le Nouvelliste*, May 25, 1999, p. 1.)

What is worse, this judicial system seems to be unaware, in many cases, of a citizen's right to freedom. A judicial system that cynically keeps innocent persons in prison is the worst thing that a nation can have. In Haiti today, the judicial system ignores the individual freedoms recognized by the Charter of the United Nations, to which Haiti is a signatory, and by the Haitian Constitution in its articles 24–27.

Let us follow our guide Joseph Guyler C. Delva:

> Many indicted persons awaiting trial end up being incarcerated for a period far exceeding the sentence that they would have received had they been found guilty.... The latest statistics provided by the Department of Prison Authorities (DAP) indicate that the prison population, in the 18 prisons throughout the country, is estimated at 3655 prisoners. According to the deputy manager of the UN/OAS International Civilian Mission in Haiti (MICIVIH), Rodolfo

Mattarollo, 80% of these 3655 prisoners are in custody; only 20% have been tried and sentenced. Mr. Mattarollo explains that of the 80% of those in custody—that is, waiting to be tried—a group quantified by MICIVIH as 1200 people are in prolonged custody.

According to the executive director of the UN/OAS Civilian Mission, Rodolfo Mattarollo, of this number, 800 prisoners have already spent between one and two years in prison, 300 have been imprisoned for more than two years and 110 have already spent more than three years in prison without being tried or sentenced. "In certain cases, let us remember, these people are held on charges for crimes that would by no means justify a detention of so long a duration, even if the charges were proven", deplores Rodolfo Mattarollo, estimating that, in most cases, it is a question of a simple offense that could have been tried and judged without too many difficulties. (*Le Nouvelliste*, May 25, 1999, p. 6.)

During the period covered by our study, nothing tangible was done to change this deplorable system, which has been used by the ruling regime to incarcerate its political opponents. In spite of many appeals by human rights organizations, the situation has remained unchanged. The recent report (August 2000) of the independent expert from the United Nations, Mr. Adama Dieng, noted this:

The disorder of the Haitian legal system is marked by a dysfunction of the penal system. A lack of independence of judges and of the attorney's office, and difficulties in gaining access to justice, continue to cause frustration not only among the population but also among international supporters. We recall that we have expressed our concern regarding non-fulfillment by the Attorney's office of provisional release orders rendered by judges, especially in delicate matters, and particularly those having political connotations. This attitude, which undermines the rule of law, had as its consequence a flourishing of cases of arbitrary detention." (United Nations, *Report on the situation of human rights in Haiti*, Document A/55/335 (28 August 2000), Section IX, par. 49.)

The State has an obligation to guard—to guarantee—the safety of the entire population. To attain this end, it holds a monopoly on the legitimate use of force, all the more so as it is its duty to administer laws—to enforce them—by using penal institutions. If the State is unable to make the justice system work, to guarantee the safety of its citizens, it *ipso facto* endangers its own existence.

In this connection, Professor Sébastian Roché writes:

The consequences of the decline in public organizations' effectiveness [in fighting insecurity] are the forced descent of the State from the supervisory position that it has occupied, and the questioning of its legitimacy to serve as supreme arbiter. If the State can no longer either guarantee security or establish what is permissible, then—since its legitimacy is justified by its capacity to do so—it saws off the branch on which it is installed. (*Sociologie Politique de l'Insécurité* [*Political Sociology of Insecurity*], p. 150.)

As natural guardians of the ideals of its founders, heads of state have a mission to ensure the survival of the nation. From that is derived their urgent obligation to ensure that public institutions are capable not only of maintaining the integrity of the territory, but also of guaranteeing the safety of the lives and property of the people.

With regard to these two obligations, the State exerts two

kinds of control: organizational and institutional.

Organizational control relates to the creation of institutions capable of protecting the territory and the people, and punishing delinquents and criminals. This control implies the organization of a professional public force—that is, army and police—the development of coercive laws and the functioning of independent courts and effective prisons. Further upstream, this control broadens to include schools as providers of basic moral and patriotic education, and of discipline regarding individual and collective behavior.

Institutional control relates to the operation of the institutions that the State creates. This control is a matter of maintaining the capacity of the public force to accomplish its mission, of ensuring the development of coercive regulations and of solving crimes and misdemeanors. This will depend on the training of the personnel involved, their working methods, their enforcement capability and the strict, prompt and uncompromising character of the punishment of deviants by the judicial system.

So far as the security of the people is concerned, the judicial system is of paramount importance: everything depends on it. As soon as citizens decide that the judicial system does not perform its task adequately, they are tempted to seek their own justice, which is something that the State must prevent, considering the serious abuses that generally result from such behavior. Citizens are authorized to seek justice only in the law courts.

Since the Constitution has abolished the death penalty in

Haiti, the dramas resulting from private applications of the self-defense formula seem more shocking. Too often, the response of self-defense is manifested in Haiti in scenes of lynching, necklacing and stoning of the kind that have been reported in this book. The purpose of the penal system of a country is precisely to prevent these antiquated forms of regulation, which are generally excessive, inopportune and irrational, and very often unjust.

The State, in theory, is legally and democratically responsible for all the unofficial executions by lynching or other means that have occurred throughout the country. It should not have left to citizens the matter of providing justice for themselves, at the risk of undermining its legitimacy.

Since the State has a monopoly on the legitimate use of force, and has the exclusive right to enact laws and then to arrest, judge and punish delinquents, it also has the exclusive right—and also the duty—to make the system function properly in order to end these antiquated practices. This monopoly is also one of the characteristics of the penal system. Let us listen to Professor Sébastian Roché:

> Let us specify the nature of the penal system: it is quite autonomous, quite free with respect to its environment. Theoretically, it occupies a position beyond competition: one cannot ignore it and seek justice elsewhere. Indeed, in the case of monopoly by a public institution, it is very difficult to bypass it: the police and judiciary are watching in such a manner that it is impossible, or almost impossible, to form one's own police force, or to obtain justice for oneself other than in the courts. (*Sociologie*

Politique de l'Insécurité [*Political Sociology of Insecurity*], p. 139.)

In order for the penal system to fulfill its mission and end the insecurity in the country, Haiti must urgently undertake an in-depth reform of its judicial system, by establishing a clear objective: the efficient and impartial dispensation of justice to the people. To achieve this goal, it is important that the executive and judicial institutions be separate, that the new role of the attorney's office be well defined, that the independence of the judges and the courts be assured, and that the prisons fulfill their purpose within the strict framework of the law. Such a project would accord with the intent of the Haitian Constitution.

a) A new concept for the Judiciary

It is important to establish the difference between the concepts of "justice" (as it is used in Haiti) and "the judiciary", which Haitians often confuse. The term "justice" has a very broad connotation that is not limited to the notion of "judicial authority". In Haiti, when it is said that "justice" is rotten, the reference is not to the judges and the courts: such an interpretation constitutes a serious mistake. It is important to understand clearly this nuance of meaning in order not to fall into regrettable misunderstanding.

The Ministry of Justice must not be regarded as an agency of judicial authority, which, according to article 173 of the Constitution, is exercised "by the Supreme Court, the Courts of Appeal, the Courts of First Instance, the Courts of Peace and the Special Courts". Only these bodies are vested with the responsibility of resolving lawsuits, punishing criminals and dispensing justice. In discussing the independence of justice here, we mean only the judicial branch of government—that is, the courts and the judges.

The task of the Ministry of Justice, a department of the executive branch of government, is to protect society against the actions of delinquents and criminals, to apprehend the authors of crimes and misdemeanors, to instigate public proceedings against them and bring them before the courts, to prosecute them, and finally to apply the sentences pronounced on them by the courts. It fulfills these tasks by the actions of the police force, the Attorney's office under the direction of the government prosecutor—currently a very powerful man in Haiti—and the detention centers.

b) A New Role for the Attorney's Office

The government prosecutor—the head of the Attorney's office—is nominated by the executive, who can also remove him or her at any time. Therefore, the prosecutor is inclined to comply with instructions received from his or her superiors, who have discretionary authority to remove him or her from office. Besides the interests of the community that, theoretically, he or she has the responsibility of defending and protecting, the government prosecutor thus behaves above all as a diligent agent of the executive branch of power.

However, governments always seek to safeguard their own interests, which is quite understandable. Consequently, a new role must be conceived for the government prosecutor, to prevent interference by the executive branch—and thus political bias—in the exercise of judicial authority. It is desirable, nay mandatory, that this senior official be confined to the duties of instigating public proceedings against delinquents, properly preparing criminal files, bringing those indicted by the examining magistrate before the courts and ensuring that convicted persons serve their sentences.

c) The Judiciary's Independence

To eliminate interference by the executive in judicial affairs, the administration of the judicial branch of government should be entrusted entirely to the judiciary, just as legislative authority belongs exclusively to the legislature. Neither the judges of the Supreme Court, nor those of the Courts of Appeal, the Courts of First Instance, the Courts of Peace or the Special Courts should receive any orders from the government prosecutor or from any office of the executive branch.

One of the objectives of this reform should be the organization of a new judicial system in which the positions of judges, legal officers and clerks are filled by applicants selected on the basis of their intellectual ability, their competence and their honesty, and not because of their membership in a clan or their loyalty to a political party or group.

These new civil servants of the judiciary, having been properly recruited, should then be granted decent salaries to protect them from the demon of corruption, which has invaded the present institutions of Haiti.

Finally, emphasis should be put on the Courts of Peace, which constitute the base of the pyramid of the dispensation of justice to a large majority of the population. A functional Court of Peace should be established in each communal section of the country, in conjunction with the application of an initiative undertaken in 1989 by the Office of Protection of Citizens, which successfully proposed to the government the institution of a legal service for law graduates in Haiti. In the same way that young physicians provide social services within the Ministry of Health, new bachelors of laws would, for a certain period, help poor people to present their complaints and ensure their defense before the courts.

d) Respecting the Law within the Prisons

With regard to prisons, reform must take into account the dignity of every prisoner, none of whom should be detained in custody while awaiting trial by a court of competent jurisdiction, except under the terms of an incarceration order from the Examining Magistrate. Governments must not be allowed to use prisons to incarcerate their political opponents.

After judgment, convicted persons must immediately go to prison to serve their sentences; but if they be recognized as innocent, they must automatically and immediately be authorized to return home, if "not retained for another cause ready to be presented to the court" (*Haitian Criminal Instruction Code*, article 290).

Moreover, constant attention should be given to the prison itself, the last element of the repressive system. The death penalty having being constitutionally abolished in Haiti, imprisonment becomes the sentence *par excellence* in the fight against crime and misdemeanor.

It thus falls to the State to create sufficient space in the detention centers or to manage them in order to release space for accommodating the most dangerous delinquents. In this regard, it would be convenient to introduce into Haitian legislation provision for automatic bail, bail hearings and "freedom on parole for good conduct". This would allow prisons to free more space for the lodging of dangerous convicts.

It is also necessary to humanize the prisons in Haiti!

In conclusion, to administer justice properly in Haiti, a democratic government would, in our view:

recognize the law courts as the only authorities over justice and imprisonment;

equip the justice system with better judges by scrupulously complying with the constitutional regulations for their nomination;

simplify the procedure for freeing accused defendants who have received "not guilty" verdicts, and eliminate the discretionary power of the Ministry of Justice in this case;

install reliable mechanisms for the orderly replacement of civil servants;

respect the principle of the lifetime tenure of judges;

create within the judiciary an office to manage its budget in order to make this branch of government autonomous;

establish a commission of ethics and discipline to deal with errant judges;

improve the expertise of the judiciary police for better preparation of criminal files;

execute all court decisions without delay;

ensure that the legal limits of police custody are observed, and establish a limit to the period of pre-trial custody following the decision of the Examining Magistrate;

manage the prisons in order to create more space to accommodate convicts;

facilitate the re-education of delinquents and the rehabilitation of prisoners;

educate the people so that they are well aware of their rights and duties in the area of justice;

institute a legal service for graduates of the Haitian law schools.

At a time when the international community is demonstrating its willingness to assist the Haitian people in the establishment of a sound national judicial system, a responsible leadership should seize this opportunity to equip the country with a judiciary adapted to Haitian culture and capable of establishing a reign of harmony, concord and peace among the people. Once this situation has been realized, the effect of these dispositions on the phenomenon of insecurity in Haiti will certainly soon become visible.

However, it is important to remember that the holding of credible elections is necessary to enable the selection of the human resources necessary to ensure the proper operation of the national judicial institutions. For, in accordance with the Constitution, institutions composed of elected officials (the Senate, the Legislative Body and local communities) have the privilege of designating not only judges, but also the members of the Permanent Electoral Council (CEP). Furthermore, elections are the only reliable means of appointing competent, honest, well-qualified, loyal, patriotic and responsible citizens to direct the political institutions of the State.

Consequently, it is essential that the results of elections always reflect the popular will. To this end, it is necessary that the electoral institutions be free of any influence from the executive branch of government or from any political party.

2. The Independence of the Electoral Council

The primary goal of elections in a country is to create and maintain an impartial State. By requiring that certain administrative positions depend on a choice made freely by the people—that is, that the positions be filled with elected officers—the Constitution intended to limit the number of nominations made unilaterally by the executive branch of government. Consequently, an executive that usurps elective functions by fraud, violence or other artifice is violating the Constitution because it destroys the goals aimed at by the fundamental charter.

The monopolization of elective functions by a government undermines the entire democratic system. It opens wide the door to corruption, nepotism, incompetence and mediocrity. It discourages the young from obtaining an education and adults from improving their skills. Thus, for the survival of democracy in Haiti, it is absolutely essential that the electoral institutions be placed beyond the reach of the influence of government officials, of the head of state and of political parties.

In 1987, the Constitution established in Haiti an independent institution devoted solely to electoral matters for the whole territory—the Permanent Electoral Council (CEP)—and composed of "nine members chosen from a list of three names proposed by each of the departmental assemblies" (article 192). While waiting for the final organization to be set up, the Constitution envisaged, in its transitional provisions, the formation of a provisional electoral council temporarily responsible for fulfilling this mission (article 289).

The formula prescribed for the formation of the provisional electoral council expressed the concern of the framers of the Constitution, who intended to avoid favoritism in the selection of members of this institution. It stipulates that eight members are to be drawn from eight entities that are independent of the public administration, with one representative per selected organization, and only one member, not a civil servant, being chosen by the executive.

The first provisional electoral council of 1987 conformed to the constitutional model. After its dissolution in November 29, 1987, it was replaced by a contingent electoral council, which carried out the elections of January 1988. This council was automatically dissolved on February 7, 1988.

In the following year, 1989, wanting to give a democratic and permanent character to the electoral institution, the government of the time, of which we were the president, convened a forum of political parties for the formation of an electoral council by consensus. The results of the workshops enabled the formation of a permanent institution with a provisional council board composed of nine members designated as intended by article 289 of the Constitution.

In 1990, the consensual electoral council of 1989 was dissolved by the new provisional government, which called upon the former members of the provisional electoral council of 1987 to organize the elections of December 1990.

Unfortunately, following this ballot, far from keeping this electoral council in operation until the formation of the permanent electoral council as prescribed by the Constitution, its members were nominated to high offices in the administration (general directorships, ministries, embassies, etc.) The electoral institution evaporated.

During the period of the *coup d'état* (1991–1994), legislative elections were organized on January 28, 1993, by another contingent electoral council formed by the putschist regime.

Then came the return to constitutional order in 1994. Pretending to apply the provisions of the Constitution designed for the formation of the Permanent Electoral Council, while local authorities—a prerequisite for the selection of members—did not exist, the Aristide government created a new provisional council remote from both the letter and the spirit of the Constitution. It selected the members thus: three designated by the Senate, three by the executive and three by the Supreme Court. The result: seven of the nine members of the new electoral council were recognized and attested as being closely associated with the restored executive.

Consequently, it was under disputed conditions and a boycott that this electoral council arranged the elections of June and December 1995 and of April 1997. The latter so shocked the political community by its many frauds and irregularities that it led to a serious political crisis: the resignation of the prime minister, Rosny Smarth, and the lame functioning of the remaining two-thirds of the Senate, culminating in the dissolution of parliament by the executive in January 2000. By the same token, President René Préval revoked all elected mayors and replaced them with new officials by decree. This is how democracy functioned in Haiti at the time of the return to constitutional order!

Facing national and international disapproval of these anti-democratic initiatives, President Préval sought a method of organizing new elections. On March 6, 1999, an agreement was signed between the government and five political parties to create a new provisional electoral council. Elections could be held only on May 21, 2000 for the Senate, deputies and administrative councils of the communal sections (CASECs). However, the results were disputed by the opposition parties, the civil society and the international community, and—surprisingly—by the five signatories to the March 6 agreement, because of fraud and unfair manipulation of the ballot. In fact, the government had allotted all the contested positions.

Outraged by this action, two of the three members designated by the five political parties of the March 6 agreement hastened to resign when requested by their party, and the president of the council, M. Léon Manus, received a death threat and was forced to go into exile. The council was thus reduced from nine to six members.

This crisis became prolonged, especially after August 28, 2000 and the appointment to parliament of officials elected in the disputed poll of May 21, in spite of complaints by the political parties and the councils of the civil society, and serious warnings from the international community.

To top everything, far from paying attention to these various remarks, President René Préval unilaterally nominated three new members to the electoral council to replace the exiled president and the members who had resigned, and then announced presidential elections for November 26, 2000. Such behavior by the executive does not augur well for the finding of a solution to the problem of insecurity in Haiti.

Such has been the course of the electoral institution since its design by the framers of the 1987 Constitution. Since 1995, the two Lavalas governments, reticent about permitting any possibility of alternation of political authority, always managed to dominate the electoral council, creating a tense situation and aggravating the climate of insecurity throughout the country.

Everyone knows that the monopolization in a country of all the political offices by one group or party leads to tyranny, dictatorship, corruption, abuses of all kinds and all the evils that can affect a nation. In this connection, let us listen to what Professor Olivier Duhamel says about the importance of fair and credible elections in a political system:

> Equipped with the considerable power to choose, the voter has in addition the right to change opinion and, by changing opinion, to change the course of events. Any system functioning by a majority must permit alternation or at least the possibility of alternation. The opposition of today is the majority of tomorrow, the date of this tomorrow being uniquely uncertain. This is what encourages the majority to show a little salutary modesty, and to restrain, at least partially, any arbitrariness. This is what gives the opposition a little hope, and restrains, at least partially, any demagogy....

> Alternation offers many other advantages. It renews elites, awakens political good-will, stimulates administrations, puts an end to entrenched clientelism, shakes up established corporatism, brings out new work sites, regenerates public discussion....

Without alternation, the leading political party becomes a mafia by governing continually. Power erodes. Power possessed for too long erodes too extensively. Power misuses. Power eternally given, eternally misuses. Power corrupts. Power enduringly monopolized, enduringly corrupts. The erosion of power, the abuse of power and the corruption of power are shaken up by alternation and are moderated by the prospect of further alternation. (*Les Démocraties* (*Democracies*), p. 320.)

Having discussed reconciliation and the independence of the judicial and electoral institutions, let us address another very significant topic in the battle against the phenomenon of insecurity: the existence of an effective, well-formed, well-equipped and non-political public force.

C. Strengthening the Public Force

One of the significant causes of insecurity in Haiti is the obvious weakness of the Haitian public force. This weakness appears in several areas: structure, personnel and equipment.

From the structural point of view, and without yet considering the absence of the military as an integral part of the Haitian public force, there is no doubt that the young national police force, the PNH, lacks several components necessary for the satisfactory functioning of a body that is responsible for ensuring the safety of the 8 million inhabitants on 27,750 square kilometers of land.

Unlike the Haitian Army (FAD'H), the institution of security and defense that it replaced, the PNH lacks a significant number of vital structures that existed within the FAD'H. It has no reliable communication networks linking the central headquarters and the stations in the cities and communal sections, no police presence in the communal sections and several important towns, no organized transportation system for moving personnel, no engineering service for establishing construction standards for police stations and prisons, no health service guaranteeing the physical condition of personnel and providing adequate care for sick police officers and agents or those wounded in the execution of their duties, etc.

On another front, although the seaboard is supervised to a very small degree by the coastguard service of the PNH, Haitian airspace is left wide open to international smugglers and drug traffickers. Nowadays, planes carrying cocaine and other noxious substances or smuggled wares land in the provincial towns to unload their goods with no concern or fear of apprehension. Their preferred landing strips are the national highways, which the gangsters clear of all traffic and other activity during the course of their reprehensible operations.

From the point of view of personnel, the national police force functions far below the level necessary to accomplish its task. The people available are far from highly skilled. Moreover, besides the fact that only a few months were allowed for preparation of the first promotions of police officers, the police institution has a personnel of barely 4–5,000 officers for the entire territory, whereas the FAD'H, which it has replaced, included 7,000 soldiers, not counting the rural police officers (section chiefs) and their assistants who supervised the 565 communal sections of the country.

In addition, the personnel of the PNH has been constantly and too frequently changed because of massive dismissals from the ranks of the young institution which, because of a lack of rigor in the selection of its first recruits, had to deal with many cases of police officers being involved in obvious violations of human rights, organized crime, assassinations, drug trafficking, robberies, etc.

In addition to these serious deficiencies, there is the great vacuum created by the absence of an army, which remains the institution constitutionally authorized to carry adequate equipment and to provide training for protecting the territory, for dealing with heavily armed criminals, assassins and terrorists who defy the police force, and for deterring drug traffickers who treat Haitian territory and airspace as their private domains.

Urgent measures should be taken to rectify the prevailing situation of inadequacy within the security forces of the country. A health service, a transport corps, a signal corps, suitable personnel, a qualified and tested leadership, a sound hierarchical structure, an adapted code of ethics, and, above all, a new military institution to fill the vacuum left by the dismantled FAD'H—these are, in brief, the framework of a new national public force capable of meeting its heavy responsibilities.

The Haitian leadership must at all costs avoid transforming the police force into a military institution of which only the name would be missing. As we emphasized in our book *From Glory to Disgrace: The Haitian Army 1804-1994*:

We think that the Haitian police should not be given the military means (weapons and training) allowing it to face security problems that are beyond the capability of a regular police force. The possession of these means will steer the new institution away from the mission for which it is designed—the protection of the lives and property of the population—and it will soon be in the same situation of hegemony as was the old Haitian Army, all the more so as it will have its tentacles spread throughout the country, like the former Army. (*From Glory to Disgrace: The Haitian Army 1804–1994*, p. 339.)

When one analyzes the situation that prevailed in Haiti at the time of the 2000 elections, one cannot deny that the national police force was overwhelmed by the belligerence of rival opposition groups at Anse d'Hainault, who disrupted election proceedings in the Grand'Anse administrative division.

In any civilized country, a similar situation would have required the use of a specialized force, differently equipped and trained, to restore order and allow the regular police force to achieve its task. For lack of this structure, the population of Anse d'Hainault suffered much loss of human life and experienced the disastrous effects of arson, which destroyed a considerable number of houses in the area.

Encouraged by this situation, apparently tolerated by the authorities, will not troublemakers in other localities decide in the future to defy the authority of the State, being assured of impunity? Are not whole sections of the population exposed to abrupt deprivation of the safety that the State has the duty of ensuring? What would occur if this kind of violent turmoil occurred simultaneously in several localities? These are questions that demand an immediate response from a responsible leadership, and that should prick the consciences of the Haitian leaders.

For these and many other reasons, we believe that the Republic of Haiti has a pressing need for a well-equipped and professional public force to guarantee the integrity of the territory and its borders, to ensure a peaceful mood among its citizens, to preserve public peace, to protect the people, to deal effectively with delinquents equipped with heavy weapons, and to intervene in social disturbances of all sizes to restore republican order.

About the necessity of the military alongside the police force, Pierre-Raymond Dumas said:

> Conceived for the maintenance of law and order, for the protection of lives and property, the national police force discovers from day to day that it is poorly equipped to fight against drug trafficking and organized crime. A reform is essential if the police are to survive so many challenges and dissatisfactions. One cannot fight against well-organized hardened traffickers and gangsters in the same way as one posts guards outside government offices....

> The "whites" who entered Haiti as saviors did not logically anticipate the development of organized crime, and did not think to prepare us to face the over-sized Dominican army.... Many extremely credible voices were very loudly raised to warn that the defense of the territory and of the border is not the job of a police force and that this weakness compared to the Dominicans is an intolerable danger that finally will cost us much if nothing be done to restore the equilibrium....

> It is not by remaining silent about the dismantled FAD'H that one

will awaken the peoples' spirit to the distressing problems of insecurity.... The necessary balance between defense of the territory, public safety and democratic stability undoubtedly lies along tested and, at the same time, new paths. Otherwise ... ("Débat sur la Force Publique en Haïti [Debate on the Public Force in Haiti]", *Le Nouvelliste*, November 29, 1999, pp. 15, 17.)

Concerning the budget necessary to accomplish the project of restoring the military, we think that the importance of the objective justifies the resources that would be required. Moreover, it has never been established, as it has been alleged on many occasions, that the military was devouring the national budget. The facts do not support such an argument. In the period before 1990, for example, the budgetary bill 1985–1986, renewed for several subsequent years, envisaged a total of 712,010,700 gourdes for the operation of all state institutions. Within this budget, the FAD'H was allocated an amount of 96,182,000 gourdes—that is, 13.5% of the total budget. (*Moniteur* 69A, September 30, 1985)

Currently, within the operational nation budget 1995–1996, totaling 5,261,980,000 gourdes and renewed each year until the present, the amount allocated to the police force amounts to 779,000,000 gourdes, without provision for presidential security, which formerly depended on the FAD'H and now has a separate budget. This amount accounts for 14.8% of the national budget. (*Moniteur* 51, July 15, 1996.)

The difference is negligible. Furthermore, Pierre-Raymond Dumas again presents the right word on this subject. He writes:

This plea in favor of the armed forces greatly dissimulates the argument concerning budgets, human resources and the place of public safety in Haiti in 2000.

In fact, although the budget of the police force continues to increase, we obtain very poor results, in spite of the increasing danger. (*Le Nouvelliste*, November 29, 1999, p. 17.)

However, the reinforcement of the police force will have no effect without the political will of the national leadership to require and ensure respect for the law by everyone. Nothing will help to fight insecurity more than strict enforcement of the law by and for everyone—both those who govern and those who are governed.

Throughout this work, we have highlighted the poignant drama often experienced by the people of Haiti at times of disorder, provoked by the inopportune irruption of the crowd onto the streets across the country. Although these situations were unlawful, they occurred with the consent, and sometimes the support, of the Haitian public authorities.

These practices must cease so that peace and safety can reign. Any effort that tends to improve the climate of security in Haiti presupposes the will of authorities to maintain the public force—army and police—far away from political alliances, and to enforce the law for everyone.

Finally, to prevent the abuses that sometimes occur between the police force and the people, who, by definition, are the ideal partners to ensure its full effectiveness, it is desirable that the Mixed Civic Service envisaged by the Haitian Constitution be applied. A civic, non-political body, harmonizing relations between the people and the public force, would help to drive out of Haiti the specter of insecurity, with its procession of difficulties: instability, economic crisis, under-employment, unemployment, etc.—all factors that increase social strains.

This last point brings us to consider another factor in the search for solutions to the problem. While insecurity can cause under-employment, chronic unemployment also generates insecurity. It is a vicious circle! Since destitution and misery are closely associated with delinquency, to address poverty and instability would undoubtedly reduce the evil of insecurity considerably. One way to fight poverty would be for the State to implement a coherent program of public investment centered on a policy of job creation for the benefit of the people.

D. Public Investment and Job Creation

"In a country like Haiti, characterized by a high degree of poverty", Haitian economist Jacques Vilgrain writes, "any economic action undertaken by the public authorities should aim to reduce unemployment and to increase people's standard of living." (*Structures, Mécanismes et Evolution de l'Economie Haïtienne* [*Structures, Mechanisms and Evolution of the Haitian Economy*], p. 79.) This reflection is also worth considering in the fight to eradicate the phenomenon of insecurity in Haiti.

Indeed, to overcome the insecurity affecting Haitian society presupposes engaging in a constant fight against the endemic situation of misery in the country. Within a new international order based on free trade and liberalization of national economies, the under-employment could be overcome if, alongside the development of a strong and competitive industrial sector and the contribution of foreign aid, a public investment plan were initiated.

This would be the most effective way to fight insecurity, for such a policy would raise people's standard of living by creating jobs for hundreds of thousands of Haitians. Since Haiti is a country still to be developed, a field ripe for cultivation, the possibilities for job creation are innumerable.

This policy would enable the State to decrease quickly the level of idleness, which very strongly promotes insecurity, and also to take some measures to feed, clothe, house, and educate the Haitian people—to provide them with adequate health care, to improve their schooling and to support the family unit.

The State can reach this goal by undertaking the construction of homes, irrigation canals, airports, sports fields, highways, terminals, schools, hospitals, administrative buildings, wharfs, public markets and amusement parks; by promoting modern agriculture, industries, arts and crafts; by undertaking the forestation of the country, etc.—in short, by transforming the country into a vast work site.

The success of such a program implies substantial international assistance. In fact, even if the criminal embargo applied against Haiti during 1991–1994 was approved, solicited and encouraged by Haitians who were anxious to return to power, the international community, having been the instrument of this policy, has the moral obligation to help this country repair the damage caused to its economic infrastructure by this unjust decision. To put Haiti back onto the path of recovery of acceptable and durable human development would require both the implementation of a true "Marshall Plan" and a responsible, patriotic leadership.

Faced with this necessity, Mme Paulette Poujol Oriol, failing to question directly the Haitians responsible for this catastrophe, wonders precisely:

To whom will the Republic of Haiti, the small black sheep of the Antilles, to whom will it have to address:

—for the damages that the international community is responsible for repairing, and from which we have not ceased suffering?

—for the fatal, unjustified and disproportionate embargo, which destabilized its economy;

—for the children of Haiti, dead because of a lack of food and medicine;

—for our industry of hired assassins, which threw thousands of families into the street, deprived of their daily bread from one day to the next;

—for the insecurity of our streets and the generalized violence; because everything is tied together: jobs lacking, unemployment increasing, the cost of living climbing, our young people in despair, drifting into drugs and delinquency;

—for these expeditions of gangs of criminals, gangsters already hardened and sentenced [by US courts] for common-law crimes, who from time to time are poured onto our shores under the pretext of "repatriating" them;

—for our army, degraded and dismantled in contempt of the letter of the Constitution, concerning which, however, so much respect, integrity and longevity was preached;

—for our currency reduced to a shadow of sorrow, a direct consequence of our moribund trade, of our destroyed export opportunities, of our polluted environment;

—for our tourism stabbed in the back by an unprecedented campaign of denigration, by the slogans posted in foreign travel agencies and even on aircraft, mis-advising potential travelers not to come to Haiti, the country being considered dangerous, insecure and unhealthy? ("Le Temps des Repentirs [The Time of the Repentances]", *Le Nouvelliste*, July 10, 2000, p. 14.)

To this legitimate and relevant list of questions, which should prompt more than one Haitian to examine their consciences, to recognize their mistakes and to make a firm resolution of repentance, we answer that these reparations will be made when all Haitians, men and women, by their responsible behavior, establish an environment that is favorable to the durable economic development of their country.

Only then will appear, as Mme Odette Roy Fombrun so ardently wishes, the miraculous combination of "the national *kombite* [gathering] of solidarity with the international *kombite* of solidarity joined together to allow the founding in Haiti of a humane democracy that will at last bring comfort and safety to all Haitians." (*Le Nouvelliste*, October 25, 2000, p. 14.)

CONCLUSION

Friends, readers, you have just made with us quite a sad journey. You have experienced the tribulations that a generalized insecurity delivers to the Haitian population. You have felt the devastating impact of unbridled violence on the development of this country. The danger to which the Haitian nation is exposed is immense, for violence constitutes a negative and destructive threat to any civilized society. As Professor Chalmers Johnson explains, generalized violence can cause a social system to disappear:

> Perfect order in a social system would be the sign that the ultimate, ideal society had been realized; generalized violence would be the indication that the system had reached its end (or that social behavior had completely lost its character of an organized system)....
>
> Society represents victory over violence. The proof is partly presented by Hobbes [the 17th century British philosopher] where he describes what life would be like without society, in this chaotic situation that he calls the "state of nature". In this state, he explains … there would be neither sciences, nor arts, nor trade, and worse: people would live in perpetual fear and in constant danger of violent death.
>
> All things considered, human life, under such conditions, would be "solitary, poor, nasty, brutish, and short". To enjoy the benefits of organized society, humankind must give up violence, because violence, more than anything else, marks with its fingerprints the "state of nature." (*Déséquilibre Social et Revolution* [*Revolution*

and the Social System], pp. 14, 15.)

In Haiti, if insecurity is not eradicated, it will destroy everything. Always possible in every community, the extent of violence in the everyday life of a nation is used by any potential investor as the best tool for determining the level of stability in a country. The degree of individual and collective safety in a community has always been used as standard for evaluating the social system itself.

As we have seen during this study, a large number of Haitians lost their lives in obscure circumstances, even though the period examined is one of full democratic experiment. The situation looks even more serious when it is noted that the number of deaths by violence listed in this work for the period 1995–2000 is far higher than that officially listed by the National Commission of Truth and Justice for the period 1991–1994, the three years of the putschist regime (1451 cases compared to 576).

In the face of this reality, we think that it is important that Haitians finally understand the need to sweep away past dissension, to get rid of rancor to make possible the unity of the Haitian family—a unity with diversity, of course, but one capable of enabling them to consider together the best way of raising their country out of the abyss into which it has been sunk.

In this book, we have tried to outline the way: effective national reconciliation, an independent judicial institution, an impartial electoral institution, a strong and neutral public force (army and police), and finally the initiation of a public investment plan centered on a policy of job creation.

Once this historical combination of objectives had been achieved, it would be necessary to have, at the helm of the country, leaders who practiced tolerance, who respected the political rights of citizens, who preached ideological pluralism and who accepted the principle of political alternation.

In this frame of mind, the country awaits a *person* of the stature of Nelson Mandela, a *patriot* who will agree to share power so that Haiti lives, who will be able to hold out his hand to his enemies to create the harmony within the nation; a native *Haitian* who will place his or her country above everything including personal ambition; a *humanist* who will choose "to forgive in order to live together".

Nelson Mandela put aside personal feelings to effect his plan for reconciliation with the South African whites, his former torturers. In South Africa, today, the results of his choice are positive. National stability is consolidated. The whites do not feel any fear of being governed by the blacks, their former victims. After the voluntary departure of the charismatic Nelson Mandela from the political scene, when he handed the torch to his colleague Mr. Thabo Mbeki, the militants of his party, the African National Congress (ANC), showed themselves worthy of their leader's efforts by banishing from their hearts all thoughts of revenge, so much so that the South Africans voters have just democratically re-elected their political party to the leadership of their country.

One highly significant point is worth emphasizing: Mr.

Mandela did not use his charisma, his immense popularity or his international prestige to destroy the multi-partisanship and political pluralism in the Republic of South Africa. At the last elections in 1999, granting victory to the new ANC leader, Mr. Thabo Mbeki, elected President of this country with 66.4% of the votes cast, the 400 seats of Parliament were distributed between several political parties: the ANC gained 266 seats, the Democratic Party (DP) 38 seats, the Inkatha Freedom Party (IFP) 34 seats; the National New Party (NNP), the party which supported apartheid, obtained 28 seats, and 12 other minority parties shared 34 seats. The possibility of alternation has not been abolished under the pretext that the African National Congress is today the most popular party in the Republic of South Africa.

This is the example recommended to our potential leaders to follow. National reconciliation must become a reality in Haiti, along with respect for democratic principles. Haiti cannot allow itself the luxury of continuing to live in error, on penalty of seeing the Haitian democratic dream disappear. We, the privileged, must work advisedly so that the people do not embrace the belief that the democratic system is incapable of facilitating peace, safety and happiness for the nation.

During six years of an experiment described as democratic, the Haitian population experienced only frustration, exasperation, suffering and sorrow. It falls to the intellectual, economic and political leaders of the country to create or reinforce in the Haitian consciousness the idea of the effectiveness of the democratic regime. They also have the privilege of offering the people a tangible demonstration that the democratic system is a catalyst of peace, safety, prosperity, truth, altruism and love.

> Democratic legitimacy, where it is firmest and most stable, has its source in a major attachment to the values rooted in the political culture of the country, and this at all levels; but it also holds, especially in the initial phase, to the effectiveness of the democratic regime and to its economic and political results: maintenance of law and order, safety of the people, arbitration and settlement of conflicts, and a minimum of foreseeability in the development and implementation of decisions." (Larry Diamond, Juan Linz and Seymour Martin Lipset, *Les Pays Développés et l'Expérience de la Démocratie* [*Democracy in Developing Countries*], p. 14.)

To attain democratic legitimacy and create the conditions needed for the development of their country, Haitians must follow all of this advice, with arbitration and regulation of internal conflicts being achieved through the effective application of a policy of national reconciliation.

Haitian families are appalled to see so many innocent lives unnecessarily destroyed by human wickedness and cupidity, to observe the devastation caused by a spirit of revenge among their fellow-citizens and leaders, to witness on television the misdeeds of crowds sowing disorder in the streets or dispensing justice for themselves. They are tired of suffering from the absence of adequate institutions for their protection, of noting the laxity of authorities regarding juvenile delinquency and organized crime, and of being victims of a lack of control among members of the police force!

While exhorting all Haitians to arm themselves with courage to face to the immensity of the task to be achieved, let us bring to mind all the destroyed homes, all the young women widowed or abruptly deprived of their children, all the orphans who have lost a father, a mother, all these people traumatized by the violent death of a brother, a sister, a relation, a friend!

Let us maintain hope, while contemplating this thought of the Bishops of the Episcopal Conference of Haiti, expressed in 1988, which is still extremely topical:

> Haiti is not a damned country, but a tested country. Certainly, our people have groaned for a long time in suffering. It is time for each one to prove that an awakening to the situation and a foundation of love for this degraded, humiliated and discredited country, finally make us find, in the union, the strength necessary to embark on the paths of development and of integral human advancement. (*Présence de l'Eglise en Haïti – Messages et documents de l'Episcopat 1980-1988*, p. 332.)

At last, let us hope that the cry of distress expressed in this book will be heard by the Haitian people, by all potential Haitian rulers and also by members of the international community who, we are certain, will not fail to offer Haiti their invaluable support for solving the thorny problem of insecurity, for the respect of life, for the reign of order and peace, and for the advent of a just, prosperous and more humane Haitian society.

APPENDIXES

THE VICTIMS OF THE INSECURITY IN HAITI

FROM 1995 THRU 2000

The sources :

LN = Le Nouvellis te

LM = Le Matin

HO = Haiti Observateur

HP = Haiti Progr ès

HM = Haiti en Marche

1- The victims for the year 1995

Date	Sources	Name	First name	Identification	Means	Location	No
7 janv.	HP 18-24/1, p. 2	Mathieu	Félix	ex-chef section	machettes	Carrefour	1
7 janv.	HP 11-17/1, p. 2	non identifié	non spécifié	paysan	machettes	Rivière Froide	1
12 janv.	HEM 18-24/1, p. 1	Cardott	Grégory	sgt Américain	balles	Gonaïves	1
12 janv.	HEM 18-24/1, p. 1	Frédéric	Aurel	ex-major	balles	Gonaïves	1
13 janv.	HO 22-29/11, p. 25	Joseph	Ali	ex-sergent	balles	P-au-Pce	1
13 janv.	HO 22-29/11, p. 25	Sans-Souci	Louis	ex-sergent	lynchage	P-au-Pce	1
19 janv.	LN 27-29/1, p. 15	Guirand	Anne-Marie	médecin	balles	P-au-Pce	1
23 janv.	HP 1-7/2, p. 3	Magloire	Thomas	non définies	machette	Hinche	1
23 janv.	HEM 25/1, p. 2	non identifié	non spécifié	non définies	balles	P-au-Pce	1
7 fév.	HP 15-21/2, p. 18	Jeanty	Robinson	mineur	balles	La Gonâve	1
11 fév.	LN 14/2, p. 1	Gracia	Henrya	ex-lieutenant	lynchage	Limbé	1
15 fév.	HP 15-21/2, p. 18	Valbrun	Pilon-Jean	non définies	balles	Delmas	1
28 fév.	HO 26/4-3/5, p. 18	Augustave	Jean	non définies	balles	Delmas	1
28 fév.	HO 26/4-3/5, p. 18	Augustave	Mme Jean	non définies	balles	Delmas	1
28 fév.	HO 26/4-3/5, p. 18	Fillette de	Augustave	mineure	balles	Delmas	1
28 fév.	HO 26/4-3/5, p. 18	Belle-soeur	Augustave	non définies	balles	Delmas	1
8 mars	HEM 8/3, p. 2	Lamothe	Eric	ex-député	balles	Frères	1
9 mars	HEM 15-21/3, p. 20	Simon	Faudener	membre MPP	balles	P-au-Pce	1
9 mars	HP 15-21/3, p. 1	non identifié	non spécifié	chauffeur	balles	Gonaïves	1
9 mars	HP 15-21/3, p. 1	non identifiés	non spécifié	passagers	balles	Gonaïves	2
15 mars	HEM 9-15/8, p. 3	Fanfan	ainsi connu	Borlette	balles	P-au-Pce	1
19 mars	HEM 22-28/3, p. 2	Augustin	Michel	commerçant	balles	Delmas	1
19 mars	HEM 22-28/3, p. 2	Augustin	Founia	fille de Michel	balles	Delmas	1
19 mars	HEM 22-28/3, p. 2	Augustin	Suzanne	fille de Michel	balles	Delmas	1
19 mars	HEM 22-28/3, p. 2	Augustin	Shelly	fille de Michel	balles	Delmas	1

25 mars	LN 27/3, p. 16	non identifiés	non spécifié	non définies	non spécifié	Cité Soleil	2
25 mars	LN 27/3, p. 16	non identifiée	non spécifié	femme enceinte	non spécifié	Bourdon	1
28 mars	HO 17-24/9, p. 20	Bertin D.	Mireille	avocat	balles	P-au-Pce	1
22 mars	LN 22/3, p. 16	Claude	Marc	ex-lieutenant	balles	P-au-Pce	1
28 mars	HO 17-24/9, p. 20	Baillergeau	Eugène	pilote	balles	P-au-Pce	1
29 mars	LN 30/3-2/4, p. 20	non identifiés	non spécifié	non définies	lynchage	Santo	2
30 mars	HO 26/4-3/5, p. 1	François	Gérard	paysan	balles	Santo	1
30 mars	HO 26/4-3/5, p. 1	Chevenelle	Pierre	ex-capitaine	lynchage	Santo	1
mars	HEM 26/4, p. 1	non identifiés	non spécifié	non définies	lynchage	P-au-Pce	97
6 avril	LN 7-9/4, p. 20	Métellus	Camélot	non définies	balles	Mirebalais	1
10 avril	LN 10/4, p. 1	St-Auguste	Altero	non définies	non spécifié	P-au-Pce	1
10 avril	LN 10/4, p. 1	Coriolan	St-Jean	non définies	non spécifié	P-au-Pce	1
10 avril	LN 10/4, p. 1	Noël	Joël	non définies	non spécifié	P-au-Pce	1
15 avril	LN 17/4, p. 16	non identifié	non spécifié	non définies	balles	Plaisance	1
19 avril	LN 19/4, p. 16	non identifiés	non spécifié	voleurs	lynchage	P-au-Pce	2
21 avril	HEM 26/4, p. 1	Eugène	Occilien	étudiant	balles	P-au-Pce	1
21 avril	HO 10-17/5, p.1	Lespinasse	Emile	commerçant	balles	P-au-Pce	1
21 avril	HO 26/4-3/5, p. 1	non identifié	non spécifié	vendeur	balles	P-au-Pce	1
24 avril	LN 25-26/4, p. 1	non identifiés	non spécifié	voleurs	lynchage	Cx-Bossales	4
24 avril	HO 26/4-3/5, p. 2	Joseph	Osselin	non définies	balles	P-au-Pce	1
25 avril	LN 25-26/4, p. 1	non identifiés	non spécifié	voleurs	lynchage	Cx-Bossales	2
25 avril	HO 26/4-3/5, p. 2	non identifiés	non spécifié	non définies	balles	Pétion-Ville	4
25 avril	HO26/4-3/5, p. 2	non identifiés	non spécifié	non définies	balles	P-au-Pce	3
27 avril	LN 28/4-1/5, p. 24	non identifié	non spécifié	non définies	balles	Gonaïves	1
30 avril	LN 3/5, p. 16	Mme Jeune	ainsi connue	non définies	machette	Marmelade	1
30 avril	LN 2/5, p. 15	Lamour	Philogène	lieutenant	balles	P-au-Pce	1
3 mai	LN 3/5, p. 16	Lamarre	Frénel	non définies	balles	Cul-de-Sac	1
4 mai	LN 4/5, p. 16	Cabrouet	Voltaire	employé Teleco	balles	Morne-Cabrits	1
5 mai	LN 5/5, p. 23	non identifié	non spécifié	commerçant	balles	Lilavois	1
5 mai	HO 10-17/5, p. 13	non identifié	non spécifié	commerçant	balles	Cx-Missions	1
5 mai	HP 10-16/5, p. 2	Lamarre	Fresnel	non définies	balles	Bon Repos	1
6 mai	HP 10-16/5, p. 2	non identifié	non spécifié	membre CEP	machette	Gonaïves	1
6 mai	HP 10-16/5, p. 2	non identifiés	non spécifié	bandits	lynchage	Mahotières	2
6 mai	HP 10-16/5, p. 2	Fabien	Joseph	non définies	non spécifié	Mahotières	1
9 mai	LN 9/5, p. 16	Jeudy	Lipsie	non définies	strangulation	Cayes-Jacmel	1

10 mai	LN 10/5, p. 20	non identifiés	non spécifié	paysans	conflits	Dessalines	5
11 mai	LN 12-14/5, p. 20	non identifiée	non spécifié	femme	balles	Pétion-Ville	1
11 mai	HP 17-23/5, p. 2	non identifié	non spécifié	non définies	balles	P-au-Pce	1
15 mai	HP 17-23/5, p. 17	Bonaparte	Clerveau	commerçant	balles	Lilavois	1
15 mai	HP 17-23/5, p. 17	Pachinau	ainsi connu	paysan	non spécifié	Léogane	1
37027	LN 19-21/5, 24	non identifié	non spécifié	non définies	lynchage	P-au-Pce	1
22 mai	LN 23/5, p. 1	Gonzalès	Michel	entrepreneur	balles	Tabarre	1
23 mai	LN 23/5, p. 20	non identifié	non spécifié	mineur	balles	P-au-Pce	1
24 mai	LN 24/5, p. 1	Hermann	Michel-Ange	ex-major	balles	P-au-Pce	1
31 mai	LN 31/5, p. 20	non identifié	non spécifié	bandit	balles	Mon Repos	1
5 juin	LM 7/6, p. 2	Moussignac	Frantz	commerçant	balles	P-au-Pce	1
7 juin	HO 7-14/6, p. 2	Turenne	Eugène	commerçant	balles	Santo	1
9 juin	LN 12/6, p. 1	Figaro	Wilfrid	médecin	balles	P-au-Pce	1
9 juin	HO 22-29/11, p.25	Blaise	Clothaire	ex- lieutenant	balles	P-au-Pce	1
10 juin	LN 12/6, p. 1	Grimard	Leslie	entrepreneur	balles	P-au-Pce	1
13 juin	LM 13/5, p. 2	non identifiés	non spécifié	non définies	non spécifié	P-au-Pce	4
21 juin	HEM 21-27/6, p.2	Boucard	Claudy	chauffeur	balles	jacmel	1
25 juin	HO 22-29/11, p.25	Kébreau	Joseph	ex-adjudant	lynchage	P-au-Pce	1
26 juin	LN 27/6, p. 16	non identifiée	non spécifié	non spécifiée	explosif	Cap-Haïtien	1
27 juin	LN 28/6, p. 1	Jean-Charles	Enock	membre KID	balles	Anse Hainault	1
28 juin	LN 28/6, p. 1	Romulus	Dumarsais	ex-colonel	balles	Delmas	1
29 juin	HEM 26/7-2/8, p.3	Dorsainvil	Joséphine	non définies	balles	Arcahaie	1
29 juin	LN 29/6, p.16	Juste	Roberson	ex-sergent	balles	Belladère	1
4 juil.	LN 5/7, p. 1	Claude	Yves-Marie	entrepreneur	balles	P-au-Pce	1
4 juil.	LN 5/7, p. 1	Beaubrun	Mario	comptable	balles	P-au-Pce	1
6 juil.	LN 5-9/7, p.20	non identifiés	non spécifié	voleurs	lynchage	St-Marc	2
6 juil.	LN 5-9/7, p.20	Maurice	Betty	commerçante	balles	P-au-Pce	1
6 juil.	LN 15-17/9, p.1	Germain	Soimilla	non définies	non spécifié	Fds-Verrettes	1
10 juil.	LN 10/7, p.20	non identifiés	non spécifié	paysans	machettes	Artibonite	2
12 juil.	HP 17-23, p.2	non identifié	non spécifié	non définies	balles	Marchand	1
14 juil.	LN 14-16/7, p.1	non identifié	non spécifié	non définies	balles	P-au-Pce	1
20 juil.	LN 21-23/7, p.1	César	Félio	non définies	balles	P-au-Pce	1
28 juil.	LN 28/7, p.1	Plaisimond	Hans	industriel	balles	P-au-Pce	1
29 juil.	LN 31/7, p.1	Marie-Colas	Etienne	Commerçant	balles	P-au-Pce	1
29 juil.	LN 31/7, p. 1	Gilbert	ainsi connu	cambiste	balles	P-au-Pce	1

2 août	LM 5/8, p. 1		Davilmar	Philoclès	non définies	lynchage	Acul-du-Nord	1
2 août	LM 5/8, p. 1		Chouchou	ainsi connu	non définies	lynchage	Acul-du-Nord	1
4 août	LN 7/8, p. 16		Mérilus	Joseph	policier	balles	P-au-Pce	1
4 août	LN 7/8, p. 11		Ernest	Franckel	non définies	balles	Carrefour	1
7 août	LN 8/8, p. 16		non identifié	non spécifié	non définies	balles	Martissant	1
9 août	HEM 9-15/8, p.18	El Gallo		ainsi connu	bandit	balles	P-au-Pce	1
12 août	LN 14-15/8, p.20	Sicard		Charles Anga	non définies	balles	Arcachon	1
21 août	LN 21/8, p.1		Thélusma	Jacqueline	non définies	balles	Carrefour	1
3 sept.	LN 6/9, p. 16		Noëo	André	non définies	machette	Verrettes	1
15 sept.	HP 20-26/9, p. 2		Lespinasse	Jacques	non définies	balles	Cap-Haïtien	1
19 sept.	LM 21/9, p. 2		Pierre	Lexius	non définies	balles	Delmas	1
29 sept.	LM 30/9-2/10, p.2	non identifié		non spécifié	cambiste	balles	P-au-Pce	1
3 oct.	LM 3/10, p. 1		Mayard	Max	ex-général	balles	Delmas	1
3 oct.	LM 3/10, p. 2		Amilcar	Odinette	non définies	balles	Gonaïves	1
13 oct.	LN 13-15/10		non identifié	non spécifié	non définies	lynchage	P-au-Pce	1
13 oct.	LM 14-16/10, p.2	non identifié		non spécifié	voleur	balles	P-au-Pce	1
23 oct.	LN 25/10, p. 1		Blanchard	Gérard	non définies	balles	Delmas	1
25 oct.	HP 25-31/10, p. 2	non identifié		non spécifié	jeune	non spécifié	Grand-Goâve	1
31 oct.	HP 8-14/11, p. 2		Colonne	ainsi connu	non définies	machette	La Chapelle	1
6 n0v.	HP 8-14/11, p. 2		non identifiés	non spécifié	voleurs	balles	Delmas	3
7 nov.	LN 8/11, p. 1		Feuillé	Yvon	député	balles	P-au-Pce	1
8 nov.	HO 8-15/11, p. 3	Sifré		Alain	Français	balles	Delmas	1
9 nov.	LN 9/11, p. 24		Estinval	Yves-Marie	dit makout	lynchage	Cayes	1
13 nov.	HO 22-29/11, p.17	non identifiés		non spécifié	bandits	lynchage	Gonaïves	5
13 nov.	HO 22-29/11, p.17	non identifiés		non spécifié	émeutiers	balles	Gonaïves	2
13 nov.	HO 22-29/11, p.17	non identifié		non spécifié	non définies	piques	Drouillard	1
14 nov.	LN 14/11, p. 1		non identifiés	non spécifié	non définies	émeutes	P-au-Pce	7
15 nov.	HO 22-29/11, p.1	non identifiés		non spécifié	non définies	balles	Limbé	2
21 nov.	LN 21/11, p. 20		Molière	ainsi connu	prisonnier	balles	P-au-Pce	1
36850	LN 21/11, p. 20		Sajous	Pierre	prisonnier	balles	P-au-Pce	1
24 nov.	HO 29/11-6/12, p.2	Thermidor		Vania	âgée de 6 ans	balles	Cité Soleil	1
24 nov.	HO 29/11-6/12, p.2	non identifiés		non spécifié	non définies	balles	Cité Soleil	2
29 nov.	HO 29/11-6/12, p.2	André		Rosemé	non définies	balles	Cité Soleil	1
7 déc.	HO 13-20/12, p.8	Mme Emile		ainsi connue	dite sorcière	brûlée	P-au-Pce	1
7 déc.	HO 13-20/12, p.8	Tania		ainsi connue	dite sorcière	brûlée	P-au-Pce	1

11 déc.	LN 11/12, p. 24	non identifiés	non spécifié	non définies	machette	Trou-du-Nord	4
12 déc.	LN 12/12, p. 1	Richemond	Jocelyn	agent sécurité	balles	P-au-Pce	1
12 déc.	LN 12/12, p. 1	Alerte	Mireille	non définies	balles	Delmas	1
26 déc.	LN 28/12, p.24	David	ainsi connu	non définies	sévices	Anse-Foleur	1
26 déc.	LN 26/12, p.24	Fleurantin	Hubert	agent sécurité	balles	Santo	1
26 déc.	LN 26/12, p.32	Volcy	Josué	chauffeur	balles	P-au-Pce	1
29 déc.	LN 3/1/96, p. 1	Dautruche	Wilner	entrepreneur	balles	Delmas	1
31 déc.	LN 3/1/96, p. 1	Mondésir	Oreste	policier	balles	P-au-Pce	1
31 déc.	LN 3/1/96, p. 1	Génord	Emmanuela	non définies	balles	P-au-Pce	1

Total of assassinated persons for the year 1995   **272**

2- The victims for the year 1996

Date	Sources	Name	First name	Identification	Means	Location	No
2 janv.	LN 3/1, p. 1	Louis	Jacquelin	non spécifiée	balles	P-au-Pce	1
11 janv.	LN 11/1, p. 1	non identifié	non spécifié	paysan	balles	P-au-Pce	1
27 janv.	LN 2-4/2, p. 23	Lucito	Jean-Robert	commerçant	balles	P-au-Pce	1
27 janv.	LN 29/1, p. 1	non identifiés	non spécifié	non spécifiée	lynchage	La Saline	6
2 fév.	LN 2-4/2, p.23	non identifié	non spécifié	bandit	lynchage	P-au-Pce	1
6 fév.	LN 62, p.24	non identifié	non spécifié	bandit	lynchage	Gonaïves	1
7 fév.	HO 7-14/2, p. 6	non identifié	non spécifié	bandit	lynchage	Cité Soleil	1
16 fév.	HP 6-12/3, p. 4	Brésil	ainsi connu	paysan	balles	Bellanse	1
21 fév.	HP 20-26/3, p.16	non identifiés	non spécifié	paysans	conflits	Gde-R. Nord	20
2 mars	HM 6/3, p.2	non identifié	non spécifié	employé APN	balles	P-au-Pce	1
4 mars	LN 4/3, p. 1	non identifié	non spécifié	jeune	balles	Carrefour	1
4 mars	LN 5/3, p.20	Dorval	Stéphane	non spécifiée	balles	Carrefour	1
4 mars	HP 20-26/3, p.3	non identifiés	non spécifié	non spécifiée	balles	Cité Soleil	9
4 mars	HP 20-26/3, p.3	non identifiés	non spécifié	non spécifiée	balles	Cité Soleil	2
8 mars	LN 8-10/3, p.1	non identifié	non spécifié	non spécifiée	balles	Varreux	1
11 mars	LN 11/3, p.1	non identifiés	non spécifié	non spécifiée	balles	P-au-Pce	4
11 mars	LN 11/3, p.24	non identifiés	non spécifié	non spécifiée	lynchage	P-au-Pce	4
12 mars	LM 12/3, p.2	non identifiés	non spécifié	non spécifiée	balles	Cité Soleil	7
14 mars	HP 20-26/3, p.5	non identifiés	non spécifié	jeunes	lynchage	Limbé	5
16 mars	HO 27/3-3/4, p.13	non identifiés	non spécifié	commerçantes	balles	Gros-Morne	4
17 mars	HO 27/3-3/4, p.6	Jeune	Julien	octogénaire	machette	Gonaïves	1
19 mars	LN 12-13/8, p.1	Jeune	Christine	policière	balles	Frères	1
20 mars	LN 20/3, p.16	non identifié	non spécifié	policier	balles	Carrefour	1
22 mars	LN 24/3, p.24	Jean	Occil	non spécifiée	machette	Léogane	1
26 mars	LN 26-30/3, p. 24	Morisseau	Charité	Borlette	machette	Mirebalais	1
26 mars	HO 27/3-3/4, p.13	non identifié	non spécifié	non spécifiée	balles	P-au-Pce	1
26 mars	LN 26-30/3, p. 24	Ladouceur	Béril	policier	balles	Petit-Goâve	1

26 mars	LN 26-30/3, p. 24	Diamand	Donald	policier	balles	Petit-Goâve	1
26 mars	LN 26-30/3, p. 24	non identifiés	non spécifié	non spécifiée	balles	Petit-Goâve	2
15/30 mar	LN 26-30/3, p. 24	non identifiés	non spécifié	non spécifiée	balles	P-au-Pce	40
1er avril	LN 2/4, p. 20	François	Raymond	policier	balles	Pétion-Ville	1
3 avril	HM 31/7, p.3	Steinmann	Hubert	Suisse	balles	P-au-Pce	1
3 avril	HM 31/7, p.3	Steinmann	Anne Kung	Suisse	balles	P-au-Pce	1
12 avril	LN 29/7/98, p.24	Paulémond	Ferdinand	non spécifiée	machette	Cornillon	1
18 avril	LN 19-21/4, p.20	Joseph	Nicole	non spécifiée	balles	Delmas	1
25 avril	LN 12-13/8, p.1	Conséant	Jean Léonard	non spécifiée	balles	P-au-Pce	1
26 avril	HO 1-8/5, p.1	Désir	Ernest	enseignant	balles	P-au-Pce	1
26 avril	HO 1-8/5, p.1	Désir	Anne-Marie	enseignante	balles	P-au-Pce	1
27 avril	LN 30/4-1/5, p.24	Elysée	Pierre-Joseph	commerçant	balles	Arcahaie	1
27 avril	LN 12-13/8, p.1	Bignac	Milcent	policier	balles	P-au-Pce	1
27 avril	LN 12-13/8, p.1	Désir	Philistin	policier	balles	P-au-Pce	1
3 mai	HP 14-20/5, p.4	Baptiste	Milcent	ex-député	balles	Cayes	1
3 mai	HP 14-20/5, p.4	non identifié	non spécifié	bandit	balles	Cité Soleil	1
3 mai	HP 14-20/5, p.4	François	Islande	étudiante	balles	Cité Soleil	1
3 mai	HP 14-20/5, p.4	non identifiés	non spécifié	non spécifiée	brûlés	Mne-cabrits	4
4 mai	LN 12-13/8, p.1	Chéry	Berthony	policier	balles	Cité Soleil	1
14 mai	HO 15-22/5, p.1	Léonard	Jean	policier	balles	Cité Soleil	1
16 mai	HO 22-29/5, p.3	Lacombe	Joannès	gardien	machette	Delmas	1
11 mai	LN 13/5, p.24	non identifié	non spécifié	non spécifiée	balles	P-au-Pce	1
20 mai	LN 20/5, p.20	non identifiés	non spécifié	non spécifiée	brûlés	Sarthe	6
27 mai	LN 12-13/8, p.1	Désir	Valcourt	policier	balles	P-au-Pce	1
27 mai	LN 29/5, p.1	non identifié	non spécifié	non spécifiée	balles	P-au-Pce	1
29 mai	HO 5-12/6, p.4	Jn-François	Erla	mairesse	balles	P-au-Pce	1
29 mai	HO 5-12/6, p.4	Dessources	Jude	policier	balles	Cayes	1
3 juin	HO 5-12/6, p.13	Elie	Pierre	employé SIN	balles	P-au-Pce	1
3 juin	HO 5-12/6, p.13	Pierre	Germaine	non spécifiée	balles	Delmas	1
3 juin	HO 5-12/6, p.13	Pierre	enfants (3)	non spécifiée	balles	Delmas	3
4 juin	LN 12-13/8, p.1	Désaubry	Marc-Holly	non spécifiée	balles	Mirebalais	1
6 juin	LN 12-13/8, p.1	Germain	Shiller	policier	balles	Martissant	1
11 juin	HO 26/6-3/7, p.1	non identifié	non spécifié	mineur 6 ans	balles	Mne-Cabrits	1
11 juin	HO 19-26/6, p.1	Jean-Philippe	Frantz	mineur	balles	Mne-cabrits	1
12 juin	LN 13/6, p.28	Michel	Marc	Hôtelier	balles	Lascahobas	1

15 juin	HO 19-26/8, p.22	Pierre	Francesca	non spécifiée	balles	Delmas	1
18 juin	LN 18/6, p. 24	non identifiés	non spécifié	bandits	lynchage	Roseaux	3
18 juin	HO 26/6-3/7, p. 6	Sérah	Jean-Victor	policier	balles	Pétion-Ville	1
19 juin	LN 19/6, p. 1	non identifiés	non spécifié	paysans	conflits	Artibonite	7
19 juin	HO 26/6-3/7, p.19	non identifié	non spécifié	bandit	balles	P-au-Pce	1
22 juin	HO 26/6-3/7, p.19	Pierre	Yves	vacancier	balles	Delmas	1
23 juin	HO 26/6-3/7, p.19	Jean	Elie	jeune	balles	Delmas	1
23 juin	HO 26/6-3/7, p.19	non identifiés	non spécifié	couple	balles	Tabarre	2
2 juillet	LN 3/7, p. 24	Saint-Cyr	Madeleine	non spécifiée	balles	Delmas	1
11 juillet	HP 06/08, p. 3	non identifié	non spécifié	technicien	machette	Pont-Sondé	1
11 juillet	HP 06/08, p. 3	Raynold	ainsi connu	non spécifiée	machette	Pont-Sondé	1
13 juillet	LN 15/7, p. 24	Antoine	Jacky	jumeau	balles	P-au-Pce	1
13 juillet	LN 15/7, p. 24	Antoine	Charles	jumeau	balles	P-au-Pce	1
13 juillet	LN 15/7, p. 24	Abraham	Alix	non spécifiée	balles	Delmas	1
13 juillet	LN 15/7, p. 24	non identifié	non spécifié	agent sécurité	balles	P-au-Pce	1
19 juillet	HEM 24-30/7, p.7	Charles T.	Emmanuel	vacancier	strangulation	Bon Repos	1
20 juillet	LN 22/7, p1	Armand	André	ex-militaire	balles	P-au-Pce	1
20 juillet	LN 22/7, p.1	Moïse	ainsi connu	cambiste	balles	P-au-Pce	1
30 juillet	LM 1/8, p.10	Leconte	Mariette	commerçantes	balles	P-au-Pce	1
1er août	HO 21-28/8. P.4	Fénélus	Orasmin	non spécifié	sévices	Jean-Rabel	1
5 août	HO 7-14/8, p.1	Charles	Joseph Rony	banquier	balles	Cap-Haïtien	1
5 août	HO 7-14/8, p.1	Joseph	Molovis	agent sécurité	balles	Cap-Haïtien	1
5 août	HO 7-14/8, p.1	Ginoh	ainsi connu	agent sécurité	balles	Cap-Haïtien	1
5 août	HO 7-14/08, p.1	Francisque	ainsi connu	agent sécurité	balles	Cap-Haïtien	1
12 août	LN 12-13/8, p.1	Lazarre	Gary	policier	balles	Cx-Bouquets	1
19 août	LN 19/8, p.1	non identifié	non spécifié	non spécifiée	balles	P-au-Pce	1
20 août	LN 20/8, p.1	Leroy	Antoine	pasteur	balles	P-au-Pce	1
20 août	LN 20/8, p.1	Florival	Jacques	politique	balles	Delmas	1
20 août	LM 20/8, p.1	Pape	Madeleine	octogénaire	balles	P-au-Pce	1
21 août	LN 21/8, p.24	non identifié	non spécifié	non spécifiée	balles	Bellanse	1
21 août	LN 21/8, p.24	non identifié	non spécifié	non spécifiée	balles	Bellanse	1
21 août	LN 21/8, p.24	non identifiés	non spécifié	non spécifiée	balles	Bellanse	3
25 août	LN 28/8, p.24	Civil	Yves Wilner	non spécifiée	balles	P-au-Pce	1
25 août	LN 26/8, p.24	Prévilon	Dieuseul	non spécifiée	balles	P-au-Pce	1
30 août	LN 30/8, p.1	Phanor	Yves Wilner	policier	balles	P-au-Pce	1

3 sept.	LN 03/9, p.1	non identifiés	non spécifié	non spécifiée	balles	Delmas	2
3 sept.	LN 3/9, p.1	non identifiés	non spécifié	non spécifiée	machette	P-au-Pce	4
3 sept.	LN 4/9, p.20	non identifié	non spécifié	non spécifiée	machette	Sapotille	1
10 sept.	Ln 11/9, p.24	Pétion	Marcel	ex-maire	balles	P-au-Pce	1
11 sept.	Ln 11/9, p.24	Coq	Hilda	avocat	balles	P-au-Pce	1
11 sept.	Ln 11/9, p.24	Charles	Jean Bernard	non spécifiée	balles	P-au-Pce	1
11 sept.	HM 11/9, p.2	non identifiés	non spécifié	paysans	machette	Artibonite	2
17 sept.	LN 21/10, p.24	non identifié	non spécifié	jeune	balles	Miragoâne	1
30 sept.	HP 9-15/10, p.2	non identifiée	non spécifié	enceinte	balles	Delmas	1
2 oct.	HM 29/11, p.17	Joseph	Renel	policier	balles	Léogane	1
2 oct.	HM 2/10, p.17	Beauplan	Eliazar	policière	balles	Cap-Haïtien	1
9 oct.	HP 9-15/10, p.2	Victor	Constance	non spécifiée	balles	P-au-Pce	1
9 oct.	LN 14/10, p.20	non identifié	non spécifié	non spécifiée	balles	Mirebalais	1
11 oct.	HO 16-23/10, p.3	non identifié	non spécifié	bandits	machette	Ravine-Sud	1
11 oct.	HO 16-23/10, p.3	Douval	Jean-Michel	bandit	machette	Ravine-Sud	1
11 oct.	LN 14/10, p.20	Sanon	Thony	ex-militaire	balles	P-au-Pce	1
11 oct.	LN 14/10, p.20	non identifiés	non spécifié	non spécifiée	lynchage	Cayes	2
11 oct.	LN 14/10, p.20	Exat	ainsi connu	bandit	lynchage	St-Marc	1
18 oct.	Ln 18-20, p.1	non identifié	non spécifié	non spécifiée	balles	Tabarre	1
3 nov.	LN 5/11, p.4	Delbal	Jean-Claude	non spécifiée	étranglé	Laboule	1
4 nov.	LN 5/11, p.20	Vincent	Edriss	entrepreneur	balles	P-au-Pce	1
4 nov.	LN 5/11, p.20	Lubin	Mario	policier	balles	P-au-Pce	1
5 nov.	LN 5/11, p.1	non identifiés	non spécifié	bandits	balles	Delmas	3
5 nov.	LN 5/11, p.1	Germain	Jean-Jérôme	bandit	balles	Delmas	1
5 nov.	ln 5/11, p.1	Salomon	Kesnel	bandit	balles	Delmas	1
9 nov.	HO 27-4/12, p.14	Vaval	Luc	management	balles	Thiotte	1
11 nov.	HO 13-20/11, p.2	non identifié	non spécifié	non spécifiée	balles	Anse-Galets	1
14 nov.	LN 19/11, p. 24	Bourdeau	Ronald	policier	balles	P-au-Pce	1
2 déc.	LN 3/12, p.24	Rouchon	Micheline	commerçantes	machette	P-au-Pce	1
2 déc.	LN 3/12, p.24	Rouchon	Fédia	mineure	étranglée	P-au-Pce	1
3 déc.	LN 3/12, p.24	non identifiés	non spécifié	Dominicains	balles	P-au-Pce	2
9 déc.	LN 9/12, p.24	non identifiés	non spécifié	non spécifiée	lynchage	Gressier	4
9 déc.	LN 9/12, p.24	Durogène	Moïse	non spécifiée	machette	Gonaïves	1
13 déc.	LN 13-15/12, p.1	non identifiés	non spécifié	non spécifiée	balles	Cx-Bouquets	10
15 déc.	LN 16/12, p.1	Harris	ainsi connu	non spécifiée	balles	Thuitier	1

15 déc.	LN 16/12, p.1	Cauvin	Serge	non spécifiée	balles	Thuitier	1
15 déc.	LN 12-13/8, p.1	Hébert	ainsi connu	non spécifiée	balles	Thuitier	1
15 déc.	LN 16/12, p.1	Thézine	Girald	non spécifiée	balles	Thuitier	1
17 déc.	HO 18-25/12, p.2	Duvernois	Edouard	non spécifiée	balles	Thuitier	1
22 déc.	HP 24-30/12, p.4	non identifiés	non spécifié	non spécifiée	balles	Tabarre	5
23 déc.	HP 24-30/12, p.4	non identifiés	non spécifié	non spécifiée	balles	P-au-Pce	9
23 déc.	HP 20-24/12, p.2	Song	Yoon Ki	Sud-Coréen	balles	P-au-Pce	1

Total of assassinated persons for the year 1996   **285**

3- The victims for the year 1997

Date	Sources	Name	First name	Identification	Means	Location	No.
3 janv.	LN 12/1, p. 1	Colbert	Georges	non définies	balles	Fragneau-Ville	1
7 janv.	HO 30/4-7/5, p. 4	Rousseau	Dumesle	mécanicien	balles	Cayes	1
16 janv.	HP 22-28/1, p. 17	Edmond	Sofli	non définies	balles	Cap-Haïtien	1
16 janv.	LN 16-19/1, p. 1	non identifié	non spécifié	non définies	émeute	Cap-Haïtien	1
2 fév.	HO 19-26/2, p. 4	Estève	Gérard M.	non définies	balles	P-au-Pce	1
2 fév.	HO 30/4-7/5, p. 4	Montalveau	Lexi Léonel	non définies	balles	Cayes	1
2 fév.	HO 5-12/12, p. 8	Pierre	Harold	bandit	balles	Cayes	1
4 fév.	LN 4/2, p. 20	non identifié	non spécifié	cambiste	balles	Cité Soleil	1
5 fév.	HO 5-12/12, p. 2	Similien	Robel	hôtelier	balles	Aquin	1
6 fév.	LN 6/2, p. 24	non identifié	non spécifié	non définies	lynchage	Gonaïves	1
14 fév.	HO 19-26/2, p. 1	Bellony	Reynold	mineur	balles	P-au-Pce	1
17 fév.	LN 17/2, p. 1	non identifié	non spécifié	non définies	émeute	Cité Soleil	4
18 fév.	HP 26/2-4/3, p. 3	Vega	Eduardo	Chilien	brûlé	Tabarre	1
24 fév.	HO 2/6-5/3, p. 1	Paraisy	Henry	cambiste	balles	P-au-Pce	1
24 fév.	HO 2/6-5/3, p. 7	Legros	Métellus	non définies	balles	St-Marc	1
25 fév.	HO 26/2-5/3, p. 1	Joassaint	Mario	policier	balles	Cité Soleil	1
25 fév.	HO 26/2-5/3, p. 3	Paul	Mondésir	agent sécurité	balles	P-au-Pce	1
27 fév.	LN 27/2, p. 1	non identifié	non spécifié	non définies	émeute	Cité Soleil	20
36585	LN 3/3, p. 28	Geatjens	Margareth	non définies	balles	Delmas	1
2 mars	LN 3/3, p. 28	Hakime	Guy	entrepreneur	balles	P-au-Pce	1
4 mars	LN 4/3, p. 28	non identifié	non spécifié	policier	balles	Delmas	1
4 mars	LN 4/3, p. 28	non identifié	non spécifié	Dominicain	machette	Belladère	1
5 mars	HO 19-26/3, p. 18	Jean	Edner	policier	balles	P-au-Pce	1
5 mars	HM 12/3, p. 2	non identifié	non spécifié	non définies	balles	La Gonâve	1
8 mars	HO 19-26/3, p. 1	Gédéon	Sony	chauffeur	balles	P-au-Pce	1
8 mars	HO 19-26/3, p.1	Mompremier	Emmanuel	policier	balles	P-au-Pce	1
9 mars	HM 12/3, p.2	non identifié	non spécifié	non définies	balles	P-au-Pce	7
10 mars	HM 12/3, p. 2	non identifié	non spécifié	non définies	balles	P-au-Pce	3

10 mars	HM 12/3, p.2	Charles	Avrinel	agt sécurité	balles	P-au-Pce	1
11 mars	LN 11/3, p. 1	non identifié	non spécifié	non définies	balles	Delmas	1
11 mars	LN 12/1, p. 1	François	Frantz	policier	balles	Cité Soleil	1
11 mars	HO 19-26/3,p. 18	Obas	Gary	chauffeur	balles	P-au-Pce	1
12 mars	LN 17/3, p. 24	Bernardin	Harrisson	non définies	brûlé	Thomassique	1
13 mars	LN 13/3, p. 1	Joseph	Lionel	bandit	balles	P-au-Pce	1
13 mars	LN 13/3, p. 1	non identifié	non spécifié	chauffeur	balles	P-au-Pce	1
27 mars	HM 2/4, p. 6	Ladouceur	Béril	policier	balles	Petit-Goâve	1
27 mars	HM 2/4, p. 6	Dormant	Donald	policier	balles	Petit-Goâve	1
6 avril	HO 9-16/4, p. 7	Chéry	Célouinord	politique	balles	Delmas	1
6 avril	HO 9-16/4, p. 2	Garotte	Emmanuel	non définies	balles	P-au-Pce	1
7 avril	HO 9-16/4, p. 2	Tarjet	Patrick	avocat	balles	Cx-Missions	1
7 avril	HO 9-16/4, p. 2	Bayard	Laureston	greffier	balles	Cx-Missions	1
7 avril	HO 9-16/4, p. 2	Ti-Papit	ainsi connu	non définies	balles	Cité Soleil	1
8 avril	LN 8/4, p. 1	Louisdhon	Célinord	non définies	balles	P-au-Pce	1
10 avril	HP 17-23/4, p. 2	Ménard	John	étudiant	balles	P-au-Pce	1
11 avril	HP 17-23/4, p. 2	Baret	Amaguel	non définies	balles	Léogane	1
17 avril	HO 23-30/4, p. 22	non identifié	non spécifié	non définies	balles	Delmas	1
18 avril	HO 23-30/4, p. 2	Jean	Fénaka	bandit	balles	Delmas	1
24 avril	LN 24/4, p. 1	Milcent	Datus	ex-député	balles	Delmas	1
25 avril	LN 28/4, p. 24	Acloque	Yvon	entrepreneur	balles	Delmas	1
2 mai	HO 7-14/5, p. 3	Désulmé	Jonas	prisonnier	balles	Cx-Bouquets	1
9 mai	LN 12/5, p. 4	non identifié	non spécifié	non définies	balles	Cayes	4
9 mai	HO 21-28/5, p. 3	Jeantiné	Onot	non définies	balles	Cayes	1
9 mai	HO 21-28/5, p. 3	non identifié	non spécifié	voleur	lynchage	Cayes	1
9 mai	HO 21-28/5, p. 3	Blaise	Ronald	voleur	sévices	Cavaillon	1
9 mai	HO 21-28/5, p. 3	non identifié	non spécifié	voleur	sévices	Cavaillon	1
15 mai	HP 21-28/5, p. 1	non identifié	non spécifié	écoliers	balles	P-au-Pce	7
15 mai	HP 21-28/5, p. 1	Ti-blanc	ainsi connu	non définies	balles	P-au-Pce	1
15 mai	HP 21-28/5, p. 1	non identifié	non spécifié	jeunes	balles	P-au-Pce	1
15 mai	HO 21-28/5, p. 13	Cadet	Alix	policier	balles	P-au-Pce	1
16 mai	LN 22/5, p. 1	non identifié	non spécifié	policier	balles	Cap-Haïtien	1
18 mai	HO 21-28/5, p. 3	Lafrance	Pascale	non définies	explosif	Thomassin	1
22 mai	LN 22/5, p. 1	non identifié	non spécifié	non définies	émeute	La Saline	10
1er juin	LN 2/6, p. 24	Athis	Jonas	non définies	balles	Arcahaie	1

ler juin	LN 2/6, p. 24	Athis	Yvane	non définies	balles	Arcahaie	1
2 juin	LN 2/6, p. 24	non identifié	non spécifié	bandits	balles	Arcahaie	2
2 juin	LN 2/6, p. 24	Hérode	Pierre	non définies	balles	St-Marc	1
3 juin	LN 3/6, p. 20	non identifié	non spécifié	cambistes	balles	P-au-Pce	3
3 juin	LM 3/6, p. 2	non identifié	non spécifié	agt sécurité	balles	P-au-Pce	2
4 juin	LN 4/6, p. 24	Jean-Louis	Elan	commerçant	balles	Delmas	1
7 juin	LN 9/6, p. 1	Célestin	Michèle	commerçante	balles	P-au-Pce	1
9 juin	LN 9/6, p. 24	Bedonet	Charles E.	non définies	balles	Gonaïves	1
19 juin	LN 19/6, p. 1	non identifié	non spécifié	non définies	conflits	Artibonite	7
20 juin	HO 25/6-2/7, p. 7	non identifié	non spécifié	non définies	balles	Cap-Haïtien	1
21 juin	HO 26/6-2/7, p. 1	non identifié	non spécifié	bandits	balles	Cap-Haïtien	3
22 juin	HO 25/6-2/7, p. 7	Dorcelin	Dieujuste	non définies	balles	Cap-Haïtien	1
28 juin	LN 23/6, p. 28	non identifié	non spécifié	non définies	balles	P-au-Pce	3
19 juin	LN 19/6, p. 1	non identifié	non spécifié	paysans	conflits	Artibonite	7
5 juil.	HO 23-30/7, p. 9	Pierre	Justin	vacancier	balles	Cap-Haïtien	1
5 juil.	HO 23-30, p. 9	Pierre	Anne-Marie	vacancière	balles	Cap-Haïtien	1
10 juil.	HO 16-23/7, p. 14	Gourgue	Ernestine	non définies	machette	Delmas	1
10 juil.	HO 16-23/7, p. 14	Frédony	Wilson	non définies	machette	Delmas	1
15 juil.	LN 16/7, p. 1	non identifié	non spécifié	bandit	brûlés	Saut-d'Eau	1
15 juil.	LN 16/7, p. 1	Kironé	Lamousse	non définies	balles	Saut-d'Eau	1
15 juil.	LN 15/7, p. 24	non identifié	non spécifié	non définies	machette	Belladère	3
21 juil.	LN 22/7, p. 1	Jean	Jn-Claude	policier	balles	P-au-Pce	1
21 juil.	LN 21/7, p. 3	non identifié	non spécifié	non définies	balles	Drouillard	3
22 juil.	LN 22/7, p. 20	non identifié	non spécifié	non définies	lynchage	Pont Sondé	3
28 juil.	LN 28/7, p. 18	non identifié	non spécifié	non définies	balles	Varreux	3
6 août	LN 6/8, p. 24 n	non identifié	non spécifié	non définies	conflits	P-au-Pce	1
9 août	HO 20-27/8, p. 10	Méus	François	non définies	machette	Savanette	1
24 août	LN 24/8, p. 24	non identifié	non spécifié	non définies	balles	P-au-Pce	1
3 sept.	LN 5-7/9, 24	Métellus	Roland	non définies	balles	CitéSoleil	1
4 sept.	LN 25/9, p. 24	Pierre	Angela	non définies	non spécifié	St M-Attalaye	1
4 sept.	LN 9/10, p. 1	Anglade	Edith S.	commerçante	balles	P-au-Pce	1
7 sept.	LN 15/9, p. 24	Joseph	Réginald	non définies	balles	Cité Soleil	1
7 sept.	LN 15/9, p. 24	Céderme	ainsi connu	non définies	balles	Cité Soleil	1
36775	LN 15/9, p. 24	Jean	ainsi connu	non définies	balles	Cité Soleil	1
7 sept.	HO 10-17/9, p. 1	non identifié	non spécifié	non définies	balles	P-au-Pce	6

12 sept.	LN 18-21/9, p. 40	Jean-Louis	Louinord	non définies	machette	Tiburon	1
12 sept.	LN 18-21/9, p. 40	Jeune	Vesta	enceinte	machette	Tiburon	1
12 sept.	LN 25/9, p. 1	Benoit	Elda	non définies	machette	St-M. Attalaye	1
12 sept.	LN 25/9, p.1	Benoit	non spécifié	fils de Elda	machette	St-M. Attalaye	1
13 sept.	LN 15/9, p. 24	non identifié	non spécifié	non définies	brûlés	Chantal	2
15 sept.	LN 16/9, p. 24	Toussaint	Pierre	vacancier	balles	P-au-Pce	1
15 sept.	HO,17-24/9, p. 5	Léger	non spécifié	mineurs	balles	Delmas	2
15 sept.	LN 15/9, p. 24	non identifié	non spécifié	jeunes	balles	Cité Soleil	5
15 sept.	LN 16/9, p. 24	Josias	Solane	non définies	balles	Cx-Bouquets	1
15 sept.	LN 16/9, p. 24	Josias	M.meSolane	non définies	balles	Cx-Bouquets	1
17 sept.	HO 17-24/9, p. 2	non identifié	non spécifié	agt sécurité	balles	P-au-Pce	1
17 sept.	Ho 17-24/9, p.2	non identifié	non spécifié	agt sécurité	balles	Pétion-Ville	1
20 sept.	LN 25/9, p. 1	Stanio	Vilus Alexis	non définies	machette	St-M. Attalaye	1
26 sept.	HO 1-8/10, p. 1	Elie	Claude	non définies	balles	Cx-Bouquets	1
6 oct.	HO 8-15/10, p. 1	Dorléans	Martine	non définies	balles	P-au-Pce	1
6 oct.	HO 8-15/10, p. 1	Auguste	Jean-Luc	non définies	balles	P-au-Pce	1
6 oct.	LN 6/10, p. 20	non identifié	non spécifié	non définies	lynchage	Bellanse	1
10 oct.	HO 12-15/10, p.10	non identifié	non spécifié	non définies	machette	Péligre	4
12 oct.	HO 12-15/10, p.10	Patrick	ainsi connu	non définies	balles	P-au-Pce	1
12 oct.	HO 12-15/10, p.10	non identifié	non spécifié	mère Patrick	balles	P-au-Pce	1
13 oct.	HO 12-15/10, p.10	Lecorps	Frantz	non définies	balles	Bedoret	1
16 oct.	LN 20/10, p. 1	Passe	Emilio	député	balles	Jérémie	1
20 oct.	HO 29/10-5/11, p. 9	Louima	Dieusibon	bandit	balles	Cité Soleil	1
20 oct.	HO 29/10-5/11, p. 9	Ti-Moïse	ainsi connu	bandit	balles	Cité Soleil	1
21 oct.	HO 29/10-5/11, p. 9	Gratien	Jean Renel	non définies	balles	P-au-Pce	1
21 oct.	LN 22/10, p. 24	non identifié	non spécifié	non définies	balles	P-au-Pce	1
24 oct.	HO 3-10/12, p. 18	Léon Joseph	non spécifié	non définies	machette	Laborde	1
25 oct.	LN 27/10, p. 1	Faustin	Jean-Saurel	policier	balles	Delmas	1
29 oct.	HO 29/10-5/11, p. 9	Lovinsky	Sévère	médecin	balles	P-au-Pce	1
30 oct.	HO 3-10/12, p. 18	Neptune	Ralph	bandit	lynchage	Camp-Perrin	1
6 nov.	HP 12-18/11, p. 7	Langlais	Germain	non définies	machette	Marigot	1
8 nov.	HO 12-19/11, p. 5	Azima	Jn-François	non définies	balles	Aquin	1
10 nov.	HP 12-18/11, p. 16	Tipa	ainsi connu	non définies	balles	Pte-Riv. (Art.)	1
10 nov.	LN 10/11, p. 1	Paula	ainsi connu	non définies	explosif	P-au-Pce	1
12 nov.	HP 12-18/11, p.16	Clergé	Penny	vieillard	balles	Cayes	1

12 nov.	HP 12-18/11, p.16	Thomas	Fontaine	vieillard	balles	Cayes	1
12 nov.	HP 12-18/11, p.16	Odette	ainsi connu	dite sorcière	brûlée	Torbeck	1
15 nov.	HO 3-10/12, p. 18	Delgrès	Dieuseul	professeur	machette	Fds-Blancs	1
11 nov.	LM 18-19/11, p. 1	Gaillard	Robert	non définies	balles	Pétion-Ville	1
11 nov.	LM 18-19/11, p. 1	Gaillard	Mme Robert	non définies	balles	Pétion-Ville	1
11 nov.	HP 12-18/11, p.16	non identifié	non spécifié	non définies	balles	St-Marc	3
17 nov.	HO 3-10/12, p. 18	Blaise	Doky	non définies	lynchage	Aquin	1
17 nov.	HO 3-10/12, p. 18	Blaise	Mme Doky	non définies	lynchage	Aquin	1
29 nov.	LN 4/12. P. 24	Augustin	Gary	policier	balles	P-au-Pce	1
30 nov.	HO 3-10/12, p. 18	non identifié	non spécifié	non définies	explosif	Léogane	1
6 déc.	LM 6-8/12, p. 2	Mérizier	Willy	non définies	balles	P-au-Pce	1
6 déc.	LM 6-8/12, p. 2	Mérizier	Alicia	non définies	balles	P-au-Pce	1
14 déc.	HO 17-24/12, p. 1	Arbrouet	Eddy	bandit	balles	Léogane	1
22 déc.	HO 31/12-7/1, p.16	Coulanges	Micheline	commerçante	balles	P-au-Pce	1

Total of assassinated persons for the year 1997   **239**

4-The victims for the year 1998

Date	Sources	Name	First name	Identification	Means	Location	No.
1er janv.	HO 7-14/1, p. 9	non identifiés	non spécifié	non définies	lynchés	Cité Soleil	3
7 janv.	HP 7-13/1, p. 2	non identifié	non spécifié	jeune	balles	P-au-Pce	1
12 janv.	LN 5/1	Thomas	ainsi connu	Telecom	balles	P-au-Pce	1
14 janv.	LN 14/1, p. 20	Dieubéni	ainsi connu	non définies	balles	Gonaïves	1
18 janv.	HO 11-18/3, p. 5	non identifiés	non spécifié	bandit	lynchés	Aquin	3
19 janv.	HO 4-11/2, p. 4	non identifiés	non spécifié	bandit	brûlés	Bonne Fin	4
19 janv.	HO 4-11/2, p. 18	non identifié	non spécifié	bandit	balles	Cayes	1
21 janv.	21/1, p. 20	non identifiés	non spécifié	non définies	lynchés	Cavaillon	2
22 janv.	LN 22/1, p. 1	non identifiés	non spécifié	non définies	lynchés	P-au-Pce	8
26 janv.	LN 26/1, p. 1	non identifié	non spécifié	jeune fille	balles	P-au-Pce	1
27 janv.	HP 4-10/2, p. 2	Toussaint	Orphélia	non définies	balles	Tou-du-Nord	1
30 janv.	HO 4-11/2, p. 1	Desmomes	Marie D.	non définies	balles	P-au-Pce	1
31 janv.	HO 4-11/2, p. 17	Bourcenet	Jean-Baptiste	agt sécurité	balles	Delmas	1
2 fév.	LM 5/2, p. 2	Thimothé	Jimmy	étudiant	balles	Carrefour	1
5 fév.	LN 6-8/2, p. 1	Dorméus	Risselin	policier	lynché	Mirebalais	1
5 fév.	HO 1-8/4, p. 8	Mérisier	Jean-Baptiste	non définies	balles	Mirebalais	1
11 fév.	LN 11/2, p. 24	Sonthonax	Norbert	non définies	balles	Gonaïves	1
15 fév.	HO 11-18/3, p. 5	non identifié	non spécifié	paysan	balles	Cayes	1
18 fév.	LM 10/2, p. 2	Kansky	Pierre	entrepreneur	balles	Delmas	1
21 fév.	LN 11/3, p. 1	François	Anneté	non définies	balles	Desdunes	1
22 fév.	HO 11-18/3, p. 3	non identifiés	non spécifié	bandit	lynchés	Cayes	2
27 fév.	HO 11-18/3, p. 5	non identifiés	non spécifié	bandit	brûlés	Cayes	7
19 mars	LN 19/3, p. 1	Etienne	Joël	non définies	balles	Jérémie	1
19 mars	LN 19/3, p. 24	Chery	Berthony	policier	balles	P-au-Pce	1

19 mars	LN 19/3, p. 24	Joassaint	Mario	policier	balles	P-au-Pce	1
19 mars	LN 19/3, p. 24	Blaise	Preneur	policier	balles	P-au-Pce	1
19 mars	LN 19/3, p. 24	Charles	Pierre-Loty	policier	balles	P-au-Pce	1
19 mars	LN 19/3, p. 24	Joseph	Robert Gary	policier	balles	P-au-Pce	1
19 mars	LN 20-22/3, p.32	Refusé	Miguel	non définies	balles	P-au-Pce	1
20 mars	LN 20-22/3, p. 1	non identifié	non spécifié	agt sécurité	balles	P-au-Pce	1
26 mars	HP 22-28/4, p. 5	Dorilien	Dieusibon	hougan	lynché	Corail	1
29 mars	LN 30/3, p. 24	Alva	Ronald	chauffeur	balles	Tabarre	1
1er avril	LM 1/4, p. 2	Lavache	Tony	non définies	balles	Pétion-Ville	1
2 avril	HP 13-20/4, p. 5	Salnave	Dézilma	bandit	lynché	P-au-Pce	1
7 avril	HP 22-28/4, p. 4	Bolville	Gérard	non définies	balles	P-au-Pce	1
8 avril	HP 8-14/4, p. 3	Azémar	Coriolan	policier	balles	Delmas	1
8 avril	LN 8-12/4, p. 1	Etienne	Renaud	policier	lynché	Cavaillon	1
8 avril	LN 8-12/4, p. 1	Enerve	Espérant	policier	lynché	Cavaillon	1
13 avril	HP 22-28/4, p. 2	Juste	Daniel	prisonnier	sévices	Jérémie	1
13 avril	HO 29/4-6/5, p.1	Morency	René	non définies	balles	Fontamara	1
20 avril	HO 22-29/4, p.1	Pétinord	Célavi	paysan	machette	Jean-Rabel	1
20 avril	HO 22-29/4, p.1	Pétinord	Mme Célavi	paysanne	machette	Jean-Rabel	1
20 avril	HO 22-29/4, p.1	Prémilus	Ilméus	bandit	lynché	Jean-Rabel	1
22 avril	HO 22-29/4, p.2	Antoine	Patrick	policier	balles	Cap-Haïtien	1
22 avril	HP 22-29/4, p.1	non identifiés	non spécifié	non définies	balles	P-au-Pce	2
22 avril	HO 22-29/4, p.1	non identifié	non spécifié	bandit	lynché	St-Marc	1
28 avril	LN 28/4, p. 5	Pierre-Louis	Raynald	non définies	balles	P-au-Pce	1
5 mai	LN 6/5, p. 1	Gracien	Chenel	non définies	balles	Borel	1
5 mai	LN 6/5, p. 1	Gracien	Mme Chenel	non définies	balles	Borel	1
9 mai	HO 13/5, p.23	Borno	Jean-Marie	non définies	balles	Kenscoff	1
11 mai	LN 11/5, p. 28	non identifié	non spécifié	étalagiste	balles	P-au-Pce	1
13 mai	LN 13/5, p. 32	non identifié	non spécifié	non définies	balles	Cité Soleil	1
21 mai	HO 27/5, p. 1	Cétray	ainsi connu	non définies	poison	St-Ls-du Nord	1
21 mai	HO 27/5-3/6, p.1	Desrivières	Madame	non définies	lynché	St-Ls-du Nord	1
24 mai	LN 25/5, p. 40	St-Fort	Guens	policier	balles	Carrefour	1
25 mai	LN 25/5, p. 1	Aristide	Charles Pelé	policier	balles	P-au-Pce	1
28 mai	LN 4/6, p. 1	Joseph	Emanie	non définies	balles	Hinche	1
28 mai	LN 4/6, p. 1	Julio	ainsi connu	non définies	balles	Hinche	1
28 mai	LN 4/6, p. 28	Molière	Lefranc	non définies	balles	Chansolme	1

Date	Reference	Nom	Prénom	Profession	Cause	Lieu	N
15 juin	HO 17-25/6, p.3	non identifié	non spécifié	bandit	lynché	Mirebalais	1
17 juin	HO 24/6-1, p.21	Jean-François	César	policier	balles	P-au-Pce	1
19 juin	HO 1-8/7, p. 1	Métayer	Jocelyn	ingénieur	balles	P-au-Pce	1
28 juin	HO 1-8/7, p. 11	Papillon	Pierre	non définies	balles	P-au-Pce	1
16 juil.	HO 22/7, p. 12	Innocent	Jean	non définies	balles	Pétion-Ville	1
17 juil.	LN 17-19/7, p.40	Mathé	Avrius	policier	balles	Delmas	1
23 juil.	HO 6/1/99, p.11	Wesh	Bernard	non définies	balles	Beaumont	1
24 juil.	HO 29/7-5, p.11	McLaney	Michael	entrepreneur	balles	P-au-Pce	1
24 juil.	LN 24-26/7, p.32	non identifiés	non spécifié	non définies	balles	Delmas	3
2 août	HO 2-12/8, p. 7	Bruno	Joudnel	entrepreneur	balles	Delmas	1
2 août	HO 2-12/8, p. 7	Domersant	Louis	policier	balles	Port-de-Paix	1
3 août	LN 3/8, p. 1	Pierre-Louis	Jean	prêtre	balles	P-au-Pce	1
5 août	LN 5/8, p. 24	Jérome	ainsi connu	non définies	balles	Arcahaie	1
5 août	LN 5/8, p. 24	Jean-Baptiste	Saurel	non définies	balles	Cabaret	1
6 août	HO 12-19/8, p.16	Exantus	Luckner	non définies	balles	Cabaret	1
6 août	LN 5/8, p. 24	Casséus	Ricardo	non définies	balles	Petit-Goâve	1
13 août	LN 13/8, p. 32	Tédal	Sorel	non définies	balles	P-au-Pce	1
21 août	HO 26/8-1, p.18	non identifié	non spécifié	bandit	balles	St-Martin	1
25 août	LN 25/8, p. 32	Jameson	ainsi connu	mineur	balles	P-au-Pce	1
30 août	HO 9-16/9, p. 20	Tiga	ainsi connu	non définies	balles	P-au-Pce	1
31 août	HO 2-9/9, p. 10	Versailles	Clothaire	non définies	balles	P-au-Pce	1
5 sept.	HO 9-16/9, p. 20	Jean-Baptiste	Jean-Robert	prisonnier	sévices	La Tortue	1
8 sept.	HEM 2-8/9, p. 18	Geatjeans	Max	antiquaire	non spécifié	Pétion-Ville	1
9 sept.	HO 16-23/9, p.18	Gilbert	Philippe	salesman	balles	Delmas	1
21 sept.	HO 23-30/9, p.22	Théodule	Onel	mineur	balles	Cité Soleil	1
26 sept.	LN 28/9, p. 1	Pierre	Marie Eric	professeur	machette	P-au-Pce	1
26 sept.	LN 1/10, p.1	Baltazar	Murielle	étudiante	sévices	Martissant	1
30 sept.	LN 30/9, p. 32	Phanor	Gary	étudiant	balles	P-au-Pce	1
4 oct.	HO 7-14/10, p.17	non identifié	non spécifié	Sud-Coréen	balles	Cap-Haïtien	1
4 oct.	HO 7-14/10, p.17	non identifié	non spécifié	chauffeur	balles	Cap-Haïtien	1
11 oct.	LN 14/11, p. 32	Altidor	Lüders	non définies	balles	Cayes	1
11 oct.	LN 12/10, p. 1	non identifiés	non spécifié	non définies	lapidation	Cx-Missions	2
11 oct.	LN 12/10, p. 1	non identifié	non spécifié	non définies	balles	Pétion-Ville	1
29 oct.	HO 4-11/11, p. 5	Diallo	Moktar	MIPONUH	balles	Delmas	1
7 nov.	HEM 18/11, p. 17	Bijou	André	entrepreneur	balles	Frères	1

9 nov.	HO 2-9/12, p.	Mehring	Kurt	Américain	balles	Pétion-Ville	1
14 nov.	HEM 18/11, p. 17	non identifiés	non spécifié	bandits	lynchage	Mirebalais	2
15 nov.	HO 9-16/12, p. 3	Baronville	Luckner	commerçant	balles	Anse-Galets	1
18 nov.	HO 9-16/12, p. 3	non identifiés	non spécifié	non définies	balles	St-Ls-du Nord	2
21 nov.	LN 24/11, p. 32	Lapin	Malherbe	messager	balles	P-au-Pce	1
21 nov.	HO 25/11-2, p. 5	Théodore	Yolène T.	non définies	balles	P-au-Pce	1
24 nov.	LN 27/11, p.40	non identifié	non spécifié	non définies	balles	Jérémie	1
27 nov.	HO 2-9/12, p. 11	Lambert	Jean Eric	non définies	balles	Pétion-Ville	1
27 nov.	HO 2-9/12, p. 11	Bernardin	Hurdon	Frère (FIC)	machette	La Vallée	1
27 nov.	HO 2-9/12, p. 11	Don Mike	Charles	bandit	lynché	P-au-Pce	1
30 nov.	LN 30/11, p. 1	non identifié	non spécifié	Hougan	lynchage	Vallée Jacmel	1
2 déc.	HP 9-15/12, p. 2	non identifié	non spécifié	policier	balles	Ouanaminthe	1
2 déc	HO 2-9/12, p. 16	non identifié	non spécifié	policier	lynché	Plaisance	1
3 déc.	LN 3/12, p. 32	non identifiés	non spécifié	agt sécurité	balles	Delmas	2
8 déc.	HP 9-15/12, p. 2	non identifié	non spécifié	paysan	conflits	Verrettes	1
11 déc.	HP 9-15/12, p. 8	Damas	Ruls	vacancier	balles	Santo	1
11 déc.	HO 16/12, p.22	Montreuil	Fritz	banquier	balles	Port-de-Paix	1
14 déc.	LN 14/12, p. 40	non identifié	non spécifié	non définies	balles	P-au-Pce	1
16 déc.	HO 23/12, p.1	non identifiés	non spécifié	agt sécurité	balles	P-au-Pce	2
22 déc.	LN 22/12, p. 44	non identifiés	non spécifié	bandit	brûlé	Delmas	4

Total of assassinated persons for the year 1998   147

5- The victims for the year 1999

Date	Sources	Name	First name	identification	Means	Location	No.
6 janv.	LN 7/1, p. 24	Paul	Hubert	bandit	lapidation	Mirebalais	1
12 janv.	LN 13/1, p. 1	Versailles	Jean-Franklin	chauffeur	balles	P-au-Pce	1
23 janv.	LN 25-26/1, p.32	Dominique	Yvel	non définies	balles	St Mic. Attalaye	1
27 janv.	LN 27/1, p. 24	non identifié	non spécifié	non définies	lapidation	Mirebalais	1
4 fév.	LN 4-6/2, p. 1	non identifiés	non spécifié	non définies	balles	Crfour-Feuilles	11
10 fév.	LN 16/2, p. 32	St-Fleur	Enks	musicien	balles	Gonaïves	1
10 fév.	HO 17-24/2, p. 1	St-Pierre	Jules	non définies	balles	Capotille	1
10 fév.	HO 17-24/2, p. 1	Présent	Théonique	non définies	balles	Capotille	1
10 fév.	HO 17-24/2, p. 1	non identifié	non spécifié	bandit	balles	P-au-Pce	1
21 fév.	LN 22/2, p. 1	Money	Joseph Simon	pasteur	balles	P-au-Pce	1
22 fév.	HO 24/2-2/3, p.5	Midi	Pierre-Marie	politique	sévices	Jérémie	1
22 fév.	HO 24/2-2/3, p.5	non identifié	non spécifié	Américain	machette	Morne Calvaire	1
23 fév.	LN 23/2, p. 1	Francis	Georges	entrepreneur	balles	P-au-Pce	1
26 fév.	HO 2-9/3, p. 18	non identifié	non spécifié	non définies	machette	P-au-Pce	1
27 fév.	LN 1/3, p. 1	Lalanne	Jimmy	médecin	balles	P-au-Pce	1
1 mars	LN 1/3, p. 1	Toussaint	Yvon	sénateur	balles	P-au-Pce	1
1 mars	LN 1/3, p. 1	Figaro	Wilfrid	médecin	balles	P-au-Pce	1
1 mars	LN 1/3, p. 1	Plaisimond	Maryse	médecin	balles	P-au-Pce	1
1 mars	LN 1/3, p. 1	Jocelyn	Fritz	Médecin	balles	Pétion-Ville	1
1 mars	LN 1/3, p. 1	non identifiés	non spécifié	non définies	balles	P-au-Pce	5
3 mars	LN 8/3, p. 24	Michelet	Dazouloute	policier	balles	Delmas	1
6 mars	HO 10-17/3, p.14	Pierre	Joceline	non définies	machette	Marigot	1
6 mars	HO 10-17/3, p.14	Pierre	Edouane	non définies	machette	Marigot	1
8 mars	LN 8/3, p. 24	non identifiés	non spécifié	non définies	machette	Marigot	2
8 mars	LN 8/3, p. 1	non identifiés	non spécifié	non définies	balles	P-au-Pce	3

9 mars	LN 10/3, p. 1	Edouard	Louis Galet	non définies	balles	Lilavoix	1
10 mars	LN 10/3, p. 1	Richard	Albert Joseph	policier	balles	P-au-Pce	1
12 mars	LN 12-14/3, p.32	non identifiés	non spécifié	non définies	balles	Cabaret	4
13 mars	HO 17-24/3, p.17	non identifié	non spécifié	agt sécurité	balles	P-au-Pce	1
13 mars	HO 17-24/3, p.17	non identifiés	non spécifié	non définies	balles	Delmas	2
14 mars	HO 17-24/3, p.17	non identifiés	non spécifié	non définies	balles	P-au-Pce	5
22 mars	LN 25/3, p. 32	Germain	Brignol	chauffeur	lynchage	Mare-Rouge	1
22 mars	LN 25/3, p. 32	Tiyoute	ainsi connu	non définies	balles	Mare-Rouge	1
26 mars	HO 31/3-7/4, p.18	Désir	Valentine	non définies	balles	P-au-Pce	1
28 mars	HO 31/3-7/4, p.18	non identifiés	non spécifié	pompistes	balles	P-au-Pce	2
30 mars	LN 5/4, p. 1	Pierre	Mme Ph.	non définies	machette	Gde Riv.-Nord	1
30 mars	HO 31/3-7/4, p.4	Smith	ainsi connu	vacancier	balles	Delmas	1
5 avril	LN 5/4, p. 1	non identifiés	non spécifié	non définies	balles	P-au-Pce	5
7 avril	HO 14-21/4, p. 3	Hervé	Jean Gérald	non définies	balles	Delmas	1
7 avril	HO 14-21/4, p. 3	Poincarré	Charles	non définies	sévices	Petit-Goâve	1
8 avril	LN 8/4, p. 32	non identifié	non spécifié	non définies	machette	Mariani	1
9 avril	HO 12-19/5, p. 3	Pierre	André	non définies	machette	Delmas	1
9 avril	HO 12-19/5, p. 3	Pierre	enfants André	mineurs	machette	Delmas	2
9 avril	HO 21-28/4, p. 10	non identifié	non spécifié	patient HUEH	balles	P-au-Pce	1
10 avril	HO 14-21/4, p. 2	Payne	Jean Ovens	policier	balles	Fontamara	1
10 avril	HO 14-21/4, p. 2	non identifiés	non spécifié	jeunes	balles	Fontamara	5
11 avril	HO 14-21/4, p. 3	non identifié	non spécifié	bandit	brûlé	Fort Sinclair	1
11 avril	HO 14-21/4, p. 3	non identifiés	non spécifié	non définies	balles	Delmas	2
12 avril	HO 14-21/4, p.24	non identifiés	non spécifié	non définies	balles	P-au-Pce	12
13 avril	HO 14-21/4, p. 2	non identifié	non spécifié	non définies	machette	Cap-Haïtien	1
14 avril	HO 21-28/4, p. 2	Mitton	Jacky	ex-capitaine	balles	P-au-Pce	1
17 avril	LN 17-19/4, p. 1	Elysée	Hippolite	bandit	balles	P-au-Pce	1

20 avril	LN 28/4, p. 1	Phyllis	Michel-Ange	Alis Boa	balles	P-au-Pce	1
28 avril	LN 28/4, p. 32	St-Georges	Milord	non définies	balles	Delmas	1
28 avril	LN 29/4, p. 5	Alcantara	Ramon	Dominicain	non spécifié	Lascahobas	1
28 avril	HO 5-12/5, p. 9	Milhomme	Dieuseul	non définies	lynchage	Dessalines	1
1er mai	LN 3/5, p. 1	Morisset	Mad	policier	balles	Tabarre	1
1er mai	HO 5-12/5, p. 8	Pierre-Louis	Bertrand	journaliste	balles	P-au-Pce	1
2 mai	LN 3/5, p. 24	Barelli	Lucas	commerçant	balles	Pétion-Ville	1
3 mai	HO 5-12/5, p. 8	Samuel	Sylvain	policier	balles	Pte Pl. Cazeau	1
3 mai	LN 3/5, p. 1	non identifiés	non spécifié	non définies	balles	P-au-Pce	6
4 mai	LN 4/5, p. 1	Johanne	ainsi connue	mineure	balles	P-au-Pce	1
7 mai	HO 12-19/5, p.10	non identifié	non spécifié	dite sorcière	lapidation	St. Ls du-Nord	1
7 mai	HO 12-19/5, p.10	Maxo	ainsi connu	hougan	lynchage	Anse-à-Foleur	1
10 mai	HO 12-19/5, p. 3	Hector	Maxime	ingénieur	balles	Pétion-Ville	1
10 mai	HO 12-19/5, p. 3	Joseph	Onius	dit sorcier	lynchage	Savanette	1
10 mai	HO 12-19/5, p. 3	Démosthène	ainsi connue	dit sorcier	non spécifié	Savanette	1
12 mai	HO 12-19/5, p. 3	non identifiés	non spécifié	non définies	lynchage	St. Ls du-Nord	2
12 mai	HO 19-26/5, p. 6	Tinès	ainsi connu	non définies	balles	St-Marc	1
12 mai	HO 19-26/5, p.10	non identifié	non spécifié	jeune	balles	Delmas	1
12 mai	LN 13/5, p. 1	Ti Boulé	ainsi connu	jeune	machette	Mirebalais	1
14 mai	HO 19-26/5, p. 6	non identifié	non spécifié	non définies	balles	Cité Soleil	1
15 mai	LM 15-17/5, p. 2	non identifié	non spécifié	non définies	balles	P-au-Pce	1
17 mai	HO 19-26/5, p. 6	Romain	Venel	footballeur	balles	Léogane	1
25 mai	LN 25/5, p. 1	non identifié	non spécifié	non définies	balles	Gonaïves	3
25 mai	LN 25/5, p. 1	Aristide	Charles Pelé	policier	balles	Gonaïves	1
27 mai	HO 2-9/6, p. 2	Jeudilien	Idilan	ex- sergent	balles	P-au-Pce	1
28 mai	LN 31/5, p. 1	non identifiés	non spécifié	non définies	balles	Crfour-Feuilles	11
31 mai	HO 2-9/6, p. 2	non identifiés	non spécifié	bandit	lynchage	Cité Soleil	2
31 mai	HO 2-9/6, p. 2	non identifié	non spécifié	chauffeur	balles	Cité Soleil	1
6 juin	HP 9-15/6, p. 2	Francis	Roseline	non définies	balles	Léogane	1
6 juin	LN 8/6, p. 24	non identifié	non spécifié	bandit	balles	P-au-Pce	1

6 juin	LN 8/6, p. 24	non identifié	non spécifié	policier	balles	Montrouis	1
6 juin	LN 8/6, p. 24	non identifié	non spécifié	bandit	balles	Carrefour	1
7 juin	LN 9/6, p. 24	Bazile	Berthony	policier	balles	P-au-Pce	1
7 juin	LN 9/8, p. 24	Adonis	Carlo	agt sécurité	balles	P-au-Pce	1
7 juin	LN 7/6, p. 24	non identifié	non spécifié	jeune	machette	Prtail-Léogane	1
8 juin	LN 8/6, p. 24	Narcisse	Pierre Richard	non définies	balles	Pétion-Ville	1
14 juin	LN 14/6, p. 24	Jean	Wisler	paysan	balles	Pierre-Payen	1
14 juin	LN 14/6, p. 24	non identifié	non spécifié	non définies	lynchage	Pierre-Payen	1
15 juin	HO 23/6, p. 2	non identifiés	non spécifié	voyageurs	balles	Morne-Cabrits	5
17 juin	LN 17/6, p. 1	Abdallah	Louis Galet	entrepreneur	balles	P-au-Pce	1
20 juin	LN 21/6, p. 32	non identifiés	non spécifié	non définies	balles	P-au-Pce	2
21 juin	LN 21/6, p. 32	Lubin	Harold	policier	balles	P-au-Pce	1
21 juin	HO 23/6, p. 2	Appolon	Volmar	comptable	balles	Cap-Haïtien	1
24 juin	HO 30/6, p.2	Bienaimé	Marie Claude	non définies	balles	Gonaïves	1
28 juin	HO 30/6, p.5	Bertin	Dérival	commerçant	balles	Carrefour	1
28 juin	HO 30/6, p.5	Loiseau	Daniel	agt sécurité	balles	Carrefour	1
29 juin	LN 21/6, p. 1	non identifiés	non spécifié	agt sécurité	balles	Cazeau	2
30 juin	HO 30/6, p.5	Léger	William	bandit	balles	P-au-Pce	1
30 juin	LN 30/6, p. 1	non identifié	non spécifié	agt sécurité	balles	Cazeau	1
2 juil.	LN 2-4/7, p. 1	non identifiés	non spécifié	non définies	balles	Titanyen	14
19 juil.	LN 19/6, p. 1	non identifiés	non spécifié	non définies	balles	P-au-Pce	2
20 juil.	LN 2-4/7, p. 1	Renard	Franciné	policier	balles	P-au-Pce	1
21 juil.	HO 28/7, p.15	non identifiés	non spécifié	bandits	balles	Léogane	2
22 juil.	HO 28/7, p.15	non identifiés	non spécifié	non définies	lynchage	Dessources	2
22 juil.	LN 23/7, p.32	Charles	Kettely	non définies	balles	P-au-Pce	1
23 juil.	LN 23/7, p.32	non identifié	non spécifié	non définies	balles	P-au-Pce	1
24 juil.	LN 26/7, p. 32	Noël	Citha	marchande	brûlé	Pétion-Ville	1
25 juil.	LN 26/7, p. 32	Pamphille	Gilbert	pharmacien	balles	Delmas	1
28 juil.	LN 28/7, p. 1	Mingot	Jérome	tailleur	balles	P-au-Pce	1
4 août	HO 11/8, p.11	Louidor	Jean Willy	entrepreneur	balles	P-au-Pce	1
4 août	HO 11/8, p.11	Benoit	Simon	entrepreneur	balles	P-au-Pce	1
4 août	HO 11/8, p.11	Max	Jean-Robert	mormons	balles	Cité Soleil	1
5 août	HO 11/8, p.11	Simon	Naomie	étudiante	balles	Delmas	1

5 août	HO 11/8, p.11	Célestin	Huguens	jeune	balles	Fort National	1
10 août	LN 11/8, p. 24	Alexandre	Patrick	policier	balles	La Saline	1
10 août	HO 18/8, p.13	Dacéus	Mme Dalismé	dite sorcière	lynchage	Pte R. Artibonite	1
22 août	HO 1-8/9, p. 7	non identifiés	non spécifié	non définies	balles	Aquin	5
24 août	^LN 25/8, p. 1	Fédel	ainsi connu	de Culligan	balles	P-au-Pce	1
30 août	HO 1-8/9, p. 23	Montalmand	Casimir	artiste-peintre	balles	P-au-Pce	1
31 août	LN 6/9, p. 1	Décatrel	Roland	commerçant	balles	P-au-Pce	1
9 sept.	LN 9/9, p. 24	Lamarre	Tira	non définies	balles	P-au-Pce	1
18 sept.	HO 22-2/9, p. 8	non identifié	non spécifié	chauffeur	balles	Cité Soleil	1
21 sept.	LN 21/9, p. 1	Charrier	Estime	non définies	balles	P-au-Pce	1
21 sept.	HO 29/9, p.1	Moïse	Frantz	bal	balles	Pélerin	1
21 sept.	HO 29/9, p.1	Thomas	Pierre Richard	non définies	balles	Pélerin	1
21 sept.	LN 21/9, p. 32	non identifié	non spécifié	non définies	balles	P-au-Pce	1
24 sept.	HO 29/9, p.1	Chéry	Edgard	policier	balles	Carrefour	1
26 sept.	HO 29/9, p.2	Chérant	Johnny	policier	balles	P-au-Pce	1
2 oct.	HO 6/10, p.16	non identifié	non spécifié	policier	balles	P-au-Pce	1
3 Oct.	HO 6/10, p.16	non identifiés	non spécifié	agts sécurité	sévices	Delmas	2
7 oct.	HO 13/10, p.11	Sidney	Jean-Robert	policier	balles	Crfour-Feuilles	1
8 oct.	HO 13/10, p.11	Léger	Mme Love	non définies	sévices	Pétion-Ville	1
8 oct.	HO 13/10, p.11	Séraphin	Cadeau	bandit	machette	Petit-Goâve	1
8 oct.	LN 11/10, p. 1	Lamy	Jean	ex-major	balles	P-au-Pce	1
9 oct.	HO 13/10, p.11	non identifié	non spécifié	bandit	balles	P-au-Pce	1
10 oct.	LN 10/11, p. 24	Georges	Eddy	entrepreneur	balles	P-au-Pce	1
13 oct.	LN 14/10, p. 32	Moïse	Nelson	non définies	balles	Cabaret	1
19 oct.	LN 21/10, p. 1	non identifié	non spécifié	non définies	balles	P-au-Pce	1
19 oct.	LN 21/10, p. 1	non identifiés	non spécifié	non définies	machette	Carrefour	5
8 nov.	LN 8/11, p. 1	Brierre	Serge	entrepreneur	balles	P-au-Pce	1
8 nov.	LN 8/11, p. 1	non identifié	non spécifié	chauffeur	balles	P-au-Pce	1
8 nov.	LN 8/11, p. 32	non identifiés	non spécifié	non définies	balles	St-Martin	2
8 nov.	LN 8/11, p. 32	non identifiés	non spécifié	non définies	machette	Bois-Patate	2
8 nov.	LN 8/11, p. 32	non identifié	non spécifié	non définies	lynchage	Tabarre	1
11 nov.	LN 4/11, p. 24	non identifiés	non spécifié	non définies	conflits	P-au-Pce	3

17 nov.	HO 24/11, p.11	Robert	Marie-Géralde	religieuse	balles	Bourdon	1
22 nov.	LN 25/11, p. 40	Jeune	Dérold	non définies	machette	Marmelade	1
22 nov.	LN 25/11, p. 40	Valcin	Vernel	bandit	lynchage	Marmelade	1
22 nov.	LN 25/11, p. 40	non identifiés	non spécifié	bandits	lynchage	Trou-du-Nord	6
27 nov.	LN 27/11, p.40	non identifié	non spécifié	prisonnier	balles	Jérémie	1
4 déc.	HO 10/12, p.3	non identifiés	non spécifié	décapités	machette	Léogane	10
5 déc.	LN 7/12, p. 1	Phanord	Edwidge	employé TNH	balles	Delmas	1
15 déc.	LN 15/12, p. 48	Hyppolite	Daniel	non définies	balles	P-au-Pce	1
16 déc.	HO 29/1, p. 19	Robert	Jean	chauffeur	balles	P-au-Pce	1
19 déc.	HO 29-5/1, p. 4	Durand	Astride	non définies	machette	Pétion-Ville	1
20 déc.	LN 20/12, p. 48	non identifiés	non spécifié	non définies	balles	Côtes-de-Fer	7
21 déc.	HO 29-5/1, p.4	Sanon	Roseline	non définies	sévices	La Tortue	1
21 déc.	HO 29-5/1, p. 4	Sanon	Milfort	non définies	sévices	La Tortue	1
27 déc.	LN 27/12, p. 40	non identifiés	non spécifié	non définies	balles	Pétion-Ville	2
27 déc.	LN 27/12, p. 40	Roland	ainsi connu	jeune	balles	Crfour-Feuilles	1
31 déc.	HO 12/1/00, p.2	St-Joy	Marjorie	non définies	balles	P-au-Pce	1

Total of assassinated persons for the year 1999   **285**

6- The victims for the year 2000

Date	Sources	Name	First name	Identification	Means	Location	No.
1 janv.	0 LN 10/1, p. 24	non identifié	non spécifié	non définies	brûlé	P-au-Pce	1
1 janv.	1 LN 12/1, p. 1	Séjour	Elison	non définies	balles	Fort-Liberté	1
12 jan.	LN 10/1, p. 1	non identifié	non spécifié	non définies	balles	Fort-Liberté	1
1 janv.	2 LN 12/1, p. 24	non identifié	non spécifié	chauffeur	machette	Verrettes	1
1 janv.	2 LN 18/1, p. 24	Mullier	Fernand	Français	machette	Jacmel	1
1 janv.	2 LN 18/1, p. 24	Mullier	Céline	Française	machette	Jacmel	1
1 janv.	2 LN 18/1, p. 24	Obin	Aspin	artiste	machette	Jacmel	1
1 janv.	5 HO 26/1-2/2, p.11	Web	Sheila	Américaine	balles	Srce Puante	1
1 janv.	5 HO 26/1-2/2, p.11	Jean-Jacques	Hyppolite	non définies	balles	P-au-Pce	1
1 janv.	5 HO 26/1-2/2, p.11	Faustin	Romain	non définies	balles	P-au-Pce	1
1 janv.	7 HO 19-26/1, p. 1	non identifiés	non spécifié	pompistes	balles	Martissant	2
1 janv.	7 LN 17/1, p. 1	non identifiée	non spécifié	Américaine	balles	P-au-Pce	1
1 janv.	9 LN 21-22/1, p.32	non identifiés	non spécifié	non définies	lynchage	St Ls.-du-Sud	3
2 janv.	3 27/1, p. 24	non identifiés	non spécifié	non définies	balles	Pétion-Ville	2
3 janv.	1 LN 31/1, p. 1	non identifiés	non spécifié	non définies	balles	Martissant	2
4 fév.	LN 4-6/2, p. 1	Piti	ainsi connu	non définies	balles	Trou-du-Nord	1
10 fév.	LM 10/2, p.2	Lhérisson	Jean-Louis	commerçant	balles	Pte Riv. Art.	1
16 fév.	LN 16/1, p. 32	non identifié	non spécifié	non définies	balles	P-au-Pce	1
21 fév.	LN 21/2, p. 24	Valcourt	Sanders	non définies	balles	P-au-Pce	1
3 mars	LN 2/3, p. 24	Jimenez	Jose	Dominicain	balles	P-au-Pce	1
3 mars	LN 3-7/3, p. 5	non identifiés	non spécifié	non définies	balles	Matheux	4
3 mars	LN 3-7/3, p. 5	non identifié	non spécifié	borlettier	balles	P-au-Pce	1
7 mars	LN 8-9/3, p. 32	Bélizaire	Ernest	policier	balles	P-au-Pce	1
8 mars	LN 8-9/3, p. 32	non identifiés	non spécifié	bandit	lynchage	Martissant	4
13 mars	LN 16/3, p. 6	Janvier	Bienheureux	non définies	balles	Moléon	1

27 mars	HO 5-12/4, p. 4	Labissière	Nelson	meurtrier	lynchage	La Saline	1
27 mars	HO 29/3-5/4, p.16	Samedi	Jean B.	non définies	machette	La Saline	1
27 mars	HO 29/3-5/4, p.16	non identifié	non spécifié	chauffeur	balles	Delmas	1
28 mars	HO 26/4-3/5, p.15	Athis	Légitime	politique	balles	Petit-Goâve	1
28 mars	HO 26/4-3/5, p.15	Athis	Mme Légitime	politique	balles	Petit-Goâve	1
29 mars	HO 5-12/4, p. 4	Jeudy	Nétula	voleuse	lynchage	St Ls.-du-Sud	1
29 mars	HO 5-12/4, p. 4	Jeudy	Jocelin	voleur	lynchage	St Ls.-du-Sud	1
29 mars	HO 5-12/4, p. 4	Jeudy	Jean-François	voleur	lynchage	St Ls.-du-Sud	1
29 mars	HO 26/4-3/5, p.16	Dorvil	Ferdinand	politique	balles	Caracol	1
3 avril	LN 1/4, p. 16	Dominique	Jean L.	journaliste	balles	Delmas	1
3 avril	LN 1/4, p. 16	Louissaint	Jean-Claude	gardien	balles	Delmas	1
6 avril	LN 10/4, p. 20	André	Guy	commerçant	balles	Pétion-Ville	1
7 avril	LN 11/4, p. 16	Sabbat	Patrick	mineur	balles	Delmas	1
12 avril	HO 19-26/4, p. 3	Déus	Mérélus	non définies	balles	Savanette	1
13 avril	LN 13/4, p. 1	non identifié	non spécifié	jeune	balles	P-au-Pce	1
14 avril	LN 14-16, p. 29	non identifié	non spécifié	non définies	balles	Delmas	1
14 avril	HO 19-26/4, p. 1	Exaüs	Emmanuel	ex lieutenant	balles	Delmas	1
16 avril	LN 19-23/4, p. 5	François	Emana	paysanne	machette	Pte Riv. Art.	1
17 avril	LN 17/4, p. 32	Jean-Claude	ainsi connu	paysan	lynchage	Pte Riv. Art.	1
17 avril	LN 17/4, p. 32	Black Kiki	ainsi connu	non définies	balles	Pétion-Ville	1
17 avril	LN 17/4, p. 32	Désir	ainsi connu	non définies	balles	Pétion-Ville	1
22 avril	LN 24/4, p. 24	Espérance	Louiné	hougan	machette	Pilate	1
25 avril	HO 3-10/5, p. 10	Ducertain	Arnaud	politique	machette	Thomazeau	1
25 avril	LN 26/4, p. 5	Kénol	Jean-Claude	non définies	balles	Carriès	1
25 avril	LN 26/4, p. 5	Kénol	Mme	non définies	balles	Carriès	1
25 avril	LN 26/4, p. 5	Kénol	enfants	mineurs	balles	Carriès	4
26 avril	LN 26/4, p. 5	Marcelin	Thierry	mineur	balles	Cul-de-Sac	1
28 avril	LN 2/5, p. 24	Laguerre	Pierre Wilfrid	policier	balles	Delmas	1
28 avril	LN 2/5, p. 24	non identifiés	non spécifié	paysans	machette	Arcahaie	2
3 mai	LN 3/5, p. 1	Belot	Lagneau	prêtre	balles	Delmas	1
4 mai	LN 5-7, p. 5	Alexandre	Michel-Ange	policier	balles	Martissant	1
6 mai	LN 8/5, p. 1	Bordes	Ary	médecin	balles	Delmas	1
6 mai	LN 9/5, p. 6	Castin	Jérôme	chauffeur	balles	P-au-Pce	1
7 mai	V2k 8/5, 5:00 p	non identifié	non spécifié	jeune	balles	Léogane	1
7 mai	V2k 8/5, 5:00 p	non identifiés	non spécifié	paysans	machette	Cabaret	2

8 mai	V2k 8/5, 12:00 p	Sénat	Elane	non définies	balles	Savanette	1
8 mai	V2k 8/5, 12:00 p	Sénat	Grégor	fils d'Elane	balles	Savanette	1
8 mai	V2k 8/5, 12:00 p	Omilien	ainsi connu	paysan	balles	Savanette	1
12 mai	LN 12-14/5, p. 40	Sanon	Branord	politique	balles	P-au-Pce	1
13 mai	LN 16/5, p. 1	Pierre	Gumane	non définies	balles	Martissant	1
13 mai	LN 16/5, p. 1	Douze	James	dit Papouche	balles	Martissant	1
13 mai	LN 16/5, p. 1	Pierre	Alain	non définies	balles	Martissant	1
14 mai	LN 16/5, p. 32	Laurent	ainsi connu	non définies	lynchage	Dessalines	1
15 mai	LN 16/5, p. 32	non identifié	non spécifié	jeune	balles	Léogane	1
20 mai	LN 23/5, p. 32	Joseph	Walter	non définies	machette	Lascahobas	1
21 mai	LN 22/5, p. 32	non identifiés	non spécifié	HUEH	balles	P-au-Pce	2
22 mai	LN 23/5, p. 1	Alophène	Jean-Michel	politique	lynchage	P-au-Pce	1
23 mai	LN 24/5, p. 32	Lebrun	Maxo	policier	balles	P-au-Pce	1
28 mai	LN 1/6, p. 24	Salnave	Amédée	12 ans	machette	Aquin	1
28 mai	LN 1/6, p. 24	non identifiés	non spécifié	meurtriers	lynchage	Aquin	2
29 mai	V2K 29/9, 8:45 p	non identifiés	non spécifié	bandits	lynchage	P-au-Pce	4
29 mai	V2K 30/5, 7:30 a	non identifiés	non spécifié	bandits	lynchage	Petit-Goâve	3
31 mai	LN 1/6, p. 1	non identifié	non spécifié	non définies	balles	Mirebalais	1
31 mai	LN 1/6, p. 24	Pierre	Wilner	quiquagénaire	balles	Léogane	1
1er juin	LN 1/6, p. 24	Laurore	Patrick	agent sécurité	balles	P-au-Pce	1
2 juin	LN 2-4/6, p. 32	non identifié	non spécifié	non définies	sévices	Carrefour	1
3 juin	LN 5/6, p. 22	St-Hilaire	S.	employé CEP	machette	Petit-Goâve	1
11 juin	V2k, 6:00 a	Beauplan	Wilmo	jeune	balles	Ennery	1
11 juin	V2k, 6:00 a	Joseph	Wilesome	trafiquant	balles	Grand-Goâve	1
11 juin	V2k, 6:00 a	Eugène	Tadaille	trafiquant	balles	Grand-Goâve	1
11 juin	V2k, 6:00 a	Lizaire	ainsi connu	trafiquant	balles	Grand-Goâve	1
12 juin	13/6, p. 24	non identifié	non spécifié	bandits	balles	Cx-Bouquets	2
13 juin	LN 13/6, p. 24	Pierre-Louis	MacKenzie	non définies	balles	Cap-Haïtien	1
14 juin	HO 27/9-4/10, p.9	Cazeau	Roger	colonel (ret)	balles	P-au-Pce	1
21 juin	LN 21-22/6, p. 32	non identifiés	non spécifié	bandits	balles	P-au-Pce	2
2 juil.	LN 3/7, p. 24	non identié	non spécifié	non définies	machette	Ile-à-Vaches	1
3 juil.	LN 3/7, p. 24	Rousseau	Gilbert	non définies	balles	Delmas	1
4 juil.	LN 4/7, p. 24	non identifiés	non spécifié	non définies	balles	Gressier	3
9 juil.	LN 10/7, p. 24	non identifiés	non spécifié	bandits	lynchage	P-au-Pce	1
11 juil.	LN 18/7, p. 6	Présumé	Darlie	non définies	balles	Cul-de-Sac	1

Date	Réf.	Prénom	Nom	Qualité	Moyen	Lieu	Nb
17 juil.	LN 17/7, p. 1	non identifié	non spécifié	non définies	balles	Jérémie	1
17 juil.	LN 17/7, p. 24	non identifiés	non spécifié	non définies	balles	Solino	2
19 juil.	LN 19/7, p. 5	Casséus	Fritznel	non définies	balles	Léogane	1
25 juil.	LN 3/8, p. 20	Alexandre	Carmen B.	commerçante	sévices	Martissant	1
3 août	LN 4-6/8, p. 24	non identifié	non spécifié	commerçant	balles	P-au-Pce	1
3 août	LN 4-6/8, p. 24	Painson	Gabriel	non définies	balles	P-au-Pce	1
3 août	LN 4-6/8, p. 24	non identifié	non spécifié	chauffeur	balles	P-au-Pce	1
6 août	LN 7/8, p. 8	non identifié	non spécifié	jeune	non spécifié	P-au-Pce	1
7 août	LN 8/8, p. 24	Lyle	Garfield	membre ONU	balles	Tabarre	1
9 août	LN 16/8, p. 32	Huguens	Jean-Paul	policier	balles	Pétion-Ville	1
12 août	LN 14-15/8, p. 24	Timanchèt	ainsi connu	bandit	lynchage	Mirebalais	1
12 août	LN 14-15/8, p. 24	non identifiés	non spécifié	bandits	lapidation	Petit-Goâve	2
12 août	LN 14-15/8, p. 24	non identifiés	non spécifié	non définies	non spécifié	Léogane	4
15 août	LN 16/8, p. 32	non identifiés	non spécifié	jeunes	lynchage	Blle-Fontaine	10
18 août	LN 22/8, p. 24	Dieudonné	Fertil	non définies	machette	St-Marc	1
20 août	LN 22/8, p. 24	non identifié	non spécifié	non définies	machette	P-au-Pce	1
19 août	LN 22/8, p. 24	Wilner	ainsi connu	commerçant	balles	Crfour-Shada	1
21 août	LN 22/8, p. 24	non identifié	non spécifié	non définies	balles	Cité Soleil	1
26 août	LN 5/9, p. 24	non identifiés	non spécifié	bandits	balles	Cité Soleil	5
13 sept.	LN 13/9, p. 24	non identifié	non spécifié	cambiste	balles	Delmas	1
13 sept.	LN 13/9, p. 24	non identifiée	non spécifié	fillette	balles	Delmas	1
17 sept.	LN 19/9, p. 24	Gousse	Patrice	non définies	balles	P-au-Pce	1
20 sept.	LN 21/9, p. 1	Toussaint	Fritz-Gérald	policier	balles	Laboule	1
20 sept.	LN 21/9, p. 1	Grégory	ainsi connu	bandit	balles	Laboule	1
25 sept.	LN 25/9, p. 32	Jeannot	Amos	ONG Fonkoze	mutilation	P-au-Pce	1
26 sept.	LN 29/9-1/10, p.32	non identifié	non spécifié	non définies	balles	P-au-Pce	1
29 sept.	LN 3/10, p. 24	Zius	ainsi connu	non définies	lynchage	Marchand	1
29 sept.	LN 3/10, p. 24	Timadam	ainsi connu	non définies	machette	Marchand	1
2 oct.	LN 2/10, p. 24	non identifiés	non spécifié	famille Alcéus	balles	Fontamara	3
4 oct.	LN 4/10, p. 24	Julien	Marcellus	septuagénaire	balles	P-au-Pce	1
7 oct.	LN 9/10, p. 24	Lirac	John	bandit	machette	Cabaret	1
7 oct.	LN 9/10, p. 24	non identifié	non spécifié	bandit	machette	Cabaret	1
17 oct.	LN 18/10, p. 24	non identifiés	non spécifié	bandits	balles	P-au-Pce	2
17 oct.	LN 18/10, p. 24	non identifiés	non spécifié	bandits	balles	Delmas	4

20 oct.	LN 20-22/10, p. 32	non identifié	non spécifié	non définies	balles	P-au-Pce	1
23 oct.	LN 23/10, p. 24	non identifiés	non spécifié	non définies	balles	P-au-Pce	3
24 oct.	LN 24/10, p. 5	non identifié	non spécifié	écolier	balles	P-au-Pce	1
24 oct.	LN 24/10, p. 5	non identifié	non spécifié	jeune (17 ans)	balles	P-au-Pce	1
4 nov.	LN 6/11, p. 24	non identifiés	non spécifié	non définies	balles	P-au-Pce	7
7 nov.	LN 13/11, p. 32	Pierre	Ednor	paysan	balles	Belladère	1
11 nov.	LN 13/11, p. 32	non identifiés	non spécifié	non définies	balles	P-au-Pce	3
11 nov.	LN 13/11, p. 32	non identifiés	non spécifié	non définies	balles	P-au-Pce	6
13 nov.	LN 13/11, p. 32	Emmanuel	Louis-Charles	écolier	balles	Carrefour	1
14 nov.	LN 14/11, p. 24	non identifié	non spécifié	bandit	lynchage	P-au-Pce	1
22 nov.	LN 22/11, p. 1	Clervil	Nickelson	non définies	explosif	P-au-Pce	1
4 déc.	LN 4/12, p. 24	Jean-Louis	Pierre	non définies	balles	Cul-de-Sac	1
6 déc.	LN 6/12, p. 24	Dantès	Louis	non définies	balles	Gonaïves	1
7 déc.	LN 7/12, p.24	Estinfil	Luc	borlettier	balles	Delmas	1
7 déc.	LN 7/12, p.24	non identifié	non spécifié	jeune	balles	P-au-Pce	1
8 déc.	LN 8-10/12, p. 28	Emmanuel	Joseph	jeune	balles	P-au-Pce	1
8 déc.	LN 8-10/12, p. 28	François	Pierre	jeune	balles	P-au-Pce	1
12 déc.	LN 12/12, p. 32	Pognon	Sénèque	non définies	non spécifié	Belladère	1
12 déc.	LN 12/12, p. 32	non identifiés	non spécifié	sorciers	lynchage	St-Ls du Sud	2
19 déc.	LN 28/12, p. 7	Denauze	Gérard	journaliste	balles	P-au-Pce	1
19 déc.	LN 19/12, p. 40	Paillère	Ernst	gestionnaire	balles	Léogane	1
20 déc.	LN 22-25/12, p. 41	Ambroise	Reynold	gestionnaire	balles	Pétion-Ville	1
20 déc.	LN 21/12, p. 40	Guerrier	Rood Ténor	ex-député	balles	Cx-Bouquets	1
21 déc.	LN 21/12, p. 40	Toto	ainsi connu	jeune	balles	P-au-Pce	1
21 déc.	LN 21/12, p. 40	non identifié	non spécifié	prévenu	tortures	St. Marc	1

Total of assassinated persons for the year 2000   223

Appendix 7- Summary

The victims for the year 1995.................................272

The victims for the year 1996................................285

The victims for the year 1997................................239

The victims for the year 1998 147

The victims for the year 1999 285

The victims for the year 2000................................223

Total of victims from 1995 to 2000........................1.431

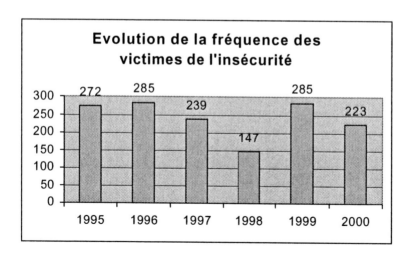

Appendix 8 - Alphabetical list of identified victims
1995 - 2000

1	Abdallah	Louis Galet	June 17, 1999
2	Abraham	Alix	July 13, 1996
3	Acloque	Yvon	April 25, 1997
4	Adonis	Carlo	June 7, 1999
5	Alcantara	Ramon	April 28, 1999
6	Alerte	Mireille	December12, 1995
7	Alexandre	Patrick	August 10, 1999
8	Alexandre	Michel-Ange	May 4, 2000
9	Alexandre	Carmen B.	July 25, 2000
10	Alophène	Jean-Michel	May 22, 2000
11	Altidor	Lüders	October 11, 1998
12	Alva	Ronald	March 29, 1998
13	Amilcar	Odinette	October 3, 1995
14	André	Rosemé	November 29, 1995
15	André	Guy	April 6, 2000
16	Anglade	Edith S.	September 4, 1997
17	Antoine	Jacky	July 13, 1996
18	Antoine	Charles	July 13, 1996
	Antoine	Patrick	April 22, 1998

20	Appolon	Volmar	June 21, 1999
21	Arbrouet	Eddy	December 14, 1997
22	Aristide	Charles	May 25, 1998
23	Aristide	Charles Pelé	May 25, 1999
24	Armand	André	July 20, 1996
25	Athis	Jonas	June 1st, 1997
26	Athis	Yvane	June 1st, 1997
27	Athis	Légitime	March 28, 2000
28	Athis	Mme Légitime	March 28, 2000
29	Augustave	Jean	February 28, 1995
30	Augustave	Mme Jean	February 28, 1995
31	Auguste	Jean-Luc	October 6, 1997
32	Augustin	Michel	March 19, 1995
33	Augustin	Founia	March 19, 1995
34	Augustin	Suzanne	March 19, 1995
35	Augustin	Shelly	March 19, 1995
36	Augustin	Gary	November 29, 1997
37	Azémar	Coriolan	Avril 8, 1998
38	Azima	Jean-François	November 8, 1997
39	Baillergeau	Eugène	March 28, 1995
40	Baltazar	Murielle	September 26, 1998
41	Baptiste	Milcent	May 3, 1996
42	Barelli	Lucas	May 2, 1999
43	Baret	Amaguel	April 11, 1997
44	Baronville	Luckner	November 15, 1998
45	Bayard	Laureston	April 7, 1997
46	Bazile	Berthony	June 7, 1999
47	Beaubrun	Mario	July 4, 1995

48	Beauplan	Eliazar	October 2, 1996
49	Beauplan	Wilmo	June 11, 2000
50	Bedonet	Charles E.	June 9, 1997
51	Bélizaire	Ernest	March 7, 2000
52	Belle-soeur	Augustave	February 28, 1995
53	Bellony	Reynold	February 14, 1997
54	Belot	Lagneau	May 3, 2000
55	Benoit	Elda	September 12, 1997
56	Benoit	non spécifié	September 12, 1997
57	Benoit	Simon	August 4, 1999
58	Bernardin	Harrisson	March 12, 1997
59	Bernardin	Hurdon	November 27, 1998
60	Bertin	Dérival	June 28, 1999
61	Bertin D.	Mireille	March 28, 1995
62	Bienaimé	Marie Claude	June 24, 1999
63	Bignac	Milcent	April 27, 1996
64	Bijou	André	November 7, 1998
65	Black Kiki	ainsi connu	April 17, 2000
66	Blaise	Clothaire	June 9, 1995
67	Blaise	Ronald	May 9, 1997
68	Blaise	Doky	November 17, 1997
69	Blaise	Mme Doky	November 17, 1997
70	Blaise	Preneur	March 19, 1998
71	Blanchard	Gérard	October 23, 1995
72	Bolville	Gérard	April 7, 1998
73	Bonaparte	Clerveau	May 15, 1995
74	Bordes	Ary	May 6, 2000
75	Borno	Jean-Marie	May 9, 1998
76	Boucard	Claudy	June 21, 1995

77	Bourcenet	Jean-Baptiste	January 31, 1998
78	Bourdeau	Ronald	November 14, 1996
79	Brésil	ainsi connu	February 16, 1996
80	Brierre	Serge	November 8, 1999
81	Bruno	Joudnel	August 2, 1998
82	Cabrouet	Voltaire	May 4, 1995
83	Cadet	Alix	May 15, 1997
84	Cardott	Grégory	January 12, 1995
85	Casséus	Ricardo	August 6, 1998
86	Casséus	Fritznel	July 19, 2000
87	Castin	Jérôme	May 6, 2000
88	Cauvin	Serge	December 15, 1996
89	Cazeau	Roger	June 14, 2000
90	Céderme	ainsi connu	September 7, 1997
91	Célestin	Michèle	June 7, 1997
92	Célestin	Huguens	August 5, 1999
93	César	Félio	July 20, 1995
94	Cétray	ainsi connu	May 21, 1998
95	Charles	Joseph Rony	August 5, 1996
96	Charles	Jean Bernard	September 11, 1996
97	Charles	Avrinel	March 10, 1997
98	Charles	Kettely	July 22, 1999
99	Charles	Pierre-Loty	March 19, 1998
100	Charles T.	Emmanuel	July 19, 1996
101	Charrier	Estime	September 21, 1999
102	Chérant	Johnny	September 26, 1999
103	Chery	Berthony	March 19, 1998
104	Chéry	Berthony	May 4, 1996
105	Chéry	Edgard	September 24, 1999
106	Chéry	Célouinord	April 6, 1997
107	Chevenelle	Pierre	March 30, 1995
108	Chouchou	ainsi connu	August 2, 1995
109	Civil	Yves Wilner	August 25, 1996
110	Claude	Marc	March 22, 1995

111	Claude	Yves-Marie	July 4, 1995
112	Clergé	Penny	November 12, 1997
113	Clervil	Nickelson	November 22, 2000
114	Colbert	Georges	January 3, 1997
115	Colonne	ainsi connu	October 31, 1995
116	Conséant	Jean Léonard	April 25, 1996
117	Coq	Hilda	September 11, 1996
118	Coriolan	St-Jean	April 10, 1995
119	Coulanges	Micheline	December 22, 1997
120	Dacéus	Mme Dalismé	August 10, 1999
121	Damas	Ruls	Decembre 11, 1998
122	Dantès	Louis	December 6, 2000
123	Dautruche	Wilner	December 29, 1995
124	David	ainsi connu	December 26, 1995
125	Davilmar	Philoclès	August 2, 1995
126	Décatrel	Roland	August 31, 1999
127	Delbal	Jean-Claude	November 3, 1996
128	Delgrès	Dieuseul	November 15, 1997
129	Démosthène	ainsi connu	May 10, 1999
130	Désaubry	Marc-Holly	June 4, 1996
131	Désir	Ernest	April 26, 1996
132	Désir	Anne-Marie	April 26, 1996
133	Désir	Philistin	April 27, 1996
134	Désir	Valcourt	May 27, 1996
135	Désir	Valentine	March 26, 1999
136	Désir	ainsi connu	April 17, 2000
137	Desmornes	Marie D.	January 30, 1998
138	Desrivières	Madame	May 21, 1998
139	Dessources	Jude	May 29, 1996
140	Désulmé	Jonas	May 2, 1997
141	Déus	Mérélus	April 12, 2000
142	Diallo	Moktar	October 29, 1998

143	Diamand	Donald	March 26, 1996
144	Dieubéni	ainsi connu	January 14, 1998
145	Dieudonné	Fertil	August 18, 2000
146	Domersant	Louis	August 2, 1998
147	Dominique	Yvel	January 23, 1999
148	Dominique	Jean L.	April 3, 2000
149	Don Mike	Charles	November 27, 1998
150	Dorcelin	Dieujuste	June 22, 1997
151	Dorilien	Dieusibon	March 26, 1998
152	Dorléans	Martine	October 6, 1997
153	Dormant	Donald	March 27, 1997
154	Dorméus	Risselin	February 5, 1998
155	Dorsainvil	Joséphine	June 29, 1995
156	Dorval	Stéphane	March 4, 1996
157	Dorvil	Ferdinand	March 29, 2000
158	Douval	Jean-Michel	October 11, 1996
159	Douze	James	May 13, 2000
160	Ducertain	Arnaud	April 25, 2000
161	Durand	Astride	December 19, 1999
162	Durogène	Moïse	December 9, 1996
163	Duvernois	Edouard	December 17, 1996
164	Edmond	Sofli	January 16, 1997
165	Edouard	Louis Galet	March 9, 1999
166	El Gallo	ainsi connu	August 9, 1995
167	Elie	Pierre	June 3, 1996
168	Elie	Claude	September 26, 1997
169	Elysée	Pierre-Joseph	April 27, 1996
170	Elysée	Hippolite	April 17, 1999
171	Emmanuel	Louis-Charles	November 13, 2000
172	Emmanuel	Joseph	December 8, 2000
173	Enerve	Espérant	April 8, 1998

174	Ernest	Franckel	August 4, 1995
175	Espérance	Louiné	April 22, 2000
176	Estève	Gérard Marcel	February 2, 1997
177	Estinfil	Luc	December 7, 2000
178	Estinval	Yves-Marie	November 9, 1995
179	Etienne	Joël	March 19, 1998
180	Etienne	Renaud	April 8, 1998
181	Eugène	Occilien	April 21, 1995
182	Eugène	Tadaille	June 11, 2000
183	Exantus	Luckner	August 6, 1998
184	Exat	ainsi connu	October 11, 1996
185	Exaüs	Emmanuel	April 14, 2000
186	Fabien	Joseph	May 6, 1995
187	Fanfan	ainsi connu	March 15, 1995
188	Faustin	Jean-Saurel	October 25, 1997
189	Faustin	Romain	January 15, 2000
190	Fédel	ainsi connu	August 24, 1999
191	Fénélus	Orasmin	August 1st, 1996
192	Feuillé	Hubert	November 7, 1995
193	Figaro	Wilfrid	June 9, 1995
194	Figaro	Wilfrid	March 1st, 1999
195	Fillette de	Augustave	February 28, 1995
196	Fleurantin	Hubert	Decembre 26, 1995
197	Florival	Jacques	August 20, 1996
198	Francis	Georges	February 23, 1999
199	Francis	Roseline	June 6, 1999
200	Francisque	ainsi connu	August 5, 1996
201	François	Gérard	March 30, 1995
202	François	Raymond	April 1st, 1996
203	François	Islande	May 3, 1996
204	François	Frantz	March 11, 1997
205	François	Anneté	February 21, 1998
206	François	Emana	16 avril 2000
207	François	Pierre	December 8, 2000
208	Frédéric	Aurel	January 12, 1995
209	Frédony	Wilson	July 10, 1997
210	Gaillard	Robert	November 11, 1997
211	Gaillard	Mme Robert	November 11, 1997

212	Garotte	Emmanuel	April 6, 1997
213	Geatjeans	Max	September 8, 1998
214	Geatjens	Margareth	March 1st, 1997
215	Gédéon	Sony	March 8, 1997
216	Génord	Emmanuela	December 31, 1995
217	Georges	Eddy	October 10, 1999
218	Germain	Soimilla	July 6, 1995
219	Germain	Shiller	June 6, 1996
220	Germain	Jean-Jérôme	November 5, 1996
221	Germain	Brignol	March 22, 1999
222	Gilbert	ainsi connu	July 29, 1995
223	Gilbert	Philippe	September 9, 1998
224	Ginoh	ainsi connu	August 5, 1996
225	Gonzalès	Michel	May 22, 1995
226	Gourgue	Ernestine	July 10, 1997
227	Gousse	Patrice	September 17, 2000
228	Gracia	Henrya	February 11, 1995
229	Gracien	Chenel	May 5, 1998
230	Gracien	Mme Chenel	May 5, 1998
231	Gratien	Jean Renel	October 21, 1997
232	Grégory	ainsi connu	September 20, 2000
233	Grimard	Leslie	June 10, 1995
234	Guerrier	Rood Ténor	December 20, 2000
235	Guirand	Anne-Marie	January 19, 1995
236	Hakime	Guy	March 2, 1997
237	Harris	ainsi connu	December 15, 1996
238	Hébert	ainsi connu	December 15, 1996
239	Hector	Maxime	May 10, 1999
240	Hermann	Michel-Ange	May 24, 1995
241	Hérode	Pierre	June 2, 1997
242	Hervé	Jean Gérald	April 7, 1999
243	Huguens	Jean-Paul	August 9, 2000
244	Hyppolite	Daniel	December 15, 1999
245	Innocent	Jean	July 16, 1998
246	Jameson	ainsi connu	August 25, 1998
247	Janvier	Bienheureux	March 13, 2000
248	Jean	Occil	March 22, 1996
249	Jean	Elie	June 23, 1996

250	Jean	Edner	March 5, 1997
251	Jean	Fénaka	April 18, 1997
252	Jean	Jean-Claude	July 21, 1997
253	Jean	Wisler	June 14, 1999
254	Jean	ainsi connu	September 7, 1997
255	Jean-Baptiste	Saurel	August 5, 1998
256	Jean-Baptiste	Jean-Robert	September 5, 1998
257	Jean-Charles	Enock	June 27, 1995
258	Jean-Claude	ainsi connu	April 17, 2000
259	Jean-François	César	June 17, 1998
260	Jean-Jacques	Hyppolite	January 15, 2000
261	Jean-Louis	Elan	June 4, 1997
262	Jean-Louis	Louinord	September 12, 1997
263	Jean-Louis	Pierre	December 4, 2000
264	Jeannot	Amos	September 25, 2000
265	Jean-Philippe	Frantz	June 11, 1996
266	Jeantiné	Onot	May 9, 1997
267	Jeanty	Robinson	February 7, 1995
268	Jérome	ainsi connu	August 5, 1998
269	Jeudilien	Idilan	May 27, 1999
270	Jeudy	Lipsie	May 9, 1995
271	Jeudy	Nétula	March 29, 2000
272	Jeudy	Jocelin	March 29, 2000
273	Jeudy	Jean-François	March 29, 2000
274	Jeune	Julien	March 17, 1996
275	Jeune	Christine	March 19, 1996
276	Jeune	Vesta	September 12, 1997
277	Jeune	Dérold	November 22, 1999
278	Jimenez	Jose	March 3, 2000
279	Jn-François	Erla	May 29, 1996
280	Joassaint	Mario	February 25, 1997
281	Joassaint	Mario	March 19, 1998
282	Jocelyn	Fritz	March 1st, 1999
283	Johanne	ainsi connue	May 4, 1999
284	Joseph	Ali	January 13, 1995
285	Joseph	Osselin	April 24, 1995
286	Joseph	Nicole	April 18, 1996
287	Joseph	Molovis	August 5, 1996

288	Joseph	Renel	October 2, 1996
289	Joseph	Lionel	March 13, 1997
290	Joseph	Réginald	September 7, 1997
291	Joseph	Robert Gary	March 19, 1998
292	Joseph	Emanie	May 28, 1998
293	Joseph	Onius	May 10, 1999
294	Joseph	Walter	May 20, 2000
295	Joseph	Wilesome	June 11, 2000
296	Josias	Solane	September 15, 1997
297	Josias	Mme Solane	September 15, 1997
298	Julien	Marcellus	October 4, 2000
299	Julio	ainsi connu	May 28, 1998
300	Juste	Roberson	June 29, 1995
301	Juste	Daniel	April 13, 1998
302	Kansky	Pierre	February 18, 1998
303	Kébreau	Joseph	June 25, 1995
304	Kénol	Jean-Claude	April 25, 2000
305	Kénol	Mme	April 25, 2000
306	Kénol	enfants	April 25, 2000
307	Kironé	Lamousse	July 15 1997
308	Labissière	Nelson	March 27, 2000
309	Lacombe	Joannès	May 16, 1996
310	Ladouceur	Béril	March 26, 1996
311	Ladouceur	Béril	March 27, 1997
312	Lafrance	Pascale	May 18, 1997
313	Laguerre	Pierre Wilfrid	April 28, 2000
314	Lalanne	Jimmy	February 27, 1999
315	Lamarre	Frénel	May 3, 1995
316	Lamarre	Fresnel	May 5, 1995
317	Lamarre	Tira	September 9, 1999
318	Lambert	Jean Eric	November 27, 1998
319	Lamothe	Eric	March 8, 1995
320	Lamour	Philogène	April 30, 1995
321	Lamy	Jean	October 8, 1999
322	Langlais	Germain	November 6, 1997
323	Lapin	Malherbe	November 21, 1998
324	Laurent	ainsi connu	May 14, 2000
325	Laurore	Patrick	June 1st, 2000

326	Lavache	Tony	April 1st, 1998
327	Lazarre	Gary	August 12, 1996
328	Lebrun	Maxo	May 23, 2000
329	Leconte	Mariette	July 30, 1996
330	Lecorps	Frantz	October 13, 1997
331	Léger	non spécifié	September 15, 1997
332	Léger	William	June 30, 1999
333	Léger	Mme Love	October 8, 1999
334	Legros	Métellus	February 24, 1997
335	Léon Joseph	non spécifié	October 24, 1997
336	Léonard	Jean	May 14, 1996
337	Leroy	Antoine	August 20, 1996
338	Lespinasse	Emile	April 21, 1995
339	Lespinasse	Jacques	September 15, 1995
340	Lhérisson	Jean-Louis	February 10, 2000
341	Lirac	John	October 7, 2000
342	Lizaire	ainsi connu	June 11, 2000
343	Loiseau	Daniel	June 28, 1999
344	Louidor	Jean Willy	August 4, 1999
345	Louima	Dieusibon	Octobre 20, 1997
346	Louis	Jacquelin	January 2, 1996
347	Louisdhon	Célinord	April 8, 1997
348	Louissaint	Jean-Claude	April 3, 2000
349	Lovinsky	Sévère	October 29, 1997
350	Lubin	Mario	November 4, 1996
351	Lubin	Harold	June 21, 1999
352	Lucito	Jean-Robert	January 27, 1996
353	Lyle	Garfield	August 7, 2000
354	Magloire	Thomas	January 23, 1995
355	Marcelin	Thierry	April 26, 2000
356	Marie-Colas	Etienne	July 29, 1995
357	Mathé	Avrius	July 17, 1998
358	Mathieu	Félix	January 7, 1995
359	Maurice	Betty	July 6, 1995
360	Max	Jean-Robert	August 4, 1999
361	Maxo	ainsi connu	May 7, 1999
362	Mayard	Max	October 3, 1995
363	McLaney	Michael	July 24, 1998

364	Mehring	Kurt	November 9, 1998
365	Ménard	John	April 10, 1997
366	Mérilus	Joseph	April 4, 1995
367	Mérisier	Jean-Baptiste	February 5, 1998
368	Mérizier	Willy	December 6, 1997
369	Mérizier	Alicia	December 6, 1997
370	Métayer	Jocelyn	June 19, 1998
371	Métellus	Camélot	April 6, 1995
372	Métellus	Roland	September 3, 1997
373	Méus	François	August 9, 1997
374	Michel	Marc	June 12, 1996
375	Michelet	Dazouloute	March 3, 1999
376	Midi	Pierre-Marie	February 22, 1999
377	Milcent	Datus	April 24, 1997
378	Milhomme	Dieuseul	April 28, 1999
379	Mingot	Jérome	July 28, 1999
380	Mitton	Jacky	April 14, 1999
381	Mme Emile	ainsi connue	December 7, 1995
382	Mme Jeune	ainsi connue	April 30, 1995
383	Moïse	Frantz	Septembre 21, 1999
384	Moïse	Nelson	October 13, 1999
385	Moïse	ainsi connu	July 20, 1996
386	Molière	ainsi connu	November 21, 1995
387	Molière	Lefranc	May 28, 1998
388	Mompremier	Emmanuel	March 8, 1997
389	Mondésir	Oreste	December 31, 1995
390	Money	Joseph Simon	February 21, 1999
391	Montalmand	Casimir	August 30, 1999
392	Montalveau	Lexi Léonel	February 2, 1997
393	Montreuil	Fritz	December 11, 1998
394	Morency	René	April 13, 1998
395	Morisseau	Charité	March 26, 1996
396	Morisset	Mad	May 1st, 1999
397	Moussignac	Frantz	June 5, 1995
398	Mullier	Fernand	January 12, 2000
399	Mullier	Céline	January 12, 2000
400	Narcisse	Pierre Richard	June 8, 1999
401	Neptune	Ralph	October 30, 1997

402	Noël	Joël	April 10, 1995
403	Noël	André	September 3, 1995
404	Noël	Citha	July 24, 1999
405	Obas	Gary	March 11, 1997
406	Obin	Aspin	January 12, 2000
407	Odette	ainsi connu	November 12, 1997
408	Omilien	ainsi connu	May 8, 2000
409	Pachinau	ainsi connu	May 15, 1995
410	Paillère	Ernst	December 19, 2000
411	Painson	Gabriel	August 3, 2000
412	Pamphille	Gilbert	June 25, 1999
413	Pape	Madeleine	August 20, 1996
414	Papillon	Pierre	June 28, 1998
415	Paraisy	Henry	February 24, 1997
416	Passe	Emilio	October 16, 1997
417	Patrick	ainsi connu	October 12, 1997
418	Paul	Mondésir	February 25, 1997
419	Paul	Hubert	January 6, 1999
420	Paula	ainsi connu	November 10, 1997
421	Paulémond	Ferdinand	April 12, 1996
422	Payne	Jean Ovens	April 10, 1999
423	Pétinord	Célavi	April 20, 1998
424	Pétinord	Mme Célavi	April 20, 1998
425	Pétion	Marcel	September 10, 1996
426	Phanor	Yves Wilner	August 30, 1996
427	Phanor	Gary	September 30, 1998
428	Phanord	Edwidge	December 5, 1999
429	Phyllis	Michel-Ange	April 20, 1999
430	Pierre	Lexius	September 19, 1995
431	Pierre	Germaine	June 3, 1996
432	Pierre	enfants (3)	June 3, 1996
433	Pierre	Francesca	June 15, 1996
434	Pierre	Yves	June 22, 1996
435	Pierre	Harold	February 2, 1997
436	Pierre	Justin	July 7, 1997
437	Pierre	Anne-Marie	July 5, 1997
438	Pierre	Angela	September 4, 1997
439	Pierre	Marie Eric	September 26, 1998

440	Pierre	Joceline	March 6, 1999
441	Pierre	Edouane	March 6, 1999
442	Pierre	Mme Ph.	March 30, 1999
443	Pierre	André	April 9, 1999
444	Pierre	André (enfant)	April 9, 1999
445	Pierre	Gumane	May 13, 2000
446	Pierre	Alain	May 13, 2000
447	Pierre	Wilner	May 31, 2000
448	Pierre	Ednor	November 7, 2000
449	Pierre-Louis	Raynald	April 28, 1998
450	Pierre-Louis	Jean	August 3, 1998
451	Pierre-Louis	Bertrand	May 1ˢᵗ, 1999
452	Pierre-Louis	MacKenzie	June 13, 2000
453	Piti	ainsi connu	February 4, 2000
454	Plaisimond	Hans	July 28, 1995
455	Plaisimond	Maryse	March 1ˢᵗ, 1999
456	Pognon	Sénèque	December 12, 2000
457	Poincarré	Charles	April 7, 1999
458	Prémilus	Ilméus	April 20, 1998
459	Présent	Théonique	February 10, 1999
460	Présumé	Darlie	July 11, 2000
461	Prévilon	Dieuseul	August 25, 1996
462	Raynold	ainsi connu	July 11, 1996
463	Refusé	Miguel	March 19, 1998
464	Renard	Franciné	July 20, 1999
465	Richard	Albert Joseph	March 10, 1999
466	Richemond	Jocelyn	December 12, 1995
467	Robert	Marie-Géralde	November 17, 1999
468	Robert	Jean	December 16, 1999
469	Roland	ainsi connu	December 27, 1999
470	Romain	Venel	May 17, 1999
471	Romulus	Dumarsais	June 28, 1995
472	Rouchon	Micheline	December 2, 1996
473	Rouchon	Fédia	December 2, 1996
474	Rousseau	Dumesle	January 7, 1997
475	Rousseau	Gilbert	July 3, 2000
476	Sabbat	Patrick	April 7, 2000
477	Saint-Cyr	Madeleine	July 2, 1996

478	Sajous	Pierre	November 21, 1995
479	Salnave	Dézilma	April 2, 1988
480	Salnave	Amédée	May 28, 2000
481	Salomon	Kesnel	November 5, 1996
482	Samedi	Jean B.	March 27, 2000
483	Samuel	Sylvain	May 3, 1999
484	Sanon	Thony	October 11, 1996
485	Sanon	Roseline	December 21, 1999
486	Sanon	Milfort	December 21, 1999
487	Sanon	Branord	May 12, 2000
488	Sans-Souci	Louis	January 13, 1995
489	Séjour	Elison	January 11, 2000
490	Sénat	Elane	May 8, 2000
491	Sénat	Grégor	May 8, 2000
492	Sérah	Jean-Victor	June 18, 1996
493	Séraphin	Cadeau	October 8, 1999
494	Sicard	Charles Anga	August 12, 1995
495	Sidney	Jean-Robert	October 7, 1999
496	Sifré	Alain	November 8, 1995
497	Similien	Robel	February 5, 1997
498	Simon	Faudener	March 9, 1995
499	Simon	Naomie	August 5, 1999
500	Smith	ainsi connu	March 30, 1999
501	Song	Yoon Ki	December 23, 1996
502	Sonthonax	Norbert	February 11, 1998
503	Stanio	Vilus Alexis	September 20, 1997
504	St-Auguste	Altero	April 10, 1995
505	Steinmann	Hubert	April 3, 1996
506	Steinmann	Anne Kung	April 3, 1996
507	St-Fleur	Enks	February 10, 1999
508	St-Fort	Guens	May 24, 1998
509	St-Georges	Milord	April 28, 1999
510	St-Hilaire	S.	June 3, 2000
511	St-Joy	Marjorie	December 31, 1999
512	St-Pierre	Jules	February 10, 1999
513	Tania	ainsi connue	December 7, 1995
514	Tarjet	Patrick	April 7, 1997
515	Tédal	Sorel	August 13, 1998

516	Thélusma	Jacqueline	August 21, 1995
517	Théodore	Yolène T.	November 21, 1998
518	Théodule	Onel	September 21, 1998
519	Thermidor	Vania	November 24, 1995
520	Thézine	Girald	December 15, 1996
521	Thimothé	Jimmy	February 2, 1998
522	Thomas	Fontaine	November 12, 1997
523	Thomas	ainsi connu	January 12, 1998
524	Thomas	Pierre Richard	September 21, 1999
525	Ti Boulé	ainsi connu	May 12, 1999
526	Ti-blanc	ainsi connu	May 15, 1997
527	Tiga	ainsi connu	August 30, 1998
528	Timadam	ainsi connu	September 29, 2000
529	Timanchèt	ainsi connu	Auguste 12, 2000
530	Ti-Moïse	ainsi connu	October 20, 1997
531	Tinès	ainsi connu	May 12, 1999
532	Tipa	ainsi connu	November 10, 1997
533	Ti-Papit	ainsi connu	April 7, 1997
534	Tiyoute	ainsi connu	March 22, 1999
535	Toto	ainsi connu	December 21, 2000
536	Toussaint	Pierre	September 15, 1997
537	Toussaint	Yvon	March 1st, 1999
538	Toussaint	Fritz-Gérald	September 20, 2000
539	Toussaint	Orphélia	January 27, 1998
540	Turenne	Eugène	June 7, 1995
541	Valbrun	Pilon-Jean	February 15, 1995
542	Valcin	Vernel	November 22, 1999
543	Valcourt	Sanders	February 21, 2000
544	Vaval	Luc	November 9, 1996
545	Vega	Eduardo	February 18, 1997
546	Versailles	Clothaire	August 31, 1998
547	Versailles	Jean-Franklin	January 12, 1999
548	Victor	Constance	October 9, 1996
549	Vincent	Edriss	November 4, 1996
550	Volcy	Josué	December 26, 1995
551	Web	Sheila	January 15, 2000
552	Wesh	Bernard	July 23, 1998
553	Wilner	ainsi connu	August 19, 2000
554	Zius	ainsi connu	June 3, 1997

BIBLIOGRAPHY

Anglade, Georges

Cartes sur Table - Itinéraires et Raccourcis, Tome I, Editions Henri Deschamps, 1990.

Association Médicale Haïtienne

Hommage au Dr. Ary Bordes, Les Éditions Areytos, 2000

Aristide, Jean-Bertrand

Aristide, an Autobiograhy, Orbis Books, New York, 1993.

Avril, Prosper

Vérités et Révélations Tome I - Le Silence Rompu, Imprimeur II, Port-au-Prince, Haïti, 1993.

Vérités et Révélations Tome III - L'Armée d'Haïti, Bourreau ou Victime?, Imprimerie Le Natal, Port-au-Prince, 1997.

Bajeux, Jean-Claude

Pour qui sont ces Serpents...?, Le Nouvelliste, October 3, 2000, Port-au-Prince.

Bordes, Ary

Au Pays de Nelson Mandela, Le Nouvelliste, January 4, 1996, Port-au-Prince.

Bertin, Mireille Durocher

La Crise Haïtienne dans le Droit International Public,

Editora Sarodj, Santo Domingo 1996.

Chavenet, Anaïse

Témoignage, Le Nouvelliste, December 30, 1996 to January 2, 1997, Port-au-Prince.

Conférence Episcopale d'Haïti

Présence de l'Eglise en Haïti - Messages et Documents de l'Episcopat 1980-1988, Editions S.O.S., Paris, France, 1988.

Dalencour, Patrice

Le Hideux Rictus de leur Démocratie, Le Nouvelliste, March 29, 1995, Port-au-Prince.

Delva, Joseph Guyler C.

Le Président Préval à la rescousse du plan de Sécurité Publique, Le Nouvelliste January 11, 2000, Port-au-Prince.

Diamond, Larry - Linz, Juan L. - Lipset, Seymour Martin

Les Pays en Développement et l'Expérience de la Démocratie, Nouveaux Horizons, Printing press of Regional Service Center, Manille, Philippines, 1998.

Dominique, Joseph

L'OCODE et l'insécurité, Le Nouvelliste, June 5 to 6, 1996, Port-au-Prince.

Duhamel, Olivier

Les Démocraties - Régimes. Histoire, Exigences, Edition du Seuil, Paris, France, 1993.

Dumas, Pierre-Raymond

Insécurité: et Demain?, Le Nouvelliste, December 30 to January 2, 1995, Port-au-Prince.

Débat sur la Force publique en Haïti, Le Nouvelliste, November 29, 1999, Port-qau-Prince.

Fignolé, Jean-Claude

1) *Criminalité?*, Le Nouvelliste, December 30, 1996 to January 2 1997, Port-au-Prince.

2) Le Nouvelliste, December 20 to 22, 1996, Port-au-Prince.

Gousse, Sabine, Olivier et Michaël

Lettre ouverte aux autorités gouvernementales, aux instances internationales et aux Haïtiens, Le Nouvelliste January 28, 1998, Port-au-Prince.

Johnson, Charlmers

Déséquilibre Social et Révolution, Nouveaux Horizons, ISTRA, Paris, 1972.

Jusma, Roselor

In Memoriam Maryse Débrosse - Se taire et laissez faire, Le Nouvelliste, February 9, 1998, Port-au-Prince.

Manigat, Leslie

Les Cahiers du CHUDAC, Centre Humanisme Démocratique en Action, Port-au-Prince, 1998.

Ménard, Emmanuel

Epître aux Elites, Cosmos Communications, Port-au-Prince, avril 2000.

Cri strident de douleur et d'espoir, Le Matin,

September 30 to October 2, 2000, Port-au-Prince.

Nixon, Richard

La Vraie Guerre, Editions Albin Michel, Paris, 1980.

Oriol, Paulette Poujol

Le temps des repentirs, Le Nouvelliste, July 10, 2000, Port-au-Prince.

Prophète, L. Jean

Inventaire de fin de Siècle, Les Editions CIDIHCA, Montréal, Canada.

Roc, François

Entre la Raison et l'Explosion, Le Nouvelliste, March 17, 1998, Port-au-Prince.

Roché, Sébastian

Sociologie Politique de l'Insécurité - Violences urbaines, inégalités et globalisation, 2nd edition, Presses Universitaires de France, 1999.

Romain, Dominique

Pour un Plan de Réforme Pénitentiaire - La Science Pénitentiaire, Histoire, Domaine et Développement, Imprimerie Le Natal, Port-au-Prince, 1989.

Toffler, Alvin

Les Nouveaux Pouvoirs, Savoir, Richesse et Violence à la veille du XXIème Siècle, Librairie Arthème Fayard - Paris, 1991.

Valet, Daly

L'Insécurité banalisée par des Diplomates, Le

Nouvelliste, March 20, 1995, Port-au-Prince.

Vilgrain, Jacques

Structure, Mécanismes et Evolution de l'Economie Haïtienne, Imprimerie Henri Deschamps, Port-au-Prince, 1995.

Le Nouvelliste

Le Matin

Haïti Observateur

Haïti en Marche

16 Décembre Magazine

Haiticonnection.com

Haitionline.com

Statedept.com

The Miami Herald

INDEX

Printed in the United States
39894LVS00002BA/354